The
Christian Science Monitor

Its History, Mission, and People

The Christian Science Monitor

Its History, Mission, and People

Keith S. Collins

Nebbadoon Press

www.NebbadoonPress.com

The Christian Science Monitor:
Its History, Mission, and People

© 2012 Keith S. Collins

Nebbadoon Press
www.NebbadoonPress.com

ISBN 978-1-891331-26-8

Library of Congress Control Number: 2011946109

Printed in U.S.A.

The following are © The Mary Baker Eddy Collection. Used with permission.

1. MBEL Accession #L00596, Mary Baker Eddy to CSBD, 7/28/1908
2. MBEL Accession #A10032, Mary Baker Eddy/Calvin Frye, 1837, "Shade and Sunshine"
3. MBEL Accession #L03064, Mary Baker Eddy to Archibald McLellan, 8/29/1903
4. MBEL Accession #L05221, Mary Baker Eddy to John F. Linscott/Ellen Brown Linscott, 5/30/1898
5. MBEL Accession #L04290, Mary Baker Eddy to John Carroll Lathrop, 5/9/1906
6. MBEL Accession #L04945, Mary Baker Eddy to Septimus J. Hanna/Camilla Hanna, 2/24/1893
7. MBEL Accession #L02279, Mary Baker Eddy to William G. Nixon, 9/13/1892
8. MBEL Accession #L02278, Mary Baker Eddy to William G. Nixon, 3/3/1892
9. MBEL Accession #L13516, Mary Baker Eddy to Augusta Stetson, 5/1/1907
10. MBEL Accession #L07590, Mary Baker Eddy to Edward A. Kimball, 6/3/1902
11. MBEL Accession #L07593, Mary Baker Eddy to Kate Davidson Kimball/Edward A. Kimball, 6/22/1902
12. MBEL Accession #L06998, Mary Baker Eddy's comments in reply to letter from John L. Wright to Mrs. Eddy, 3/12/1908
13. MBEL Accession #L07146, Mary Baker Eddy to Archibald McLellan/Allison V. Stewart, 5/3/1908
14. MBEL Accession #L07268, Mary Baker Eddy to Board of Trustees of The Christian Science Publishing Society, 8/8/1908
15. MBEL Accession #L06474, Adam H. Dickey to Archibald McLellan, 8/12/1908
16. MBEL Accession #L07269, Adam Dickey to Board of Trustees of The Christian Science Publishing Society, 8/14/1908
17. MBEL Accession #L03212, Mary Baker Eddy to Archibald McLellan, 2/21/1909
18. MBEL Accession #L14824, William R. Rathvon to William P. McKenzie, 1/4/1910
19. MBEL Accession #L13516, Mary Baker Eddy to Augusta E. Stetson, 5/1/1907
20. MBEL Accession #L04847, Mary Baker Eddy to William P. McKenzie, 10/2/1894
21. MBEL Accession #V03307, Adam H. Dickey to Archibald McLellan, 11/24/1908

Additional permissions:

Extracts for "Alexander Dodds, Autobiography and Story of the Founding of the Monitor" (manuscript), 1917: Original in the Longyear Museum collection, Chestnut Hill, Massachusetts. Permission granted by Longyear Museum.

Quote from the *Boston Herald* used with permission.

Passages from *Kay Fanning's Alaska Story* quoted with permission of Epicenter Press, Kenmore, Washington.

Passages from Edmund Stevens quoted with permission of Edmund Stevens, Jr.

Passage from "A toxic threat arises amid northern Iraq's prosperity" in *The Christian Science Monitor*, December 24, 2004, quoted with permission of Annia Ciezadlo.

Passage from "Selling War: the British propaganda campaign against American 'Neutrality' in World War II" quoted by permission of Oxford University Press.

Passage from Robert Peel's *Mary Baker Eddy: Years of Trial* quoted with permission of A.W. Phinney.

Passages from the *Anchorage Daily News* quoted with permission.

Passages from Erwin Canham's *Commitment to Freedom* quoted by permission of Carolyn Dain.

Passage from *The Christian Science Way of Life* quoted with permission of DeWitt John, Jr.

Passages from Richard Nenneman's *A Spiritual Journey: Why I Became a Christian Scientist* quoted with permission of Nebbadoon Press.

Cover design: John Kehe.

Cover photo credits:

Scott Bauldauf and Kenyan Girl. CS Monitor Photo ID 5748992
Melanie Stetson Freeman / © 2008 The Christian Science Monitor

Willis J. Abbot. CS Monitor Photo ID 329576
Photographer and date unknown
Courtesy of The Christian Science Monitor

Charlotte Saikowski.   CS Monitor Photo ID 762715
© 1972 The Christian Science Monitor

Erwin Canham and President Dwight Eisenhower.
CS Monitor Photo ID 344624
© 1954 The Christian Science Monitor

Mary Baker Eddy. MBEL Accession Number P00217
Clara Shannon / © 1936, renewed 1964 The Mary Baker Eddy Collection

Globe Lamp in Hall of Ideas. CS Monitor Photo ID 18445063
John Kehe / © 2011 The Christian Science Monitor

For Téa

**Who blesses the world every day
with her vision, patience, courage, and love**

"The object of the *Monitor* is to injure no man, but to bless all mankind."

> Mary Baker Eddy, Founder of
> *The Christian Science Monitor*

"To the extent that one prays in [a] spiritually assertive way, one can help lift a little corner of the blanket of fear that often seems to smother the world in regard to many situations."

> Takashi Oka, foreign correspondent,
> *The Christian Science Monitor*

Author's Note

I believe that the world is a better place because *The Christian Science Monitor* is in it. That's a positive way of saying that this book is not an unbiased history. I can't pretend to be neutral on a subject I care so much about. I want the *Monitor* to succeed, because I believe it has the tools to change the way people think about human events.

I hope, though, that what I have written is fair. After having lived with so many of the key individuals in the *Monitor*'s history for the years I have spent writing this book, I am convinced that every one of them acted from his or her highest motives. Some of the people were selfless, compassionate, and wise. Some, not so much. But in fairness, every person was sincere in his or her attempt to help the *Monitor*, and everyone loved the paper. That is one reason why I believe it is still around.

The objective of the *Monitor*, in the words of its founder, is "to injure no man, but to bless all mankind." I have written this book with that spirit in mind.

February 1, 2012
Keith S. Collins
Geneva, Switzerland

Contents

Introduction

By ten o'clock in the morning on September 11, 2001, lobbyists, lawyers, government officials, and policy wonks were flooding the streets of Washington, D.C. Television images of planes hitting the World Trade Center had already crashed deep into American consciousness. The dark cloud rising from the Pentagon across the Potomac River confirmed that the news was not just happening in New York City.

As I left my office at a trade association and joined the crowd rushing through Farragut Park toward the subway, I looked back at the White House. The sky above was a deep autumn blue and wide open. I shuddered at what I imagined coming through it.

In the subway car, I sat with my back to Pennsylvania Avenue. If the White House was to be the next target, I just hoped, in my growing fever of fear, that the fire would stop before it reached me. I closed my eyes and counted the seconds as we moved farther and farther from downtown until, emerging at Friendship Heights station, I hurried up the escalator, through Hecht's department store, and out of the parking lot to my home across the street.

As I burst through the door, I grabbed the TV remote and told my wife she wouldn't believe what had happened. She watched as I turned to one of the networks, then she went back to what she was doing. I slipped lower into the sofa, sick with horror.

By the afternoon, I couldn't move without my back shooting pain throughout my body. My wife turned off the news and helped me into bed. She had been through wars and terror in her native country, so this was not new to her. But for at least one American, the experience was paralyzing.

It would take me three days to recover enough to walk, but it would take more than two years to root out the fear and anger brought on by the attacks. My freedom came when I was forced, for my own survival, to finally look outside myself.

By that time—late 2003, six months after the American invasion of Iraq—I was in Baghdad as an employee of a company trying to reform the health-care system in the country. Attacks on foreigners were growing, and mental paralysis was settling in. As on September 11, I felt like a moving target as I crossed the street from the company's hotel or drove through the neighborhoods of Baghdad. This time, however, I also felt an urgent need to keep my head up.

I made notes about the joy being kept alive by foreigners and Iraqis alike—the American boss who was determined not to let a meeting pass without at least one laugh, the Iraqi hotel staff who made extraordinary efforts to make guests feel at home (ice cream bars!). Like everyone, I was aware of the fear and hate that seemed always ready to explode, but the joy felt stronger than the fear.

I turned the notes into essays, at one point sitting with my laptop on the floor beneath the window of my hotel room, listening to a gun battle rage in the streets. By bringing alive, in stories of hope, the peace I saw around me as well as what I was becoming convinced was the powerlessness of fear and hate to defeat it, I found courage. I felt a strength that I can only describe as a divine presence, keeping me and, I believe, those around me safe. (There were no casualties that night, I learned later.) The next step was logical, at least to my way of thinking: I published the essays in *The Christian Science Monitor*.

At that point, I felt my September 11 experience was complete. I had grown from narrow self-concern to a measure of rebirth, and I was certain that, in some small degree, there had been healing. Some of the fear that had gripped so many people on that terrible day, at least the fear that had gripped me, had been dissolved. And through the pages of the *Monitor,* I had found a way to communicate my experience to the world.

■ ■ ■

A decade and a half earlier, the *Monitor* seemed near death. Published by the Christian Science church, the famous newspaper was losing circulation and had apparently been scheduled for closing by a group of church officials that decided the future of the news media lay in television. The officials spent half a billion dollars trying to make broadcasting work, many angry church members objected, and the *Monitor*'s Pulitzer-Prize-winning editor and some of its most distinguished correspondents quit in protest. The church's Board of Directors finally realized it had made a mistake, and with what amounted to an apology to the members, it allowed the newspaper to continue. But the paper faced serious financial problems, and the future still looked cloudy.

Limping along, the *Monitor* kept losing readers until circulation stood just above 50,000, a quarter of its peak a few decades earlier. The Board of Directors finally felt it had to take action, and in 2009, it made a dramatic move. It seemed to work. Closing the print daily and switching everything to the Web, except for a weekly print edition, the church created a *Monitor* that started to grow again. Millions of people in the United States and a million more around the world started reading its articles every month. Most of these readers were passersby, just clicking on an article or two. It was a bit of a comedown for what was once one of the world's premier newspapers—it has won seven Pulitzers along with many other awards for excellence. But considering what the *Monitor* had been through, it was an accomplishment.

Since its early days, the *Monitor* has had a reputation as a trustworthy news source, especially for international stories ignored by other media. It has tried to present the world in a way that is honest but unspectacular, realistic but encouraging about humanity's problems. It can be comforting during crises, energizing in promoting reforms, and occasionally, even inspiring.

From its first issue, however, the paper has also struggled with a tendency toward naiveté, pedantry, and predictability. Since the television debacle in the 1980s, the paper has tried to regain the respect of the government officials, journalists, and academicians who used to read it regularly, but with limited success. Some *Monitor* reporters are still highly regarded, but there are fewer at the top of their profession than there used to be.

Why, then, bother to write this book?

Because the world needs *The Christian Science Monitor*.

When Mary Baker Eddy founded the *Monitor,* in 1908, she defined its objective as "to injure no man, but to bless all mankind." [1] The church itself, which she had established in 1879, was formed, in her words, to "reinstate primitive Christianity and its lost element of healing." [2] If humanity is someday to rise out of its immense troubles, it would not be a bad thing to have a news source that reports reliably, perceptively, and compassionately on what those troubles are, with the conviction that healing will come.

It takes an understanding of Mrs. Eddy and her approach to religion to know the *Monitor.* (In keeping with what most Christian Scientists call her, the *Monitor*'s founder will be referred to as "Mrs. Eddy" throughout this book.) Mrs. Eddy taught that God's love is an ever-present help, and that His love can be proved through healing by anyone who follows sincerely the teachings of Christ Jesus. The *Monitor* is designed to be part of that healing work, helping its readers overcome the greed, fear, and other tendencies, in themselves and others, that cause so many problems that end up in the news.

The church structure Mrs. Eddy established is key to how the *Monitor* functions. At the top is The Christian Science Board of Directors, who themselves take direction from the *Church Manual* that Mrs. Eddy left as the controlling document for church governance. The church runs The Christian Science Publishing Society, which is overseen by a Board of Trustees and publishes the *Monitor* along with church magazines, books by Mrs. Eddy, and other publications. The Directors and Trustees have had their differences over the years.

The Christian Science church has no clergy, but there are groups of people who are seen as authorities. One is Christian Science practitioners, professional healers who charge a fee for their services. Christian Scientists turn to them when they can't heal themselves. Many people, including *Monitor* journalists, have become Christian Scientists because of healings they or their family members have experienced, with and without the help of Christian Science practitioners.

Another group of authority figures is Christian Science teachers, who conduct classes each year on the deeper teachings of the religion, including how to heal through prayer. Teachers play important roles in the history of the *Monitor*, with four having served as editors. Being a teacher has been no guarantee of success. One teacher was perhaps the most successful editor of all. Another almost caused the paper to collapse from the weight of his ego.

Christian Scientists also run schools, the most well-known being The Principia, which operates a grade school and high school in St. Louis and a college in Elsah, Illinois. Principia has no formal relationship with the church, but many *Monitor* journalists have been graduates, especially of Principia College.

The rank-and-file members of the church have also played a prominent role in the *Monitor*'s history as its core readership. A church member once wrote, ". . . if I find myself reading the *Monitor* just for information, I stop and remind myself that the reason I'm reading it is that I have a commitment to pray—to do something about the problems." [3]

This is, in fact, the primary way the *Monitor* tries to bring healing: through the prayers of its readers. For readers to remain cynical or fearful is more difficult if they read the *Monitor* with the spirit Mrs. Eddy intended. And, the thinking goes, it is more difficult for the rest of the world to remain in its pit of despair if *Monitor* readers are engaged and actively praying.

"The *Monitor* isn't just a group of people in a newsroom," one staff editor says. "It's a commitment by a community to a way of interacting with the world." [4]

Then there are the journalists. Their stories form the crux of this book. With hundreds of them having moved through the *Monitor* since 1908, it would be impossible to do justice to everyone of significance in a single book. *The Christian Science Monitor: Its History, Mission, and People* focuses on a relative handful of them as representative of both a larger number and a type of person who tends to do well at the *Monitor*: someone with good professional skills and an ego under control, who is perhaps not a Christian Scientist but has enough compassion "to injure no man, but to bless all mankind."

It should be noted that *Monitor* journalists have won many prizes over the years, but the prizewinners the book focuses on are the Pulitzer winners. This is done because the Pulitzer Prize is regarded as American journalism's highest award. The fact that not all *Monitor* prizewinners are mentioned does not imply that their work is less noteworthy.

Some of the best *Monitor* journalists have burrowed beneath the surface of daily journalism to explore the range of Mrs. Eddy's vision. They have tried to bear witness to the beauty and goodness they see around them as a reflection of God's presence and to uncover evil as a lie about God and His true nature—a core belief of Christian Science. Journalists who do this are rare, even at the *Monitor*, but when they appear, they create *Monitor* journalism at its most compelling, helping to lift human thought and action to a level where the news can get better.

When the paper forgets its healing mission, it crashes. The biggest disasters that have befallen the *Monitor* over the years have come when editors or church officials have either let fear or pride guide them or have misunderstood what the *Monitor* is supposed to do. On the other hand, when the church has united behind Mrs. Eddy's idea for the *Monitor* and allowed the paper to tackle the big problems of the world with a deeply healing sense of what it means "to bless all mankind," the *Monitor* has built an excited staff and a dedicated following both inside and outside the church. At those times, the *Monitor* has risen to a level of almost Biblical sublimity.

■ ■ ■

Not surprisingly, the *Monitor* started with a healing. On a summer night in July 1908, Mary Baker Eddy lay in her bed in Chestnut Hill, Massachusetts, stricken with intense pain. She had been under verbal and mental assault for many years for the presumed heresy of her teachings and of the church she had founded. In the eighteen months prior to her illness, two famous publications—the muckraking *McClure's Magazine* and the feisty newspaper owned by Joseph Pulitzer, *The New York World*—had published sensational and absurdly distorted articles about Mrs. Eddy and her church. The articles were full of breathtaking and unproven accusations exemplary of the yellow journalism of the period, and the *World* had even secretly financed a lawsuit against Mrs. Eddy, which had eventually collapsed.

The virulent press attacks were largely over, but Mrs. Eddy—now in her eighty-eighth year—was struggling. She had tried without success for two weeks to heal the undiagnosed illness through prayer, the method of healing she had adopted for herself and her church, and the situation seemed hopeless. Her secretary noted in his diary that she "despaired of living until morning." [5]

All that changed at midnight. A call came into her home from a *Boston Herald* reporter, asking what time Mrs. Eddy had died. The secretary noted that "when this telephone was rec'd it revealed cause of attack & [she] felt much relief." [6] Mrs. Eddy and those around her knew now what they had to address in their prayers: the press-fueled desire, conscious and unconscious, to see her dead.

The incident seemed to crystallize things for Mrs. Eddy. As early as 1883, she had written that she wanted to publish "[a]n organ from the Christian Scientists." [7] By 1896, when she republished the article as part of a book, she had changed "organ" to "newspaper." [8] In the interim, she had created denominational magazines, while the newspaper idea kept maturing. The Christian Science "movement" kept maturing too, spreading beyond the United States by the turn of the century and attracting more and more of the world's attention.

Her followers, known as Christian Scientists, faced the demand to address humanity's problems as well as their own.

Mrs. Eddy had to do something to keep her church going in the right direction. On the morning she recovered from her illness—July 28, 1908—she took the step she reportedly described as the most important since writing her main work, *Science and Health with Key to the Scriptures*: She gave instructions to the Board of Directors of her church to start *The Christian Science Monitor.* [9]

1

Journalism to Heal the Nations

Mary Baker Eddy had been coloring her gray hair for some time in an attempt to mirror the youth and energy she felt inside. Around 1890, for the first time, she began letting her real color show.[1]

It was a sign not that she was surrendering to age but that she had reached a new phase of leadership in the Christian Science church. Now in her late sixties, she was moving beyond her role as a personal leader—an intelligent, deeply religious, determined, and often lonely New England woman who had overcome adversity to start a popular religious movement. The church she had founded and led for the past decade now needed a more mature leader for the future, one who could point her followers away from her personality.

For much of her life, Mrs. Eddy had battled poor health, a lack of formal education, and the persistent roadblocks erected before anyone of her gender and ambition in the nineteenth century. In more recent years, she had met heavy resistance to her idea that the Comforter that Christ Jesus promised had made itself known through Christian Science. She herself had healed many people of sickness, in person and through her writings, and so had many of her followers. But as the last decade of the nineteenth century approached, the challenges to Christian Science were increasing, and her church did not yet have all the tools it needed to survive.

In 1890, she finished a major revision of *Science and Health with Key to the Scriptures*, the book in which the teachings of Christian Science were laid out most clearly. Not personally but through *Science and Health* and other writings she would guide her followers, helping them to understand Christ Jesus' teachings and showing them how to put the teachings into practice by performing the healing works that Jesus did. Through this healing power of Christ, she explained, they would establish and spread Christian Science to the "millions of unprejudiced minds" [2] that she felt were looking desperately for hope.

The founding of *The Christian Science Monitor* was still seventeen years away, but she was preparing the ground not only through *Science and Health* and other writings but also through a major reorganization of the church, the development of church magazines, the nurturing of Christian Science healers and teachers in the United States and abroad, and the steady address of the world's problems through both church avenues and her own articles in secular publications. She didn't need to color her hair to prove that the church had a Leader for the ages.

A tough and gentle faith

Born into a devoutly Congregational family in the small town of Bow, New Hampshire, in 1821, Mary Baker found herself caught in the theological conflict between the loving religious sense of her mother and the stern Calvinist convictions of her father. The faith she developed had elements of each.

When she turned twelve years old and it came time to be admitted to her family's church, she wrestled with the requisite affirmation of the doctrine of predestination. How could she consent to be saved when it meant her brothers and sisters, who had not professed any interest in religion, would be damned? In her desperation, she fell into a fever. As she related the incident later:

> *My mother, as she bathed my burning temples,*
> *bade me lean on God's love, which would give me rest,*
> *if I went to Him in prayer, as I was wont to do, seeking*
> *His guidance. I prayed; and a soft glow of ineffable joy*

came over me. The fever was gone, and I rose and dressed myself, in a normal condition of health. . . . [T]he "horrible decree" of predestination—as John Calvin rightly called his own tenet—forever lost its power over me. [3]

When it came time for her examination for church membership, she boldly told the minister that she "was willing to trust God, and take my chance of spiritual safety with my brothers and sisters, . . ." [4] Her stand was so sincere that he relented and took her in, she said, "and my protest along with me." [5]

The positive response to her integrity gave her confidence and lifted her sights; she was determined to learn as much as possible about the world. Her formal education extended only to high school, common for girls in rural New England at the time, and most of her school years were only partial because of persistent illness. She read widely, however, and she developed a special interest in public affairs. The local newspaper, the *New Hampshire Patriot and State Gazette*, was constant reading material and discussion fodder in the Baker home.

Her father was active in local government, serving at times as county coroner, surveyor of roads, justice of the peace, selectman, and member of the school board. Her older brother Albert studied law with the future President Pierce and, in 1839, was elected to the New Hampshire state legislature.

Albert, to whom Mary was close, represented hope for her that someday she also might play an important role in the world beyond small-town New Hampshire. He tutored her when he was home, and he helped train her in writing. His public life also showed her what a prominent role in the world might cost. Before he was elected to the legislature, Albert developed a powerful enemy in the person of Isaac Hill, former editor of the *New Hampshire Patriot*, who obtained a charter to build a railroad to Concord, New Hampshire, near Bow. Albert defended the rights of the farmers across whose land the tracks would run, and Hill attacked Albert mercilessly in the pages of his new paper, *Hill's Patriot*. Even after Albert died, in 1841, at age thirty-one, breaking Mary's heart, Hill did not let up.

Mary figured her mission was to be a writer. When she was sixteen years old, she wrote in a poem that she longed to "people earth with visions of my own," [6] but she was also aware of the moral demands that this longing placed on her. In another poem, she asked to be free "From vanity, folly, and all that is wrong—With ambition that binds us to earth." [7]

After her first marriage, in 1843, to George Washington Glover, a builder from Charleston, South Carolina, she moved to the South, where her perspective and opportunities broadened. As Mary Baker Glover, she contributed theater reviews as well as poems and other material to newspapers in Charleston and Wilmington, North Carolina, where she and her husband lived for short periods. When he died, in less than a year from yellow fever, she dived briefly into the 1844 political campaign on behalf of the Democratic Party, at one point sending a political jingle to the newspapers and at another writing toasts for a party dinner.

After moving back to New Hampshire later the same year, seven months pregnant, she taught school and continued her budding writing career, publishing an elegy to Andrew Jackson in the *New Hampshire Patriot* and poems in the *Concord Monitor* about American glory in the Mexican-American War. Over the next twenty years, she sustained a modest living, publishing pieces on both personal topics and public affairs, trying to blend Christian ideas with secular themes. In the fall of 1863, she began writing a regular column for *The Portland Daily Press* on issues ranging from the Civil War to the harmfulness of slander. Her health, however, was a constant thorn. When the editor of *The Independent* asked her to write for his publication, she declined, pleading continued illness.

She was also realizing that what she was publishing was never going to rise far enough above conventional writing to fire people's hearts and hopes the way she had wanted to. Her style was gentle and sincere, but it showed little individuality or deep thought. She was writing what editors would pay for. She hadn't yet put off the fears and ambitions that "[bound her] to earth" and kept her from embracing more original ideas.

Meanwhile, her poor health caused her to experiment with alternative methods of healing. Nothing worked for long, and her search reached a crisis in the winter of 1866. Falling on a patch of ice in Lynn, Massachusetts, she was carried nearly unconscious to a nearby house, then to her home in Swampscott. She lay incapacitated for several days with severe internal injuries until, in desperation, she turned to the Bible and a story of one of Jesus' healings. Contemplating its meaning, she was quickly healed.

The incident proved a turning point in her life. She started a period of deep Bible study to learn what had cured her, eventually calling it the Science of Christianity, or Christian Science. She began teaching classes and healing others through prayer, and she eventually formed a church. (She also married Asa Gilbert Eddy, in 1877, taking his name.) Christian Science, not writing, became her principal calling, and ironically, her writing became clearer and stronger. She came to believe that her mission to establish Christian Science in the world was God-given. "As Mary Baker Eddy I am the weakest of mortals," she would later tell one of her followers, "but as the Discoverer and Founder of Christian Science I am the bone and sinew of the world." [8]

This is the Leader she wanted her followers, then and in the future, to see. In 1891, she published her autobiography, *Retrospection and Introspection*, in which she laid out her vision of where the Christian Science movement was headed and what it would take to get there:

> *I am persuaded that only by the modesty and distinguishing affection illustrated in Jesus' career, can Christian Scientists aid the establishment of Christ's kingdom on the earth. In the first century of the Christian era Jesus' teachings bore much fruit, and the*

Father was glorified therein. In this period and the forthcoming centuries, watered by dews of divine Science, this "tree of life" will blossom into greater freedom, and its leaves will be "for the healing of the nations." [9]

To live daily the qualities of Christ was to do much good for oneself and one's neighbors, she had found. But for the teachings of Jesus to fulfill their potential to meet the broader needs of humanity—for there to be an end to disease, an end to war, an end to the fear that paralyzes people and nations—the Christly qualities had to be exercised in healing, as she believed Jesus showed they could be. That healing had to address not only personal illness but also the larger problems of society, including the deepest sins of humanity. Such a broad healing and redeeming mission involved collective as well as individual effort.

The Church of Christ, Scientist—Mrs. Eddy's church— had much to accomplish.

Publishing and healing

Eight years before her autobiography came out, in 1883, Mrs. Eddy had started *The Christian Science Journal* as "an independent family paper, to promote health and morals," (the subtitle of the early *Journals*) serving initially as its principal writer as well as editor. She focused its contents primarily on individual concerns of sickness and sin, and she indicated in an editorial in the first issue what she had learned so far, that what needed to be addressed was not physical but mental:

After looking over the newspapers of the day, very naturally comes the reflection that it is dangerous to live, so loaded seems the very air with disease. These descriptions carry fears to many minds, to be depicted in some future time upon the body. This error we shall be able in a great measure to counteract, for at the price we issue our paper we shall be able to reach many homes. A great work has already been done, and a great work yet remains to be done. [10]

Mrs. Eddy made it clear that the role of all publishing in her church was to support spiritual healing. As one of her associate editors put it, every publication, including, eventually, *The Christian Science Monitor*, "was designed to bring life to all; to enter into the history of each individual, to rehabilitate his experience, and to shape his destiny." [11] Writing and other means of human communication, she believed, were "temporal" ways to establish a religion. Doing it through spiritual healing was permanent.[12] Even her own writings, she believed, would not have their force were they not backed by her own healing work.

This was not to say that skillful writing was irrelevant. Mrs. Eddy made clear, in a letter to one editor, what kind of content she expected from the publications of her church:

> *Our periodicals stand for a system to be established and a Science to be demonstrated. They are not to amuse or to entertain so much as to instruct the public. They should contain only what tends to this result . . . We need cultured writers to make the abstract interesting; and sound subjects to make our readers satisfied. . . . Wit and wise repartee are sometimes auxiliaries to this end; and sarcasm blent with love may gain a strong point in human thought. Unlettered novices in [Christian Science] are not the writers that we need.* [13]

Healing writing was strong writing—not merely competent but of the highest quality and deepest insight. Mrs. Eddy had no interest in the self-righteousness, doctrinal nitpicking, or shallow pleasantness one might see in some religious publications. Neither did she want her publications to preach in a pushy sense. She once wrote, "Christian Science cannot be carried as anti-slavery and temperance are or have attempted to be. *Agitation* injures our Cause. We should always be . . . Christlike." [14] Her goal was to produce publications of a quality that could stand toe-to-toe with the finest in the world, but with the added benefit that they transformed thinking and led to healing.

Much about Mrs. Eddy's view of Christian Science publishing can be inferred from how she approached it herself. The *Journal* was the only publication she ever took a direct role in producing, serving as editor from its first issue, in April 1883, to August 1884.

There is an audacity of tone in these early issues of the magazine, which disappeared quickly when she left the editorship. Her confidence in her message was never far from the surface, as if she were saying, "These are things you may not understand, but you should, and you eventually will." Her aim was clearly to help people grasp and practice Christian Science for themselves as well as on behalf of those who came to them for healing.

In her selection of content, Mrs. Eddy chose a mixture of essays, poetry, experiences, supporting quotes, occasional news items, and even humor. She once said that Truth "entertains" as well as elevates and invigorates mind and body,[15] and the *Journal*'s humor always had a point—usually, the haplessness of conventional medicine:

> *"Ah!" said the pastor, "your father is dead, then: did he have a doctor?"*
> *"No sir," said the boy; "he died himself."* [16]

Everything in the *Journal* under Mrs. Eddy worked toward a single purpose—to reduce readers' fear of matter and improve their understanding of what it means to live a moral life and demonstrate Christian Science. Showing her unconventional concept of religion, there were no stories of ordinary people saying or doing good things to make life a little more pleasant. Mrs. Eddy had no illusions that mere pleasantness was the goal of Christianity. Human life was a process of putting off the flesh, she believed, and everything in the *Journal* was intended to forward this result. The point was to help people grow out of the limitations of matter, not to be more comfortable in them; not to think more positively but to think more critically.

The most cogent arguments and sharpest vision came from Mrs. Eddy herself. Her articles, poems, sermons, and instruction, one or more of which appeared in every issue during this time, burned with moral fire. She was determined to expose evil as powerless—a foundational point of Christian Science and something she believed humanity would eventually accept.

Mrs. Eddy was always trying to take her readers to a less encumbered view of themselves and the world. In the second issue, she reprinted one of her sermons, "The People's God: Its Effect on Health and Christianity":

> *Proportionately as the people's belief of God, in every age, has dematerialized and impersonalized has their Deity become good: no longer a personal tyrant or a molten image, but the divine and spiritual model of eternal Life, Truth, and Love, . . . This more perfect Deity, held constantly before the people's mind, must have a benign and elevating influence upon the character of nations as well as individuals, . . .*[17]

The distinctiveness of her writing and of the issues of the *Journal* during her editorship came not so much from verbal skill, topical knowledge, or varied content, although all were present in some degree. It came from uncovering strains of thought she felt others did not see, along with the marshaling of facts to counter them. She addressed the continuum of issues from the personal to those of organizations, nations, empires, systems, "the race," and "the people." Her writing was always shaped by the conviction that thought influences action at every level, divine thought being the most powerful of all. In fact,

God to her was the only real Mind. Again and again, she made the point that humanity progresses only as individuals put off material-mindedness and become more moral and spiritual, moving closer to the divine reality of man as God's idea.

As the *Journal* moved into 1884, its circulation grew, and Mrs. Eddy decided it was time to develop other talent. She needed an editor to take over who could combine a mature understanding of Christian Science, and of her, with a clarity of thought that could communicate the scope of the religion. The public often knew little about Christian Science and was sometimes confused by people who had left the church to teach their own versions of Mrs. Eddy's ideas. Her next editor should be someone who was humble enough not to push personal opinions and ambitions.

He or she also had to feel the same sense of urgency about healing as did Mrs. Eddy. This quality wasn't easy to find. She wrote to one of her household workers, ". . . I mourn over the ease of Christian Scientists, . . ." [18] Cherishing the peace and joy that often came with Christian Science was understandable, but that wasn't enough, especially in those who took leading roles in the church.

Finding the right editor became a process of trial and error for Mrs. Eddy. Soon after she installed her first choice, Emma Hopkins, the tone of the magazine turned from audacious confidence to insecurity and pugnaciousness. The content became more insular, airing members' dirty laundry and lashing out at critics. Mrs. Eddy had tried to appeal to a higher state in her readers, lifting them up. Hopkins's *Journal* was feisty, but it lost the tone of quiet, spiritual authority.

Hopkins was gone in a little over a year. After retaking the reins briefly, Mrs. Eddy hired a former clergyman as editor, then another, then returned to the first. She had hopes that the men could bring more intellectual energy to the *Journal* and find new ways to convey the radical insight of Mrs. Eddy's teachings. They had studied with Mrs. Eddy and admired her, and they were good writers. But there was a problem: They did not consistently practice the healing that was the essential proof of the religion. To them, Christian Science was more of an intellectual fascination than a transformative theology, and they clashed with her over what they felt was their superior understanding of Christian doctrine.

Having concluded that she couldn't find her ideal editor among outsiders, she then turned to a man who was loyal to a fault. It turned out, however, that he idolized Mrs. Eddy, a sure sign that he did not understand her or Christian Science.

The whole process of overseeing flawed editors drained Mrs. Eddy's time and attention. No one was stepping up to help her. She could have jumped back into the fray again herself, at least till the ship was righted, but instead, she did the opposite. Believing that a main reason her editors had not been able to come up to her standards was that they had depended too much on her, she gave notice in 1890 that she should no longer be consulted as to what should be published in the periodicals. "My students must learn sooner or later to guard themselves," she wrote to a follower, "to watch and not be misled." [19]

Her new approach didn't make finding a good editor any easier. In 1892, she hired a charming Christian Scientist named Julia Field-King, but a magnetic personality is rarely helpful in Christian Science publishing or healing, and Field-King lasted only five months.

Finally, Mrs. Eddy settled on Septimus J. Hanna. Known as Judge Hanna, because as a young man he had worked for a brief time as a judge in Iowa, he had pursued a law career in Colorado before finding Christian Science. His approach to the religion was clear and logical, and much of his writing had the flavor of a carefully reasoned judicial opinion. It radiated intelligence without being demeaning or flying off into esoteric subjects. She asked him and his wife to come to Boston and work for her, Hanna as editor and his wife as associate editor.

The couple quickly became aware of the built-in tensions in their new positions. In a letter that shows, at least in part, why her previous editors could not keep their jobs, Mrs. Eddy wrote the Hannas a few months after they arrived in Boston, "The personal Mrs. Eddy is pliant as wax, the impersonal impregnable to wind and wave." [20] It took an extraordinary understanding of Mrs. Eddy as both a woman and as the Discoverer and Founder of Christian Science to work successfully for her.

Business and Christian Science publishing

From the initial issue of the *Journal*, Mrs. Eddy welcomed advertising. At first, it was just from professional Christian Science practitioners, or healers. But by 1885, the *Journal* carried ads for everything from a piano company and a glass company to printers, attorneys, and even dentists.

There was no conflict in Mrs. Eddy's mind between practical Christianity and practical business. Business to her was not a distinct discipline, separate from Christian Science, that helped make the religion and its followers more worldly and successful. Business was—or should be—the demonstration of Christian Science itself, applied to the field of enterprise, meeting human needs through practical Christianity. This approach, she felt, would ultimately be more profitable because it would demonstrate God's affluent goodness and love.

Christian Science business had to reflect the deepest spiritual integrity. In 1889, by that time having withdrawn from the day-to-day publishing activity, Mrs. Eddy appointed William G. Nixon, a South Dakota businessman, publisher of the *Journal*. She hired him for his talents and energy, which were considerable, but she was wary of what she called his "worldly material means." [21] If an approach relied more on human schemes than divine inspiration and failed to recognize the healing character of Christian Science publishing, she believed, it would ultimately fail.

In a talk given between 1889 and 1892, Mrs. Eddy laid out her view of business in the context of her church:

> *Personal combinations, human thought and effort, material ways and means whereby to establish and maintain the Church of Christ are weak, vacillating,*

temporal, subject to divisions, actions, feuds, and all the etcetera *of mortal and material phenomena. . . . What is your model business man—the real Scientist who plants in Mind, God, who sows in Mind and reaps in Mind, or he who begins with political economy, human plans, legal speculations, and ends with them, dust to dust?* [22]

Nixon got off on the wrong foot. When he assumed his new post, he told the *Journal* editor, Julia Field-King, to focus not on content but on circulation, assigning her the task of traveling around the country to raise subscriptions. But numbers in and of themselves never impressed Mrs. Eddy. She wrote Nixon, "If she gets *10000* subscribers for the Jour. it will not change my views. They will be lost again unless the Jour. deserves them."[23] In her opinion, editorial quality determined the success or failure of a Christian Science publication. The business side only existed to make sure the content was financed and spread as widely as possible. And business operations had to reflect the same spiritual and Christian attitude as the content. They were all part of the one, undivided message that Christian Science was sending to the world.

Nixon, although he embraced Christian Science as a personal healing method, never understood what Mrs. Eddy wanted. His idea of a Christian Science publisher was a smart businessman who believed in what Mrs. Eddy was trying to do and could turn a profit from subscriptions and advertising, which she could then use to further her cause. But she needed something more: the deep spiritual integrity that put the demonstration and dissemination of God's word before any personal or business priorities.

Mrs. Eddy's ultimate goal was to spread Christian Science, not just to sell periodicals or books. Spreading Christian Science meant spreading the understanding and practice of it, not just spreading its name and the letter of its teachings. The readers she wanted were those who had the character and deep longing that would open their thought to a new approach to life and religion. These people might at first simply be healed by what they read, but eventually they would take the ideas, digest them, expand them further through study of the Bible and her writings, then make the ideas even more tangible by healing others and bringing practical Christianity to the world.

Reaching these people could be expensive and required smart business thinking, but as with everything else in Christian Science, it was ultimately a demonstration of God's universal love and healing power that would make the church's work successful. Business workers, along with writers and editors, who had a practical understanding of Christian Science were ultimately the ones who could make her plan work.

Toward the end of 1892, Nixon resigned in frustration.

Taking on the news

Notwithstanding Mrs. Eddy's difficulties in finding good editorial and business managers for her publications, the Christian Science movement was growing. Believing the church needed to address more quickly both the distortions of Christian Science that were also growing and the problems of the world that Christian Scientists were too often ignoring, she started *The Christian Science Weekly,* in 1898, renaming it *Christian Science Sentinel* a year later. Mrs. Eddy was not involved in the *Sentinel's* editing or production, but she took a strong interest in the magazine and contributed occasional articles.

The *Sentinel* quickly became a kind of window onto the world for the church. Mixed with denominational reports and articles defending Christian Science were regular columns of world news. The news was included, as the first issue stated, "to keep the busy workers fairly well informed as to the more important facts of general interest." [24]

News coverage was generally reprinted from other sources. The issue of August 2, 1900, for example, gave readers basic facts about a race riot in New Orleans, a new regulation of the Chicago City Council on billboards, a new record for the amount of gold held by the U.S. Treasury, the assassination of

King Humbert of Italy, and the apparent end of a drought in the Midwestern United States. The lead feature for that week, taken from the *Concord Evening Monitor*, described preparations for the 1901 Pan-American Exposition in Buffalo. The coverage was brief and general.

Mrs. Eddy continued trying to lead the way, through her own writing, on how church members should deal with public affairs. She was never neutral about important issues. "I reluctantly foresee great danger threatening our nation," she wrote in 1899, looking ahead to the twentieth century, "imperialism, monopoly, and a lax system of religion. But the spirit of humanity, ethics, and Christianity sown broadcast—all concomitants of Christian Science—is taking strong hold of the public thought throughout our beloved country and in foreign lands, and is tending to counteract the trend of mad ambition." [25]

She made clear, however, that politically, she was nonpartisan. She once told a follower, "Avoid being identified pro or con, in politics. If you do otherwise it will hinder our cause, . . . Give all your attention to the moral and spiritual status of the race. God alone is capable of government; you are not, I am not, . . ." [26]

To Mrs. Eddy, the most powerful means of addressing the problems of humanity were not political or advocatory but metaphysical. Her deepest convictions on issues—the ones she drew from the Bible and pointed to as the basis of prayer and healing practice—come through most clearly in *Science and Health*:

> *One infinite God, good, unifies men and nations; constitutes the brotherhood of man; ends wars; fulfils the Scripture, "Love thy neighbor as thyself;" annihilates pagan and Christian idolatry,—whatever is wrong in social, civil, criminal, political, and religious codes; equalizes the sexes; annuls the curse on man, and leaves nothing that can sin, suffer, be punished or destroyed."* [27]

She wanted her church to get to the point where her followers could prove that God's government is infinite, stretching from the individual to the universal. The "scientific" fact was that, although humanity may seem to be in deep trouble, God's law of Love is always the same, preserving man forever. Ideally, Christian Science publications would help lift people to see that fact and apply it in their personal as well as public thoughts and lives. Turning readers into tougher Christians, active in resisting evil, gentle in compassion, accurate in their understanding of God (even if that understanding was elementary), and as a result, able to heal themselves, others, and the world through prayer, would be a powerful means of bringing hope and healing to the nations.

These readers would be the key to fulfilling the varied purposes of Mrs. Eddy's publications. She praised the "right thinker" who labors "to awake the slumbering capability of man." [28] Later, The Christian Science Publishing House, built to house all Christian Science publications, including, eventually, *The Christian Science Monitor*, had this verse from Psalms carved into its façade: "The Lord gave the word: great was the company of those that published it." [29]

Mrs. Eddy saw it as her job, as long as she was with them, to rouse her followers to the immense mental task of being practicing Christians in a suffering world.

Management by keeping people awake

As the twentieth century dawned, Mrs. Eddy was making few public appearances. But for her editors and other church officials, she was still a strong personal presence. One of her biggest challenges was to keep them alert to the subtle ways in which they might be influenced to act in opposition to the best interests of Christian Science—and, she believed, humanity. "Many sleep who should keep themselves awake and waken the world," she told her church in 1902. [30]

If to most of the world Mrs. Eddy was a kindly, if eccentric, old lady, to her executives she was steely and demanding, although her austerity was apparently tempered with gentleness when needed. One of the Trustees of The Christian Science Publishing Society wrote of her "rebuking mistakes with a clarity which produced not resentment but enlightenment." [31] It was a generous view of her management style. Her meetings, in fact, were not for the faint of heart.

Henry P. Nunn, a former newspaper man who worked for the *Journal* and *Sentinel* under Judge Hanna, once attended a meeting at which Mrs. Eddy was presiding. He was new to the staff and didn't know what to expect. As his wife wrote later, Nunn "was shocked at the rugged, vehement manner in which [Mrs. Eddy] talked to the others." She spoke "in thundering tones of Sinai," telling those in the meeting to rouse themselves, Mrs. Nunn wrote. At one point, a chastised Hanna said it seemed she had given him too much responsibility, and she nearly shouted at him, "Don't you say that to me." She then turned to Nunn "with an absolutely changed expression, one of extreme kindness, even tenderness, [and] remarked: 'This is strong meat for one so young in the fold as you.'" [32]

Mrs. Eddy was well aware that, in the midst of the everyday demands of professional work, it can also be hard to keep growing spiritually and "putting off the flesh." But that's what she expected of workers in her church. "Never absent from your post, never off guard, never ill-humored, never unready to work for God, . . ." is how she once described the effective Christian Scientist. [33]

Mrs. Eddy once asked a church manager to have an address of hers published, telling him that if he allowed a single error to occur in the publication of the discourse, he would lose his position. He managed the task successfully. For her, he noted, "To have in her employ persons who had the willingness, the character, moral strength and general qualifications to do the first time and without repeated trials what her mission required was an absolute necessity . . ." [34]

It's easy to see why some of her editors wilted under the pressure.

Mrs. Eddy ultimately decided that Hanna was not the

long-term editor she needed—he would sometimes panic and make poor decisions—and in June 1902, she removed him from the editorships of both the *Journal* and *Sentinel.* "I must have an advocate," she wrote another executive of the church at the time, "the cause must have an advocate, in those at the head of our publications and not *dodge* when they should fire and not fire when it is unwise." [35]

She replaced Hanna with Chicago attorney Archibald McLellan, implying in a letter to one of her followers that McLellan was "a born editor." [36] McLellan had the worldly experience she needed, the unflappability that Hanna lacked, and the humility to obey but not idolize her. Whether McLellan was tough enough spiritually to help Mrs. Eddy move the church forward was not yet clear, but she felt there was promise. For his part, an exhausted Hanna admitted that he was "fagged out" [37] from the demands.

Managing a growing church, keeping its key people awake, dealing daily with the intense opposition to her and her movement were demanding on Mrs. Eddy. As any leader does, she battled her own weaknesses as well as those of her followers. At one point, when one of her students showed her a portrait that the student had had painted of Mrs. Eddy, the Christian Science Leader commented, "I cannot see why artists always want to make me look so confoundedly pleasant." [38]

To those who couldn't stand the heat, Mrs. Eddy had a mercurial temper. One worker once described her as being "in wild tumult raging with Elizabethan frankness." [39]

Those who stayed, however, spoke of her with profound respect. What Mrs. Eddy demanded, they said, was simply spiritual maturity. She knew that only workers who had mastered their own principal failings could help the church rise above the general level of human institutions and contribute to solving the great problems of humanity. She wanted editors and others who could help spread Christian Science with quiet, commanding, and healing authority.

Challenge and growth

By this time, Christian Science had started to grow in Europe, first in Great Britain, then in Germany, where Christian Scientists were performing dramatic healings. For the German audience, Mrs. Eddy started *Der Herold der Christian Science.*

Her publishing operation had now grown to three magazines (as well as her books), each intended to play a role in acquainting the world with Christian Science: The *Journal,* to record and communicate the deeper metaphysics of Christian Science; the *Sentinel,* to lift readers out of their naiveté and defend the church from those who would distort or oppose its teachings; and the *Herold,* to demonstrate the universal appeal of the religion.

The magazines didn't always reach their ideals. In the same way, however, that consistent success in Christian Science healing was about spiritual growth—constantly getting rid of pride, selfishness, jealousy, and other sinful traits and replacing them with the qualities of Christ—so success in Christian Science publishing was about putting off material limitations. "Every step of progress is a step more spiritual," [40] Mrs. Eddy had written in *The People's Idea of God.*

Such spiritual growth, along with the human progress that inevitably accompanies it, often came through hard experiences. Mrs. Eddy herself now faced one of her deepest challenges. Living by this time in seclusion in New Hampshire, she was writing less for publication and working more on organizational issues, keeping in close touch with church executives. The world, however, intruded. In 1906, Joseph Pulitzer's *New York World* and then *McClure's Magazine,* famous for exposing monopoly abuses at Standard Oil and U.S. Steel, published "exposés" on Christian Science, which said more about the nature of the yellow journalism of the period than about Mrs. Eddy or her church. Typical of the tone was the *World*'s initial headline, in October:

MRS. MARY BAKER G. EDDY DYING:
FOOTMAN AND "DUMMY" CONTROL HER

None of it was true, but it made for sensational reading.

If it were only the articles that were the problem, they could perhaps have been swatted away with aggressive truth-telling. But right behind came a lawsuit charging that Mrs. Eddy had lost control of her church and fortune and was being controlled by others. Former New Hampshire Senator William E. Chandler became lead attorney for the suit and roped in Mrs. Eddy's naïve son, George Glover, who now lived in South Dakota, as the plaintiff, along with Glover's daughter and other relatives. Ironically, one of the people who helped Chandler was William G. Nixon, Mrs. Eddy's former publisher, who was desperate for money and had turned against her.

The suit was, in fact, initiated and financed by the *World* itself, although there is no evidence Pulitzer knew about it. It was not the finest hour for American journalism. The judge appointed a Master of the court to determine Mrs. Eddy's competence, and with his judgment that she was sane and in control of her affairs, the case collapsed.

It has been assumed that this very unpleasant incident finally soured Mrs. Eddy on newspapers and led to the creation of *The Christian Science Monitor,* a little over a year later, as a way to set a better example. But there is no reason to think she suddenly turned into a crusader for good journalism. Her focus was the church, not the press. What this incident told her was not just that the world needed better newspapers but that Christian Scientists needed to be bolder in their involvement with the world. For them to sit back complacently, be good people, and heal just their own problems would never be enough. Not only her editors and publishers but the church as a whole needed to be awakened.

As usual, she had to lead the way. She loved the beauty and tranquility of her New Hampshire estate, but she was tired of battling "the mental force here so benumbed by materiality."[41] In the middle of 1907, she had representatives search out a new residence in Massachusetts. She settled on one in Chestnut Hill, a short drive from Boston, and made the move in January 1908. She was now eighty-six years old.

Two months after moving to Chestnut Hill, Mrs. Eddy received a letter from John L. Wright, a Boston newspaperman and Christian Scientist, who explained what many church workers had been discussing, that it was time to start a daily newspaper run by Christian Scientists. "I am not thinking of a daily official Christian Science paper," he said, "or one containing in its title the words Christian Science, but of a general newspaper owned by Christian Scientists . . . ; so presenting news more as Christian Scientists would like it presented than any newspaper now presents it." [42]

Mrs. Eddy drafted a reply to Wright's letter that was apparently never sent but that indicated her thinking:

> *I have had this newspaper scheme in my thought for quite a while and herein send my name for our daily newspaper*
>
> The Christian Science Monitor
>
> *This title only classifies the Paper and it should have departments for what else is requisite* [43]

At the same time, she drafted another note, this one to *Journal*, *Sentinel*, and *Herald* editor McLellan and her publisher, Allison V. Stewart: "The time has come when we must have a daily paper entitled Christian Science Monitor. Allow no hesitation or delay on this movement. I will loan you all the money I can raise to help do it." [44] This note was also never sent. She was evidently holding back because a new Christian Science Publishing House was being built and needed all the funds that could be raised. But one thing was clear: Despite Wright's suggestion, she was convinced that the paper should have Christian Science in the title.

Then, on July 14, she got sick and was confined to her

bed. After two weeks, her situation appeared desperate. But as often happens in Christian Science healing, she finally had a breakthrough when she saw the problem in mental terms, in this case as an attack on her and her teachings, understood that the omnipotence of God was with her, obliterating even the belief in the problem, and felt her fear and that of those around her dissolve through what she was sure was the power of Christ.

She recovered quickly, and the next morning, she sent a note to the church Directors: "So soon as the Pub. House debt is paid I request the C.S. Board [of] Directors to start a daily newspaper called *Christian Science Monitor*. This must be *done* without fail." [45]

Mrs. Eddy's lifelong desire to "people earth with visions of my own" had gone through a painful transformative process, first in her assertion of theological independence in childhood, then in gentle poetry and prose that got lost in the flood of published journalism, then in her own healing of injury in the fall on the ice, an event that led to her conclusion that healing was the foundational proof of Christianity. She began to heal others, then to teach them how to practice what she had discovered, then wrote a book to reach even more people. It sold phenomenally well.

In order to establish Christian Science in the broader society as well as in the minds of her students, she had started a church and begun publishing magazines. The magazines helped explain the teachings and practice of Christian Science, and they even addressed the news on occasion. But they did not really spread Christian Science beyond the ranks of the faithful. Most of these people were sincere and lived moral lives, but the level of Christian Science demonstration was still immature, and the world at large was still out there, not knowing Christian Science at all, needing, in Mrs. Eddy's view, the knowledge of Christ to escape the miseries of human life. Her followers, she believed, were only dimly aware of the extent of the need.

She could not allow this gulf between Christian Science and the world to stand. In the *Monitor,* Mrs. Eddy was creating a vehicle for her church to learn about and intersect fully with the world. Part of the point was to convey accurate information about humanity's problems, but the larger point was to create a unity of spirit that encircled the globe, spreading the understanding and demonstration of God's government not just to Christian Scientists but to all who were receptive. "The government of divine Love derives its omnipotence from the love it creates in the heart of man; . . ." [46] she had written. The *Monitor* would not explain the letter of Christian Science but demonstrate its spirit. It would capture not just the minds but also the hearts of readers.

Much of the world that knew Christian Science believed that the religion, with its insistence that God does not know evil, was out of touch with reality and had no heart. The *Monitor* would prove them wrong. Other newspapers, the good ones, offered the spirit of sympathy and righteous anger about the world and its problems. The *Monitor* would add the spirit of hope and healing. Readers didn't need to know anything about the religion. They just needed to be open to another way of looking at things—more gentle, more perceptive, less emotional, less impressed with the fireworks of the world, and more dedicated to reform, not of systems but of thought.

For Mrs. Eddy, "the healing of the nations" could now begin in earnest.

2

Thunder and Lightning

Reverend William P. McKenzie closed the door behind him and stepped into the 4 A.M. darkness.

He and his wife, Daisette, dedicated Christian Scientists, had been spending their summer vacation at a friend's farm in Dublin, New Hampshire. The welcome respite from a demanding life in Boston had come abruptly to an end, however, when McKenzie received a telegram asking him to attend an urgent meeting of the Board of Trustees of The Christian Science Publishing Society, of which he was a member, the next morning. He had no idea what the meeting was about, but he knew he had to be there. It was August 10, 1908.

Crossing the property, McKenzie found the dirt path that headed north toward East Harrisville and began walking. A train would be passing the station three miles away before long, and he was determined to be on it.

The former Presbyterian minister loved the predawn hours. Long ago, he had become used to praying when the world around was asleep. He had once written the following lines, in a poem called "A Song of the Dawning":

> *Even now the light-spires dazzle and the note of Hope is heard,*
> *Man is learning God's new language, building letters to a word;* . . . [1]

As a boy in Ontario, Canada, he had wrestled with the doctrine of Presbyterianism as Mrs. Eddy had with

Congregationalism, wondering how to reconcile hope with the terrors of a cruel God. His father was a minister, and though the elder McKenzie died early, William's mother fully expected her son to follow a career in the church. She didn't know how desperately he was searching for an alternative.

After graduating from Toronto University, in 1884, he spent a year in Saskatchewan, covering the Northwest Rebellion as a reporter for the Toronto *Daily Mail*, then returned to Toronto to study theology in preparation for a career in the ministry. The church elders, however, saw not a smart and questioning young man but a potential renegade, and they denied him a church of his own. He was not unhappy with the verdict, as he was growing in his discontent with Presbyterian theology, but his mother was beside herself.

The church elders finally agreed to give him a small and theologically liberal congregation in Avon, New York. But constant guilt over his mother's disappointment finally led to a nervous breakdown, and he entered a sanatorium in Dansville, New York, for treatment. Lying on a couch on the roof one night, fighting his anguish, it came to him that God is Love.[2]

In a short time, he was back in his parish. Nothing had been resolved about his career, but he was at peace. Out of curiosity, he attended a talk one day on Christian Science and afterwards sat with the speaker, Daisette Stocking, for four hours discussing the religion. He began travelling to Toronto on Sundays, after preaching in his own church, to hear Stocking preach at the Christian Science church there.

Meanwhile, he started writing for *The Christian Science Journal*, and Mrs. Eddy became interested in one of his poems about the mother-love of God:

> *Gently hath a sweet voice spoken:*
> *One thing needful must ye choose;*
> *O ye weary and heart-broken,*
> *Can ye still this call refuse? . . .*
>
> *And that love, the one thing needful,*

Bringeth life and conquers death;
Oh, let hearts be still and heedful,
Hearing what the sweet voice saith. [3]

Mrs. Eddy wrote him that he had "touched my heart of hearts,"[4] and she invited him to visit her in her home in New Hampshire on Christmas Day, 1894. He had already told his mother he would come home for Christmas, and he knew what a change in plans—especially this one—would mean.

He agonized over the decision, then chose New Hampshire. His family was angry, but he said later, "I have never had an experience so heavenly; I am her man now forever." [5]

Knowing it would devastate his mother one more time, he finally gave up his pastorate in Avon, in 1895. A number of people in his Avon congregation joined him in leaving the Presbyterian church for Christian Science. Others became openly hostile. One of McKenzie's friends, a lawyer, said, "I hope I shall not finish my career until I have seen one of those Christian Scientists hanged." [6]

McKenzie and Stocking together—by now they were more than just friends—visited Mrs. Eddy the following year. After the visit, they returned to Toronto to find the atmosphere more charged than ever. At one point, McKenzie was reading a newspaper article attacking Christian Science and felt his anger rising. Soon he was physically ill, too weak to call for help. He remembered something Mrs. Eddy had told the couple, that in her initial writing about Christian Science, she had faced so much resistance that she had had to move eight times in eight months, sometimes finding her belongings thrown onto the sidewalk. But she had learned, she said, not to fight back. "A man would have been more apt to resist," she told the couple, "and to resist would have been fatal. I had to learn the lesson of the grass. When the wind blew, I bowed before it, and when mortal mind put its heel upon me, I went down and down in humility and waited,—waited until it took its heel off, and then I rose up." [7]

"I immediately repented of my anger and indignation," McKenzie said later, "and asked the divine Presence to forgive and heal. A beautiful relief came to me, and very soon I was myself again. I believe that if I had remained in that state of resistance and resentment for a short time longer, I would not be here to tell you this." [8]

In 1896, Mrs. Eddy asked McKenzie to come to Boston to work at the church, and his self-purification continued. He wrote Mrs. Eddy at one point:

> *I have learned how my whole human mentality with its poetic idealism, aesthetic love, hero worship, pride of seeing hidden things, glory in mental power, has been a subtle spiritualizing of matter—a putting of divine wisdom into human mind. The uncovering was terrible & for a time I seemed to lose my consciousness of Good. Then the intricacies of personality have been revealed as never before & after a long agony I seem to find myself alone with God. I never had any idea before what was unconsciously in mind ...* [9]

Mrs. Eddy called what McKenzie had been through spiritual growth, and she expected it of her followers. She had gone through it herself, and she knew it would not only make him a better healer but would give him the strength to help her guide the Christian Science movement.

The same year she asked William and Daisette, who were now engaged to be married, to come see her again in New Hampshire. As they concluded their conversation, she told the gentle young couple:

> *There is an etiquette in a soft voice, but I want my students to speak out. Do not recede before error. Ask God to guide you. Say, 'Take my hand.' Do not be afraid. God always keeps His promise. Spiritualize your thought.* [10]

She wanted courageous workers, who could see beyond the material view of things. In 1898, she appointed McKenzie a Trustee of The Christian Science Publishing Society, and he helped start the *Sentinel*. Soon thereafter a disaffected student sued Mrs. Eddy for libel, and the case threatened to pull the whole church down. McKenzie became part of a group of followers who prayed around the clock, and he set his alarm for 4 A.M. every day to do his shift. He was no stranger to the early morning hours.

"Let there be no delay."

The first rays of the sun began filtering through the maples and birches as McKenzie crossed Nubanusit Brook. He could see the East Harrisville station now. He quickened his pace, and soon he heard the train in the distance. Reaching the platform in time, he signaled the engineer, who brought the steaming engine to a halt. McKenzie climbed aboard.

In the decade and a half since learning of Christian Science, his concept of God's love had grown. It included as much a faithful fatherhood as a gentle motherhood. He had written a poem that had been turned into a church hymn and began:

> *Trust the Eternal when the shadows gather,*
> *When joys of daylight seem so like a dream;*
> *God the unchanging pities like a father;*
> *Trust on and wait, the daystar yet shall appear.* [11]

The deep prayer and conviction that God was giving him strength were now making him useful for Mrs. Eddy's publishing operation. She needed basic skills in her workers, and McKenzie had the writing and journalistic experience to at least understand the professional needs of publishing. But she needed more than skills. She also needed spiritual strength, and McKenzie had progressed to the point where he could put his spiritual understanding into practice and help neutralize the opposition that was biting at Mrs. Eddy's heels. He could assist her in raising the church and its publishing beyond religious passion to spiritual communication, where both he and she believed that God spoke directly to His children.

By 10:30 A.M., McKenzie arrived in Boston and went straight to the conference room in the Publishing Society. There he greeted fellow Trustees Clifford P. Smith, a former lawyer and judge from Iowa, and Thomas W. Hatten, a Christian Science practitioner from Kansas. Also at the table sat Archibald McLellan, now chairman of The Christian Science Board of Directors as well as editor of the *Journal, Sentinel,* and *Herald.* [12]

The two boards were integral to the church's management. In 1898, Mrs. Eddy had created the Board of Trustees in a Deed of Trust "for the purpose of more effectually promoting and extending the religion of Christian Science . . ." [13] They now managed all property of the Publishing Society "exclusively for the purpose of carrying on the business, which has been heretofore conducted by the said Christian Science Publishing Society, in promoting the interests of Christian Science; . . ." They were to conduct the business "energetically and judiciously . . . on a strictly Christian basis, . . ." [14]

The financial demands on the Trustees were clear: They should "keep accurate books," and "[o]nce in every six months the trustees shall account for and pay over to the treasurer of 'The First Church of Christ, Scientist, in Boston, Mass.,' the entire net profits of said business." [15] They should incur no liabilities that they could not liquidate promptly from current revenue. They also had to be loyal Christian Scientists.

McKenzie and the other Trustees soon discovered why they had been called in. McLellan read them a letter from Mrs. Eddy that had been sent three days before:

Beloved Students:

> *It is my request that you start a daily newspaper at once, and call it the Christian Science Monitor. Let*

there be no delay. The Cause demands that it be issued now.

> *You may consult with the Board of Directors, I have notified them of my intention.* [16]

The meeting soon adjourned. There was much to digest. The next morning, the two boards met again, agreeing that the Trustees would manage the start-up of the paper, while the Directors would provide the location for publishing it. The ultimate authority for any decisions would rest with the Directors.

Everyone knew from experience that the *Monitor* would have to be more than just a newspaper, just as the church itself was more than just an organization. Mrs. Eddy had given "church" a dynamic definition in *Science and Health*, reflecting what she felt was the meaning Jesus had given it:

> *The Church is that institution, which affords proof of its utility and is found elevating the race, rousing the dormant understanding from material beliefs to the apprehension of spiritual ideas and the demonstration of divine Science, thereby casting out devils, or error, and healing the sick.* [17]

The closest any of the Trustees had come to newspaper work was McKenzie's stint as a reporter in Saskatchewan. None of them had started a business. Yet they knew the publication had to be financially successful from the start, with no encumbering debt, as the Directors depended on the Publishing Society to help finance the church. There was no provision for deficit financing from church funds.

After the meeting with the Directors, the Trustees sent a letter to Mrs. Eddy that put on a brave face:

> *Beloved Leader:*
>
> *Your letter of August 8th was delivered to us yesterday. The announcement contained in your letter is*

good news. We are confident that this move is timely; that the Monitor will be a mighty instrument for the promotion of Christian Science; and that it will be a success from a business standpoint. We rejoice to have this additional opportunity of assisting you in your plans for the welfare of humanity. [18]

The task was huge. The new Publishing House, just completed, was too small for a newspaper operation and had to be extended. This meant demolishing a block of three-story apartment buildings and relocating the tenants, some of whom were away on summer vacation. Printing machinery and other equipment had to be ordered and installed. A staff had to be assembled to operate not only news gathering and editing but also advertising, circulation, accounting, and other elements of the news business.

The Directors had asked Mrs. Eddy for more complete guidance as to what kind of paper she wanted, but in keeping with her conviction that leaving her workers free to pray and get inspiration directly from God was best for everyone, she declined to give suggestions.

But that didn't mean she wasn't engaged. On August 12, just two days after the Trustees had first heard about the project, but more than two weeks since she had informed the Directors of her plans, Adam Dickey, her secretary, wrote a note to McLellan with a clear tone of urgency:

Mr. Frye [Mrs. Eddy's secretary] has suggested that you prepare a fully printed sample newspaper such as you expect the Monitor to be, and present it to our Leader in order that she may have an intelligent idea of what you propose to do. She has been expressing a great deal of anxiety about the outcome of your efforts, and is somewhat impatient at the seeming delay. [19]

McKenzie noted years later that Mrs. Eddy "expected the newspaper to make its appearance immediately, and it had to be explained how the printing office and presses must be constructed first, and how much machinery must be assembled, and how many men recruited." [20]

It is doubtful that her ignorance of the newspaper business was the sole, or even the main, reason for her impatience. Urgency, for her, was not so much in terms of time as in terms of spiritual alertness. The idea for a Christian Science newspaper was popular in the church, but she knew that her concept of the *Monitor* went beyond most people's conception and would be opposed in subtle ways. She needed managers who were alert to the opposition, which might influence them to delay things, and who could meet the opposition in mental terms. This, she believed, would determine the business and journalistic outcome. Again, she was managing by keeping people awake, urging her executives not to let their mental guards slip.

She finally agreed to a delay—it would take ninety days alone for the printing equipment to be delivered—but she encouraged the Directors and Trustees to start the paper as soon as possible.

Her officials charged ahead. Nothing was too grand for their Leader and Christian Science, and they were determined to produce a fully formed major newspaper on the first day. On August 13, they detailed for Mrs. Eddy the expected start-up costs, about $300,000, showing clear concern whether the church could afford the new enterprise as they envisioned it:

> *The revenue from the Publishing Society paid to the Church has been about $90,000 a year. If we were to expend as much as that in one year on this enterprise we would have nothing for the Mother Church which now depends somewhat upon this revenue. We have no larger fund to draw upon if we are to keep the business in the proper state of solvency. Nevertheless we know the newspaper can be financed, since you see it to be the right time for the enterprise.* [21]

Again, Mrs. Eddy could not restrain her concern. Dickey wrote back:

Dear Brethren: -

Your letter of the 13th instant addressed to Mrs. Eddy comprising the report of your plans for starting a Christian Science daily paper is at hand. After reading this report our Leader expressed surprise at the amount of capital that would be required. Her original thought on the subject was, that you should proceed to get out a small paper of about eight pages and with a circulation of about fifty or sixty thousand copies, at a much less outlay than the amount stated in your letter. Her intention was not to branch out at once into metropolitan greatness, but rather to begin in a comparatively small way and grow into bigger things with the progress of time.

That said, she backed off again:

However, she does not wish to hamper your movements by placing restrictions on the amount you shall spend, but wishes you to go ahead with wisdom and economy as your guide. [22]

As with the issue of time needed to launch the enterprise, her concern was not only with the size and cost of the paper. It was also whether the church had the mental and spiritual resources to make a success of it. To be heroic is one thing; to be wise, another. One could be confident in God's unlimited goodness and yet also be wise in scaling the expression of that goodness to the demonstration of Christian Science that had so far been achieved. There was major risk in making a large claim on the faith of the church and the public without the accompanying proof. The modesty Mrs. Eddy urged was not a modesty of spiritual ambition but of human ambition.

The Trustees seemed to learn somewhat from her admonition. They wrote her back and outlined their vision, which was now closer to Mrs. Eddy's:

> *Beloved Leader: Your communication written by Mr. Dickey under date of yesterday is before us. We are planning an eight-page afternoon or evening paper, and expect to start it with a circulation of 50,000 copies, and to do this without unnecessary expense and without delay.* [23]

The tension between humility and ambition would play itself out again and again for the *Monitor* and the church in the coming decades. At this point, there was only so much Mrs. Eddy could do.

A fine pleasure

There were obstacles. The composing room equipment, including type, cabinets, makeup tables, and other items that had been ordered from a company in New Jersey, sank to the bottom of Long Island Sound when the ship they were on collided with another one. The company, however, quickly reshipped the order. Western Union informed the *Monitor* that it could not provide the wire service it had promised, as telegraph lines stopped a block and a half short of the Publishing House and couldn't be extended in time. The church reached out to Colonel Robert Clowry, president of Western Union, who happened to be interested in Christian Science. He told his staff to make sure the *Monitor* got what it needed, and it did.

Perhaps the biggest obstacle to Mrs. Eddy's vision, as often happened, came from within the church. McLellan, managing editor Alexander Dodds, and others were insistent that the words "Christian Science" be removed from the title of the paper. They believed that identifying the paper with the church would keep it from being accepted by outsiders. At one point, McLellan and others secured a meeting with Mrs. Eddy where they made their case. In a few moments, the editor emerged and said, "Mrs. Eddy is firm, and her answer is, 'God gave me this name and it remains.'" [24]

Mrs. Eddy wanted a name, editorial writer John Flinn said later,

> *. . . which would leave no doubt regarding the exact identity of the newspaper which she was engaged in founding. . . .*
>
> *. . . [S]he was understood to be immovable in the position that to evade or to attempt to evade the issue would not only be unwise but unscientific; that here as at all times, and in every particular, the Truth must be expressed and adhered to. The impression that we all received of Mrs. Eddy's attitude toward the name of the newspaper was: That since the Monitor was to represent Christian Science in journalism, the only thing, because the right thing to do, was to stamp it at once with its proper designation.* [25]

McLellan accepted Mrs. Eddy's verdict, but whether he understood completely why she insisted on the name is open to question. In an editorial in the October 17, 1908, *Sentinel*, he explained his concept of the new paper:

> *It will be the mission of the* Monitor *to publish the real news of the world in a clean, wholesome manner, devoid of the sensational methods employed by so many newspapers. There will be no exploitation or illustration of vice and crime, but the aim of the editors will be to issue a paper which will be welcomed in every home where purity and refinement are cherished ideals.*[26]

Unusual and welcome though it may have been, a newspaper whose main purpose was to be "clean" would hardly justify the importance Mrs. Eddy placed on the *Monitor*. The

Boston Herald expressed the skepticism of many at the idea that a merely sanitized newspaper would be a hit: "Good luck to the coming Christian Science newspaper. Starting a daily paper is an enterprise that usually tests the courage and resources of the bravest and most resourceful souls. The graveyards are full of their remains." [27] A writer at the New York *Herald* mocked, "Readers afflicted with heart trouble may open up the newspaper with absolute safety." [28]

The next issue of the *Sentinel*, October 24, carried an article from McKenzie called "Newspaper Possibilities." It took a more perceptive stand on what the *Monitor* represented:

> *When some man has made the ideal practical, the news thereof may well be made known universally, for in emulation there is a fine pleasure; also the story of successful goodness enables ten thousand strugglers to "pluck up their courage." It makes them work with hope. There seems to be therefore a great field for a paper devoted to exploitation of positive goodness, usefulness, and success, one which will not consider the abnormal to be news, but which will minister to man's legitimate interest in "the good that men do."* [29]

Whereas McLellan praised the lack of the "exploitation or illustration of vice and crime" in the coming *Monitor*, McKenzie discussed the paper's power to spread practical ideals. One approach was passive. It supported, however unintentionally, the idea that has bedeviled Christian Science since its founding: that Christian Scientists simply ignore evil. The other approach was active. It was based on the idea that Christian Science and every element of its church exist for one purpose: to forward the demonstration of practical Christianity. The main purpose of this newspaper was not to satisfy curiosity or spread mere knowledge, but it was also not to help people avoid the dark alleys of human life. The purpose was to inspire people to greater heights of healing and thereby build humanity's hope.

The lightest of all days

By mid-November, the staff was in place. Dodds, who, with McLellan's responsibilities as a Director and editor of the *Journal, Sentinel,* and *Herald,* had become the newsroom leader, explained to them his concept of the *Monitor*'s approach to journalism. As Erwin Canham, a later editor, related, "Mr. Dodds told them they were to turn traditional newspaper practice upside down. That is to say, instead of emphasizing sensation, passion, conflict, and disorder they were to record the important and constructive developments in the news, whether local, national, or worldwide." [30]

The staff was enthusiastic, if a bit smug. Paul Deland, a young staff member, said later that "it wasn't long before we found that we were not turning things upside down. We were turning things right side up." He wrote:

> *We were instructed to devote our efforts to making as interesting as possible all events of intrinsic merit and permanent value. This was a relief and satisfaction to a newspaper man who had previously been required to glorify out of all proportion the transient and inconsequential happenings that, as has been aptly said, were to be 'ashes' the next day . . . Each story was discussed, and while the general form was that of the regular newspaper, what a difference in the substance and treatment!* [31]

Meanwhile, subscriptions were coming in, and it seemed that the "clean" *Monitor* had an eager audience. A woman in Nebraska wrote:

> *. . . I have prayed for years that God would send us a good clean daily newspaper. Oh! What a comfort it will be to sit down midst our children or friends and read a newspaper that is not filled with flourishing headlines, depicting vice, crime, disaster, and death, magnifying*

evil and minimizing good. God bless the 'Monitor.' [32]

On November 23, two days before the first issue, McLellan sent Mrs. Eddy a trial copy of *Christian Science Monitor*. She wrote back through Dickey, insisting that *"The"* be included in the name,[33] but otherwise expressing satisfaction with the appearance of the paper. She directed that an article on Christian Science be included in every issue,[34] a clear indication that the paper had a religious purpose, even though it was a "real" newspaper.

Rather than an island of religion in a secular sea, this article on Christian Science, which continues today as "A Christian Science Perspective," was a window into the thought behind the paper, an introduction to the way of approaching the world that Christian Science represented. In some sense the article would be the central feature of the paper and, ideally, make everything else in the paper clearer. It would be a key to seeing the news as Christian Science saw it, as an opportunity for healing, and it would marshal ideas for readers that would help make that healing possible.

When Archibald McLellan and Alexander Dodds delivered the first issue to Mrs. Eddy, at her office, on November 25, according to Daisette Stocking McKenzie, "she came forward with both hands extended and received the paper and clasped it to her heart. They reported that the scene was most moving. Her great hope which she had cherished so long had at last found expression." [35]

Later, Mrs. Eddy assembled her household staff. Almost as if she expected it—her accomplishments had never come without significant resistance—she asked if the day was dark. Someone replied that "a heavy fog makes it darker than usual." Mrs. Eddy, who could see for herself the gloom outside the window, was always looking to contrast what the senses said to what she believed God wanted and saw. She replied: "This, in truth, is the lightest day of all days. This is the day when our daily paper goes forth to lighten mankind. . . !" [36]

What she saw was the paper's potential. The actual

product before her that morning wasn't necessarily her ideal. In fact, the news in that first issue of the *Monitor* reflected more the attitude of positive thinking that seemed to predominate in those putting the paper together than it did actual Christian Science.

Don't worry

The editors featured good news on their first front page. They de-emphasized bad news or presented it in a way that made it seem under control or at least safely detached from the lives of readers.

The lead story was one of local interest:

Construction Work Rapidly Progresses on Great Dam Across the Charles River Basin

Sufficient progress has been made on the Charles river dam to warrant the statement that the work will be in a very satisfactory condition before severe weather compels a partial cessation of work on this enormous piece of construction.

The article went on to show in detail the evidence of progress: "The lower lock house is well along . . ."; the upper house "is nearing completion"; the concrete work "is nearly finished." The lock gates "are the first of this type to be used in America and are notable specimens of engineering skill." [37]

Other lead articles that day covered the refusal of Andrew Carnegie to testify before a Congressional committee (minimizing the obvious conflict between Carnegie and the chairman of the committee), the attempt of a local shoe manufacturer to stop union members from harassing scab workers at his factory, and the attendance of President Roosevelt at a ceremony honoring a Civil War hero.

The rest of the page, in the style of newspapers of the day, was packed with short articles on a variety of topics both local and international. One covered the quelling of an anti-Austrian student protest in Rome. Another reported on the recovery by the City of Boston of illegal profits from the sale of cemetery land to the city. Another noted that a ship survived a storm near Guam. The fact that 37,000 turkeys—a record—had arrived from Cincinnati for Thanksgiving did not escape the notice of *Monitor* editors. About a dozen other items completed the page.

It was a fair summary of some of the day's news from the perspective of a Boston newspaper. And yet, despite the similarity in appearance to other papers, the *Monitor* was clearly different in tone. All stories of suffering had happy endings but one, and that one—a report on the burning of the cruise ship Sardinia, when "many lives . . . were lost" —bore the headline "Sardinia Beached Because of Fire," as if the ship had simply run aground with no further problems. The dominant theme came through clearly in the lead story on the Charles River dam: Don't worry; despite what you may hear and see, mankind is making progress!

It is not fair to assume that the editors were simply shutting their eyes to evil. They knew, from their own practice of Christian Science healing, that evil could be destroyed only by facing it, not by ignoring it. They also knew that making evil into something fearsome was irresponsible and that doing so in a mass circulation publication would only add to the weight of human misery. Their task was huge; they were trying to give a view of human events that would help humanity, not hurt it. They were breaking new ground, with no model and little guidance. It is not surprising that the result on that first day was far from perfect.

And yet, taken as a whole, the news on the first *Monitor*'s front page did not help readers demonstrate God's love for humanity as much as it gave support to the belief that ignoring evil would help destroy it. It was the opposite of Christian Science. There was a long way to go to reach the ideal of *Monitor* news coverage.

The contrast with the *Boston Herald* and *The New York*

Times that day is subtle, but telling about where the *Monitor* stood in relation to the rest of American journalism.

The *Herald*, one of the two major Boston papers in 1908, published twenty-seven articles on the front page of its November 25 issue. Only two of them—"Anti-Austrian Riots" and "Carnegie Likely to Decline"—overlapped with the *Monitor*'s front page.

In coverage of the "riots" in Rome, the *Herald*'s story began:

> *Italians are showing intense resentment against Austria and Austrians, because of the anti-Italian riots which have taken place at Vienna.*

The four-paragraph article ended by noting that the Italian Chamber of Deputies believed "war is inevitable."

The *Monitor* took a different tack. Heading its story "Call Troops to Quell Students," the article's first sentence read:

> *Troops had to be called to aid police in suppressing an anti-Austrian student demonstration this afternoon.*

The *Monitor* focused on the suppression of the incident and called it a demonstration rather than a riot. Peace seemed to be the theme, even if the peace was at the point of a gun and there was little peace under the surface. The *Monitor*'s story also cited the chamber of deputies but noted its demand that Italian foreign minister Tittoni "be openly anti-Austrian." The paper clearly did not want to put in print the belief that war was inevitable, since everything Christian Science stands for says that evils such as war are never inevitable.

Which angle was more helpful to readers, the more observable—but fatalistic—view that war could erupt soon, as it did in a few years, or the more comforting—but misleading— view that war could be controlled by aggressive state power?

The former contributed to a public acceptance that war could not be avoided, hardly a helpful message, but the latter, at best, gave readers a false sense of security that emotions could be bottled up, akin to a Christian Scientist believing that sickness could be healed by quieting fear with a drug.

There was no attempt by either paper to deal with the underlying thoughts of revenge and hatred that were pushing the world toward war.

The New York Times did not address the Austrian incidents on its front page that day. The thrust of its coverage of other major events, however, provided an interesting contrast with both the *Herald* and the *Monitor*.

The *Times* led with a story of the determination of New York Governor Hughes to fight for more independent government in the state, free from the partisan favoritism of political "bosses." "Oh, the hours that are wasted in the discussion of whether a thing will take," he said, "instead of considering the question whether it is right!" [38]

Another major headline shouted, "Three Men Lynched after 'Legal' Trial." Three "negroes" had been accused of killing a deputy sheriff in Tennessee. The reporter noted that the lynching "gained a semblance of legality" when a trial was hastily arranged, and that a man who pleaded with the mob to let the law take its course "met with a long growl of disapproval." [39]

It was a nasty incident, but the *Times* felt it was important for readers to know about it. To give the readers perspective, the article communicated not only the facts of the lynching but also the implied moral views of the reporter.

The tone in this article, and throughout the *Times*' front page that day, is one of reform. Ironically, the paper seemed to cover the mental and moral landscape of the news with more assurance than the *Monitor*, which was the more logical publication to stake out that territory.

Times uncovered evil and took it to task.

The *Monitor* did not uncover it but simply sketched its outlines, trying to minimize the fear of it.

The *Herald* merely told the objective facts without agenda. It gave no regard to how the news influenced readers. It even printed, at the bottom of its front page, a one-paragraph story about a chauffeur who fell from the seat of his taxicab and "was probably fatally injured." It was this kind of irresponsible news coverage, writing about a potential tragedy as if it were inevitable, thus contributing to public fear and fatalism, that so disappointed Christian Scientists and led to their desire for a paper like the *Monitor*.

Deeper purpose

The *Monitor* was trying to be different by doing no harm. It was indeed "clean." But was that what Mrs. Eddy was aiming for? There had been no provision for comment from her in the first issue, but in a letter to McLellan on November 11, she asked him to make space. He did so on the editorial page.

She used, as a jumping-off point, a letter sent to her by a Christian Scientist who was an editor at another paper:

> *Dear Leader—As a newspaper man I thank you for* The Christian Science Monitor *in prospect, and I feel sure that such will be the sentiment of hundreds of newspaper workers all over the land when* The Monitor *in fact shall have demonstrated the feasibility of clean journalism.*
>
> *A definition of "monitor" is, "One who advises," and I foresee that when this* Christian Science Monitor *shall have proved that there is such a thing as newspaper success along non-sensational lines, there will follow a widespread readjustment of news policies, for which I am sure none will be more truly thankful than an army of honest, conscientious toilers in the ranks of newspaperdom.*

Gratefully yours,

Frank Bell
Managing Editor Harrisburg Telegraph [40]

Bell's letter described well how many other readers saw the newspaper at the moment. Mrs. Eddy, however, went further, linking the paper to the religious mission of the church and its entire publishing operation:

> *The gentleman, Mr. Frank Bell, has caught my thunder; therefore he will not object to the lightning which accompanies it.*
>
> *I have given the name to all the Christian Science periodicals. The first was* The Christian Science Journal, *designed to put on record the divine Science of Truth; the second I entitled* Sentinel, *intended to hold guard over Truth, Life and Love; the third,* Der Herold der Christian Science, *to proclaim the universal activity and availability of Truth; the next I named* Monitor, *to spread undivided the Science that operates unspent. The object of* The Monitor *is to injure no man, but to bless all mankind.* [41]

The wording of the *Monitor*'s main purpose was not original with Mrs. Eddy. She had taken it from Alexander Pope's "An Essay on Man":

> *All are but parts of one stupendous whole,*
> *Whose body, Nature is, and God the soul;*
> *That, chang'd thro'all, and yet in all the same,*
> *Great in the earth, as in th'ethereal frame,*
> *Warms in the sun, refreshes in the breeze,*
> *Glows in the stars, and blossoms in the trees,*
> *Lives thro' all life, extends thro' all extent,*
> *Spreads undivided, operates unspent, . . .*

The pantheistic flavor of the passage—the idea that matter is a part of God—was not Christian Science, but as in many other instances, Mrs. Eddy borrowed the phrasing of a thinker and reinterpreted the meaning.

"To bless all mankind"—this idea was something new, however, in connection with her publications. The word "bless" had deep meaning for Mrs. Eddy. Rather than a religious rite or a weak human attempt at soliciting the favor of God, "blessing" for her was closer to Jesus' "Love your enemies, bless them that curse you." [42] For Mrs. Eddy, God's love included both tenderness and rebuke. She believed that one of the worst sins of mankind was to conceal evil when it should be exposed, to be passive rather than active in destroying its influence. She noted how Jesus rebuked the evil he saw in people before he healed them. She had written in *Science and Health*, "You uncover sin, not in order to injure, but in order to bless the corporeal man; and a right motive has its reward."[43] Whether the healing work was on the individual or collective level, how could one bless others if one allowed them to wallow in sin?

Merely spreading good news could never perform the healing that could be accomplished by uncovering and destroying evil with spiritual truth, as Christian Scientists understood the process. Minimizing bad news, writing about it without alarm or avoiding it altogether when there was nothing positive to say, could be helpful in the way that avoiding certain topics helps keep peace in a family. But it could also lead to complacency. It was not the same as changing the news through healing.

The *Monitor* was, in a way, a new tool of Christian healing. It could inspire people to take the mental steps that would help bring about reform on the deepest levels of human thought. Inspiring readers to overcome evil with good, in their own lives and then in the world around them, would help transform the earth and, in the word used in Genesis, give mankind "dominion" over it. It would bring real hope. And it could help turn readers into bolder, tougher, wiser thinkers, not just happier ones.

To Mrs. Eddy, the need was not so much for gentle sunshine as for "lightning." The tone of the *Monitor* could be kind in its treatment of people and events, but the content was not to be a watered-down version of Christian thinking, condescending to the supposedly immature spiritual understanding of the masses. It was to be the culmination of Christian Science, placing the spirit of Christ squarely in the arena of ideas and actions, and demanding that its healing power be demonstrated. It was to be the vehicle for the ultimate proof Mrs. Eddy had always insisted be part of Christian Science: the proof, through healing, that God loves all His creation without division and without exhaustion. Her own healing works, and those of her followers, had helped establish that proof in the individual bodies of those who came to them for cure. Now was the time to lift sights higher and begin establishing the proof for "all mankind."

3

Beyond Clean

How to make the *Monitor* a demonstration of the power of Christ to heal the world's problems, as opposed to just sanitizing the news, was the challenge facing the editors and staff, even if they were not always fully aware of it. Their early efforts were crude. They had to invent *Monitor* journalism as they went along.

Paul Deland had taken a pay cut of $5 from his job at the *Boston Traveler*, earning $25 a week as a copy editor with the *Monitor*. "I had about decided to give up the type of newspaper work we were doing [at the *Traveler*]," he said later, "because it seemed as though crime and disaster were about all we handled." [1]

Before the *Monitor*'s first issue, as practice, he and his editing and reporting colleagues took stories that had been published in other papers and rewrote them:

> *We eliminated or minimized the sensational and the unnecessarily discordant details and endeavored to bring out in bold relief the helpful and healing angles that were so often minimized. . . . Among other things we were told to avoid such traditional newspaper words as "struck, blow, blast, hit," especially in our head writing. Instead of merely recording disaster or socially destructive action, we were told to seek the rescue and reconstruction and preventive and let that be the dominant note in our stories. To let our stories so far as possible encourage not discourage people.* [2]

Everyday management of the paper fell to Alexander Dodds as managing editor. He was a serious student of Christian Science, with a streak of insecurity, which led him toward the formulaic in news writing. At one point, he took Mrs. Eddy's statement "If you wish to know the spiritual fact, you can discover it by reversing the material fable, be the fable *pro* or *con*, – be it in accord with your preconceptions or utterly contrary to them," [3] and he concluded, "so – in establishing a working rule at the beginning [for *Monitor* news writing] it was clearly a matter of analysis":

> *. . . [w]ould the exact reverse of the daily press give the standard? Crime, scandal, disaster are the three common features in the display headings of the daily press. The reverse are law-abiding, good tidings, and the opposite of disaster or destruction which is construction. This was the key which would unlock the great mine of unpublished news of the world, and should be the standard established. This was my key for the news policy of the* Monitor, *and I counted word by word the stories of crime, scandal and disaster, and substituted in exact ratio, stories of constructive effort throughout the world.* [4]

To make sure the right ideas were communicated, writers were told not to use direct quotations. As Deland put it, "The reporter was to present the story in his own words to be sure that it was accurate, balanced, in good perspective, and written from a Christianly Scientific standpoint." [5]

The kind of paper that came out was not surprising: pleasant, untroubling, easy to digest—and rather inconsequential.

Gratitude

Dodds was a sincere and unpretentious man. After completing his only year of high school, in his native

Pittsburgh, he took a job with a pharmacy, clinging to the dream of becoming a doctor. He began to see, however, what he called the "underside" of physicians' lives—a constant use of stimulants to keep their energy up—and quit. Next, having known some reporters and written a few articles for the local papers, he decided to try his hand at journalism.

He liked it well enough, and it became his new profession. He worked incessantly to overcome his lack of education and turn himself into the best newspaperman he could be. He eventually became night managing editor—the youngest in the city—of the *Pittsburgh Dispatch*. His health, however, which had never been good, broke down—it is unclear what the cause was—and he had to resign. Looking for a change of environment, he bought a half interest in the Sharon, Pennsylvania, *Daily Telegraph* and moved to Sharon, where he came across *Science and Health* and was healed.

As he did with every other new road in his life, he started down this one with enthusiasm. As a new Christian Scientist, he stopped "social" drinking right away. "I studied faithfully," he said, "attended the church services and in every way strove to grasp the principle which I knew must underlie Mrs. Eddy's wonderful book, *Science and Health*." [6] After two years he felt he had a breakthrough. He stopped smoking, wearing glasses, and taking medicine.

He returned to journalism in Pittsburgh, moving from paper to paper, then married a Christian Scientist. On a trip to Boston, in 1906, he met Archibald McLellan. Two years later, McLellan asked Dodds to come to Boston to discuss the new *Monitor*. Only thirty-four, Dodds impressed the Directors and Trustees with his knowledge of what it took to produce a daily paper. He returned to Pittsburgh but continued to give help to the new venture. "Everything that you send is of value, . . ." William McKenzie wrote Dodds. "We are grateful for your enthusiastic co-operation, and hope to have more of it." [7]

A full-time job offer with the *Monitor* came in September. Dodds left his latest employer, the *Pittsburgh Sun*, and began helping oversee preparations for the Trustees. He felt that he had found his calling:

> *To myself who oft had had, when working in other papers, a vision of a clean newspaper, helpful and truthful, untainted by political ambitions, it came as a fulfillment in some degree of that vision. No man of righteous desire and aim can look upon the world as it seems today and not be heart sick over the vice and crime, the horrors of human living and "doleful dying"* (Science and Health), *and not long to do something to alleviate, to soften, nay to heal the woes of mankind:* [8] . . .

Obedience

Dodds and Deland were journalists, and their motives, in part, were to create a new day for journalism. The goal of Archibald McLellan, the paper's editor, was different. With no journalism background except a few years as editor of the church's religious periodicals, he was not so much interested in news as in helping Mrs. Eddy. He knew she had not started the *Monitor* to change journalism any more than she had started it for financial gain, political influence, or even public spiritedness. Her whole thought and life were directed toward one goal, to establish Christian Science as a permanent fixture in the world, and McLellan realized that, if he was to succeed at the *Monitor,* he had to subordinate everything to that goal. Newspaper expertise was important for the paper to function, but others could supply that. The primary responsibility of the editor was to be responsive to Mrs. Eddy.

McLellan was a careful and thoughtful man who tended toward the stodgy. A fellow church worker, W. L. Johnson, described him as "not hampered by emotionalism." This was a compliment. Mrs. Eddy, Johnson said, ". . . wanted her students to accept and practice her teachings in a clear, logical and comprehensive manner, never emotionally, and thus remain with both feet well fixed upon a solid foundation." [9]

Canadian by birth, the youngest of seven children, McLellan had worked as a traveling salesman in New York, then as a corporate lawyer for what eventually became Dun and Bradstreet in Chicago. One of the associate editors of the religious periodicals, William McCrackan, wrote of him:

> *In appearance McLellan suggested the prosperous banker or broker. He was always carefully dressed, somewhat formally as befitting one who was apt to be called at any moment to visit Mrs. Eddy in her home. . . . When talking he had a characteristic habit of looking off into the distance and of causing his eyelids to flicker in a sort of a blinking fashion, as though the light which he saw was too bright for his eyes. He talked with much deliberation and very much to the point, but searchingly as though constantly feeling his way for the next words to come. His voice was gentle, yet what he said seemed to have an inherent power of penetration derived from his obvious conviction that he was right in his judgment.* [10]

Before he came to Boston, McLellan had had some contact with journalists. One of his principal tasks for the church was to serve as the one-man Committee on Publication for Illinois, and he had been successful in getting newspapers to correct mistakes in articles on Christian Science. When Mrs. Eddy had decided to move to the Boston area from New Hampshire, in 1908, she asked McLellan, now working for the church in Boston, to take the lead in finding a new home for her, but to keep it all a secret. She knew the move would prompt attention in the press, and in fact, the evening before her arrival, two reporters appeared at the door of the new house, demanding information. McLellan talked them out of publishing the scoop.

Mrs. Eddy took note. She had written him earlier that the good results of his work in Illinois had been achieved "not through aggression, but through love." [11]

His calmness was impressive to anyone who knew him.

Fred Birchall, assistant managing editor of *The New York Times*, who got to know McLellan on a tour of Glacier National Park, in 1912, wrote of an afternoon when the whole party seemed "out of joint." Birchall felt impelled to seek out McLellan and found him quietly reading. He seemed very much at peace. He put his book away and chatted with Birchall. "I realized then that of us all he alone had a place of refuge. . . ." Birchall wrote later. "Never shall I forget his influence, for as no other man I have ever met he lived what he professed." [12]

Mrs. Eddy valued McLellan's character. While he would not produce a newspaper of eloquence or radical creativity, neither would he embarrass her or the church. He spoke of the *Monitor* as making "favorable appeal to a large portion of the reading public, namely, those . . . who desire to look upon the brighter and more wholesome side of things." [13] That was enough for him and apparently satisfied Mrs. Eddy for the present.

Changing thinking

Did McClellan's and Dodds's effort to sanitize the news actually mislead readers into thinking events were less serious than they were? In July 1909, when King Alfonso of Spain took action against rioters in Barcelona and Melilla and against rebellious army troops who refused to fire on them, the *Monitor* headed the story "All of Spain Today is Declared Under 'War Law' by King" and reported in the first paragraph:

> *King Alfonso this afternoon, by imperial decree, proclaimed martial law throughout Spain and suspended the constitutional decrees. This action immediately followed his return to the capital from San Sebastion, when he had a hurried conference with his ministers.*

Only toward the bottom of the article did the writer mention that "a battle between the fanatical Moorish tribesmen and the Spanish garrison at Melilla was resumed this morning and is still being waged with heavy casualties on both, . . ." [14]

By contrast, *The New York Times* headed its story, "Spain Verges on Civil War," with the subheads "'Down with King' Cry Mobs in Barcelona" and "Gen. Pintos and Other Officers Killed—Casualties Exceed 200—Severe Previous Losses Reported." The story went on to paint a picture of chaos and death, with "four or five soldiers…shot daily for insubordination." [15]

It almost seemed as if the papers were talking about two different incidents.

With the *Monitor*, a knowledgeable reader would understand that a declaration of "war law" by the king revealed a serious internal problem, but the reader could also conclude that the king's "hurried conference with his ministers," featured as it was in the lead paragraph, indicated a situation more or less under control. For the *Monitor* to accomplish its purpose of blessing mankind, it would have to inspire the prayer of its readers, yet it is debatable if a busy reader would see the need for serious prayer after reading such a report.

The *Times* story, more graphic, leaves the reader alarmed but also sympathetic. If a *Times* reader was inclined to pray, he would have the motivation as well as the information. The risk, as a Christian Scientist might see it, would be that he might also be overwhelmed by the seriousness of the situation and become paralyzed by anger or fear and thus be ineffective in his prayer.

Knowledge versus emotion, calm versus anger, distance versus immediacy: One can argue the virtue of each approach, but on the *Monitor*'s own terms, one wonders if the report on events in Spain really helped "to bless all mankind" or if it merely calmed readers with soothing news. When Mrs. Eddy once asked some of her students what it took to heal instantaneously and she didn't receive a satisfactory answer, she said, "I will tell you the way to do it. It is to love! Just live love—be it—love, love, love. Do not know anything but Love. Be all love. There is nothing else. That will do the work." [16] Did the *Monitor*'s story inspire love? Did it provide the spark to ignite the healing power of loving prayer for a desperate situation? Did it change readers' thinking?

Changing thinking was constantly on Mrs. Eddy's mind. A primary interest of hers was altering how humanity thought about God and religion, for she believed that a change in thinking about God would lead to broader societal reform.

The *Monitor* was clearly part of Mrs. Eddy's reformist mission. How the news pages could contribute to human progress beyond simply minimizing tragedy and highlighting positive news, however, seemed to puzzle McLellan and his staff. They were somewhat less stymied when it came to the editorial page, where opinion and interpretation were more easily accepted. Then again, most of the editorials were written by Johnny Flinn, the most experienced writer—and in many ways, the most profound thinker—of the *Monitor*'s founding group.

Humility

Born in Ireland, in 1851, Flinn had come to Boston as a young man and then found his way to the Midwest, where he settled into professional newspaper work. Beginning in 1873 as a night editor and then as a legislative correspondent at the *St. Louis Globe*, he moved to Chicago in a few years and became an editorial writer for the *Chicago Daily News,* then became managing editor of the *Chicago Mail* and *Chicago Times*.

In the late 1880s, Flinn left daily journalism to start Flinn & Sheppard, and the Standard Guide Co. He wrote and published a history of the Chicago police as well as the *Official Guide to the World's Columbian Exposition in the City of Chicago*, which he took to the fairgrounds and sold himself.

Like Mrs. Eddy, Flinn was impressed by the surge of inventiveness at the end of the nineteenth century. He had written in the Fair's guide, "It is presumed at the outset that the great majority of visitors are those who seek to enlighten themselves regarding the progress which the world has made in the arts, sciences and industries."

His own progress, though, was stymied by a longstanding problem. A heavy drinker, he came home one night completely drunk. His next-door neighbor was a Christian Scientist, and she talked to him until he fell asleep. When he awoke, he felt rejuvenated. He never took another drink. [17]

Flinn's later writings for the Christian Science religious periodicals show a little of what he began to go through at that point:

> *Among the first things the earnest beginner learns in Christian Science is that he starts out at once with an unexpected patient on his hands, and one of the most troublesome he will ever have to deal with. None can come to him in the future who will demand more of his attention, none who will be more difficult to manage, none who will be more insistent, more unreasonable, or more selfish. This patient, of course, is he himself; . . .*[18]

Flinn realized he had to make deep changes to get his career back on track. What he finally reached, he said, was "a humble desire to be about God's business."

> *It is not difficult for the average mortal to be self-assertive, to wish to control others, to talk long and often upon what he imagines to be the right side of every trivial question; it does, however, require spiritual strength, forbearance, love, reliance upon God, to enable one in the midst of heated controversy to seal his lips and know that the wisest course is mentally and humbly to depend on Principle, through complete self-surrender, so that the one Mind may settle everything harmoniously.*[19]

By 1898, he had returned to newspaper work, becoming an editorial writer at the *Chicago Inter-Ocean*, where he remained until he was asked to help start the *Monitor*. He was offered $82.50 per week, plus moving expenses, if he would come to Boston as chief editorial writer.

Flinn brought with him not only a hard-earned humility but also an approach to journalism that was noticeably deeper than that of many others at the new *Monitor*:

> *. . . we have learned through progressive steps that Mind's unlimited power can and must be applied to the solution of problems that concern the universe, as well as to those that concern humanity; to problems that concern the mass, as well as to those that concern the individual; and that it can and must be applied not only to the correction of wrong conditions,—moral, social, religious, industrial, and political,—but to the elimination of all the suppositional causes underlying these various and varied conditions.* [20]

Flinn's vision went far beyond "clean" journalism. As he saw it, the *Monitor*'s only path to success in the marketplace was to become the best newspaper in the world at spiritual healing:

> *. . . since the* Monitor *could not, or would not, enter into competition with its contemporaries in some respects, it must excel them in others. It must find a field of its own and occupy it. It must demonstrate its capability of meeting a need in journalism of which thinking people everywhere, and newspaper people among them, were cognizant, and in doing this it must get far away from the methods of the insipid if uplifting dailies that had preceded it in the reform field, and which had expired in an effort to be good without being useful.* [21]

Flinn probably understood better than most what Mrs. Eddy was trying to do with the paper, reforming not just society and journalism but human thought and action, because he had achieved a deep measure of reform himself. "It is not by pressing self to the forefront," he said, "but by overcoming self, that we make headway." [22] Eventually he became a practitioner and teacher of Christian Science.

Given his understanding of the *Monitor*'s deeper purpose, Flinn might have made a good chief editor. But for what Mrs. Eddy was looking for, McLellan made more sense. She was a risktaker, but only when she was sure her ideas would be carried out. She could trust McLellan to take no step that was not in line with her wishes.

There was also the matter of learning styles. Flinn seemed to grow mostly through suffering. McLellan, starting with his decision to follow Christian Science out of rationality rather than healing, progressed more through logic. Both tendencies were valid, but the lessons from suffering, when learned on the job by those who managed church affairs, came at too high a price for Mrs. Eddy.

Change in the air

In 1910, nearly two years after the *Monitor*'s launch, McLellan gave a talk about the paper. His concept seemed little different from what it had been at the beginning. The paper, as he saw it, was

> *. . . extending the hand of encouragement and the word of cheer to the hosts of newspaper men throughout the world who are hoping that the day will come when the daily newspaper everywhere shall be less a purveyor of bad or shocking news, and more a medium for the telling of the good news of the world.* [23]

He noted proudly that the *Monitor* reached many people well past the day of publication but was still eagerly read. News of crime and tragedy was cabled around the world, he said, and everyone knew it, but the good news was not known and thus stood up over time. There was logic to this, but his definition of good news was simply things that did not disturb. Instead of news of crime, he said,

> *. . . the traveler, . . . would much rather read of a new bridge being built or a new public building erected in his home town, and see a picture of it, showing a portion of his own old-time main street. This is what a man wants who is reading a paper which is or should be of interest to all home-loving people, and this is what he gets in the* Monitor. *Do you not think he prefers to read such items, rather than the details of an accident or brawl in some portion of the globe, bringing into prominence for the moment some one of whom he never heard and in whom he has not a particle of interest?* [24]

Extreme parochialism would never fulfill the paper's promise, and Mrs. Eddy seemed to sense McLellan's problem. She wanted him to manage the paper's birth, but the future needed broader vision. On November 27, 1908, only two days after the first issue of the paper had appeared, she instructed McLellan to bring Frederick Dixon—"our star in England" [25] — to take charge of the editorial page. Dixon was a journalist and Christian Scientist of cultured mind and skillful rhetoric, who had taken on critics in the British press on behalf of the church with great success. He was also a sophisticated and educated observer of public affairs, with extraordinary relationships with some of the leading political figures in England and the United States. As a writer, he was sometimes obscure in his historical references and over the top in his language, but he would clearly bring a broader perspective to the *Monitor*.

Mrs. Eddy didn't give much attention to feelings when it came to finding the right people to help run her church. McLellan would have to live with the appointment. "He [Dixon] would make a splendid Editor," she wrote McLellan, with clear implications for the future of both men at the paper, "but we do not want to change our present chief Editor." [26]

Dixon arrived in December and took the title of associate editor. Mrs. Eddy asked that his name be placed on the paper, so for the first time, in late January 1909, the names of senior editors began appearing on the *Monitor*'s masthead.

Rather than taking Mrs. Eddy's move as a goad to upgrade their view of *Monitor* journalism, McLellan and Dodds interpreted it as a slap. It didn't help that Dixon was very aware of his own star quality. Very soon, Mrs. Eddy realized that the turmoil the move was causing could hamper the paper's early growth and retreated, asking Dixon to return to England. In April 1909, he left to take charge of the *Monitor*'s London bureau. She did not bring him back again, but it was clear she had a different ideal for editor.

In terms of production and circulation, though, the paper was getting off to a good start. As later editor Erwin Canham wrote in his history of the *Monitor*:

> *Its Thanksgiving issue in 1910 carried seven tons of newsprint to London. Shipments went to Australia, China, Japan, Egypt, South Africa, and of course all of Western Europe. With the aid of gift funds the* Monitor *in its earliest years was available in every leading American consulate throughout the world, in foreign steamship booking offices, in public libraries, and many other public places.* [27]

Mrs. Eddy did not judge the *Monitor*'s success solely by its numbers, but she was apparently satisfied that at least some of those in charge had the right idea. In a letter McKenzie wrote her in early January 1910, he referred to the *Monitor* as "a most genial persuader of men," and she exclaimed as she read it, "That is the spirit I have enjoined upon them from the start!" [28]

In April, eight months before her death, McKenzie, still one of the Trustees of The Christian Science Publishing Society, saw her for what proved to be the last time:

> *She appeared as one who had been through conflict, . . . Her first question was, 'Did you know me?'.*
> *. . I began to tell her of the welfare of the Publishing*

Society. I spoke of the many puzzling problems which had come up in our work so greatly enlarged in scope with the issuing of a daily newspaper and how much we had wished her both to advise us and to direct us—how we had asked her for this help a good many times, but she had not elected to give it and so to the best of our ability we had to seek earnestly for the guidance of Mind. Once again I saw her rare smile as with deep earnestness she said to me, 'That is just what I wanted you to do.' [29]

On December 3, she died, and the struggle to define the *Monitor*'s identity began in earnest.

4

To the Barricades

It was August 3, 1914, the eve of World War I, and the *Monitor* was not giving up hope that peace could be restored in Europe. "The political situation is bad," the front-page article said, "but not hopeless."

Inside the paper, the lead editorial concluded that the problem was not so much political as moral. European governments, it said, needed to be shaken out of their arrogant complacency.

Arrogance was indeed a major contributor to the appalling death and destruction of the war that followed. Since Christian Science teaches that all physical problems are, at base, mental, it was logical that the destructive attitudes ruling European thinking were taken to task in the *Monitor*. The purpose was to help readers pray effectively. The writing lacked the spirit of forgiveness and love, which Christian Science teaches must also be present to heal, and the lack was a sign of big problems to come. But the approach was at least more helpful than presenting, for example, a bland report that things were not as bad as they seemed.

A new era had begun at the *Monitor*. At the head of the paper since June was none other than Frederick Dixon, who had stormed back into Boston as if he had been Mrs. Eddy's choice all along for the next editor. From all appearances, it may have been true.

The lead editorial, clearly written by Dixon, eagerly

took up the subject of religion in connection with the threatening war:

> *The inconceivable has occurred. In the twentieth century of the Christian era the nations of Europe have drawn the sword with no more respect for the teaching of the Sermon on the Mount than was displayed by the Roman legionaries on Calvary. The sceptic demands, with unconcealed contempt, whether the event is the result of twenty centuries of Christian practise. The question is perhaps natural, but it is none the less not a little shallow. Christianity is no more responsible for war in Europe today than Epicureanism was responsible for the persecu-tion of Marcus Aurelius; but what is termed religion was, and is, largely responsible for both. You cannot convert the cathedral into something approaching the temple of Janus, nor can you indulge in dithyrambs concerning consecrated battleflags, without reducing your Christianity to the region of the Cromwellian maxim, "Trust in God and keep your powder dry."*

The editorial continued:

> *The simple fact is that if the energies of Christendom had been directed more to the demonstration of practical Christianity—that is to say, to the healing of the sick—war would long ago have become impossible.* [1]

The editorial was energetic, articulate, breathtaking in its self-confidence, brutal in its honesty, and almost giddy in its wide-ranging and sometimes obscure historical references. It put Christian Science squarely into the middle of debate on the causes of the war and what to do now.

The prospects on the whole for the *Monitor* seemed promising. Under McLellan and Dodds, Erwin Canham pointed out, the paper was "a trifle amateurish, folksy, scrapbookish. . . . [and] often parochial. It needed its sights lifted." [2] Under Dixon, it adopted a strong international perspective, along with a more aggressive application of Christian Science to the news. For him, when it came to public affairs, Christian Science was not, in words Mrs. Eddy once used to describe an insipid sense of love, "something put upon a shelf, to be taken down on rare occasions with sugar-tongs and laid on a rose-leaf." [3]

Rather than treating difficult news as a disease, which one had to turn readers away from to minimize their fear, Dixon approached the problems of the world as sin, calling out what he saw as the underlying errors of thought and exposing their hidden ways of doing evil. He believed Christian Scientists had an important role to play in pointing up and condemning sin and in helping the world work in more productive directions. And he respected his non-Christian Science readers enough to expect them to follow his reasoning.

Since Mrs. Eddy had invited Dixon to the paper as an editor in 1908 and then asked him to leave the next year, after what amounted to a culture clash with McLellan and Dodds, Dixon had written articles for the paper and run the European news bureau for the *Monitor* out of London. He also had worked professionally as a Christian Science practitioner and, since December of 1910, had taught classes in Christian Science as an official teacher of the religion.

When the Directors decided to bring Dixon back, this time as chief editor, telling him of their "conviction that by your ability and your demonstration of Christian Science you are particularly fitted for this position," [4] McLellan and Dodds balked again. But times had changed, and the Directors felt that the *Monitor* needed a bolder hand at the helm. "Clean" journalism was out, at least as it had been practiced. Dixon believed that readers were, or should be, as willing as he was to wade into the messy details of human conflict, especially when it came to international events that affected millions.

He may have overestimated the appetite of *Monitor* readers, who were still mainly Christian Scientists, for difficult subjects. He may also have overestimated their appetite for him personally.

"We are for the right"

Dixon had begun his journalism career in his native England, in 1888, with *Macmillan's Magazine*. He became a Christian Scientist a decade later, serving the church as the one-man Committee on Publication for Britain, doing the same press-relations work McLellan had done in Chicago. After his brief move to Boston in the paper's first year, he began writing astute and articulate articles on world affairs from London, which were several notches above those of anyone else at the paper, and he eventually established the paper's famous system of foreign correspondents, which still gives its international coverage distinction.

Dixon developed strong relationships with many political leaders on both sides of the Atlantic. He could get private meetings with American presidents (he talked frequently with President Woodrow Wilson and his assistant, Colonel Edward M. House) as well as with German and British ambassadors and other leading figures, and he served as an informal liaison between the British and American governments. He did not hesitate to give advice to political leaders and advisors, and it was apparently taken.

Dixon cherished his contacts and the access they brought him, but his main interest was metaphysical, namely, the evil men do and how to correct it. Neutrality in the face of wrongdoing, he insisted, is immoral. He rejected the automatic objectivity that was assumed by many to constitute good journalism. He felt that the *Monitor* had to interpret news from its unique standpoint or there was nothing to set the paper apart from other good publications. If the *Monitor* didn't bring hope and healing based on the application of Christian Science, he insisted, it would inevitably fade into the background of, in Flinn's phrase, "insipid if uplifting dailies."

Dixon was modest on the surface. He worked

intensively and disliked personal publicity. But he was also very sure of his moral positions. Longtime staff member Walter Cunningham wrote, "I remember in the early stages of World War I when a group of our German readers challenged his attitude on the war, which was definitely pro-British, he answered them in this way: 'This is not a war between the British and the Germans. It is a question of right and wrong. We are for the right.' From this position he never yielded an inch." [5]

After the sinking of the Lusitania, in 1915, the Directors approved an editorial that clearly took sides in the conflict, but Dixon went beyond partisanship to call *Monitor* readers to their own battle stations:

> *We believe that the people of the United States, standing outside the storm of mental conflict which today is convulsing Europe, can, by a firmness of purpose and an appreciation of the facts, do much to quiet the passions of the world, and to put a stop to methods, which even undisciplined human consciousness has hitherto regarded as illegitimate warfare.* [6]

Dixon understood the *Monitor*'s purpose to energize uplifted thinking, even if the German Christian Scientists, a significant segment of the international membership of the church, were not happy with the *Monitor*'s positions.

Mrs. Eddy undoubtedly had loved the self-confidence that made Dixon's writing stimulating and enabled him to see a larger purpose for the *Monitor* than merely giving a pleasant recitation of the news. His absolute conviction that Christian Science is truth made him an effective Christian Science practitioner and teacher. But his certainty in his own opinions also raised hackles.

"I must have complete authority"

When Dixon arrived in June 1914, immediately upon

receiving the Directors' formal offer of the editorship, he laid out for them his conditions:

> *. . . I feel that if I am to undertake the work, which will make me largely responsible for the paper in both hemispheres, I must have complete authority. . . .*
>
> *I must feel that everybody wants me, and I must feel that I have the right always to appeal to the Directors, as the ultimate court, for assistance and guidance.*
>
> *I want my relation to the Trustees also clearly defined, and I want to feel that in such matters as specifically affect them, I can refer also to them.*
>
> *The Christian Science Monitor, as I see it, has got to be made the organ of the universe. I cannot sit permanently in an office in Boston, and keep in touch with the world. I must have the right, if necessary, to visit other countries, and I must visit Europe at least as often as, and for longer periods than, I have been in the habit of visiting Boston.*[7]

To Canham, the letter showed arrogance, that Dixon expected to hold the power, not the Directors, a situation contrary to the Board-managed governance Mrs. Eddy set up for her church. But the interpretation is unfair. Dixon knew at least some of what it would take to make the paper as great as the Directors wanted it to be, and he felt obligated to tell them. He recognized the Directors as the ultimate authority, but he had to be sure lines of communication ran both ways. He had to be free to travel both to gather information from sources he knew well and to keep the *Monitor*'s flag high. He also realized that, as an Englishman working for an American publication and at a period when England was on one side of impending troubles in Europe, he needed unquestioning support from the Directors.

The Directors gave no indication that they resented his straightforwardness, and they stood behind him for a long time.

Dixon followed through on his part of the bargain. Later, when his relationship with the Directors had become strained, he reminded them, "You all know that when I became editor I made the stipulation that I should have the right to come to the Board for help and advice at any time I wanted it, and I have always carefully adhered to that, and have never worked out any great problem without consultation with it." [8]

Tension grows

With Dixon's energy, understanding of international relations, and unequivocal moral stands on the issues of the day, the paper now had a worldwide circulation of more than a hundred thousand, a budget of more than a million dollars per year, and a readership of influential people. Behind the scenes, however, things were not happy.

On July 16, 1917, Dixon wrote Washington bureau chief Charles Warner, who had become his closest confidante:

> *Now here is something deadly serious. The paper has reached the place where the jealousies surrounding it are colossal, and now is the time above all that none of us who know what we are doing should blow its trumpet, especially inside the movement. . . . When the Monitor counted for very little, nobody cared much about it. Now that it has become a great power in the land, they all want their fingers in the pie. They did not understand what it meant, nor did they want to bear the burden and heat of the day, now they are all Jack Horners, in search of the plums.* [9]

For a time Warner was supportive of his boss. A representative of the Emergency Peace League came to see him and told him that "Christian Scientists cannot support the government [on the war] and be Scientists." When Warner disagreed and tried to show her that Mrs. Eddy herself had acknowledged the importance of the military, the woman left in a huff and started spreading rumors that Warner had thrown her out of the office. "She is a dangerous person," he wrote Dixon. [10]

The woman, however, was just the tip of a very large iceberg. Staffers with similar sympathies moved in and out of the *Monitor* office in Washington, spreading complaints about the *Monitor*. One man came to Dixon in August of 1917 to say "terrible things" about the Washington office. Dixon defended Warner and dismissed the visitor as "a mean little gentleman, if ever there was one." [11]

Then one of the ugliest memories in the church's history began to resurface. It was rumored that the *New York World*, which had attacked Mrs. Eddy a decade earlier and tried to wrest away control of her fortune, was preparing a new attack on the church as being secretly pro-German. Dixon, as editor of the most visible activity of the church, was blamed by church officials in the "field"—especially Committees on Publication, who were dealing with the press and state governments, trying to head off attacks and restrictive legislation—for causing the controversy and hurting the church's image, even though Dixon was anything but pro-German.

Dixon's convictions, however, were not subject to compromise. He wrote an editorial on December 1, 1917, called "Feet of Brass," speaking of the war as "between human tendencies," with German "Kultur" on one side and "republicanism and democracy" on the other. As usual, however, his real theme was metaphysical, and he saw the war as the "sifting out of the hearts of men before the judgment seat of Principle":

> *Armageddon . . . is the inevitable result of the influence of false appetites and of the acceptance of wrong ideals, . . . in order that, through their destruction, adherence to purer conceptions and spiritual ideals may be achieved.* [12]

He quoted the "Battle Hymn of the Republic," with its apocalyptic view of the Civil War, and then words from

Revelation about "one like unto the Son of man" with "feet like unto fine brass":

> *The feet of brass are surely trampling through the battlefield of Armageddon today, causing men to lay down through suffering those animal beliefs they clung so tenaciously to in days of sensual ease. For what is being crushed in the battle is not nations or people, but the material instincts which are hiding Principle from men.* [13]

He was right in his theme and in the direction of his conclusions, and his approach echoed Lincoln in his writing on the Civil War. Dixon's tone, though, fell far short of Lincoln's compassion and forgiveness.

What Dixon had seen as jealousy of the *Monitor*'s success was turning into resentment of him personally, and pressure on the Directors from offended Christian Scientists was growing. Dixon continued to nurture his relationship with the Directors as well as the Publishing Society's Board of Trustees. In February 1918, the Trustees raised Dixon's salary to $15,000 and gave him a bonus of $3,000. [14]

A rift, however, began developing between the Trustees and Directors that had nothing on the surface to do with Dixon but that may have developed in part because of his success with the *Monitor*. The Trustees insisted on their right, under the 1898 Deed of Trust, to manage the Publishing Society, including the *Monitor*, as they saw fit, and the Directors insisted on their prerogative, under the *Church Manual*, to direct the whole church, including the Publishing Society.

Dixon knew trouble was brewing, but he plowed on in the certainty that he and the *Monitor* were doing too much good to stop. On March 23, 1918, he wrote an editorial that brought a simmering issue to a head. It had offended Dixon that Pope Benedict XV had issued a plan for peace that called for laying down arms without dealing with what, in Dixon's view, were the main causes of the war. To Dixon, religion that kept peace by avoiding the hard question of sin was worse than useless. To be neutral, he believed, was to be complicit in war, or at least in this one. The particular incitement of the editorial was a statement by a member of the Canadian parliament criticizing the *Monitor* for anti-Catholic bias. Dixon defended himself and his paper:

> *The moment the Roman Catholic church descends into the public forum, it makes itself legitimately liable to criticism like any other political body. And for Mr. Murphy [the Canadian Member of Parliament] to object to this is childish. The thousands of people tortured in the dungeons of the Inquisition, or burnt at the stake, by command of the Inquisition, suffered purely and simply for religious views they had a perfect right to hold, . . .*[15]

For the Committees on Publication, who intensively cultivated good relations with other churches, the editorial, especially its defiant tone, was intolerable. They complained once again to the Directors, but the Directors, although sympathetic to the Committees, saw a larger picture. In a statement in the *Sentinel* for April 6, they wrote:

> . . . The Christian Science Monitor *demands for, and extends to, every religion the toleration it claims for itself and has no conflict with any form of religious teaching. It does, however, maintain its right to record and analyze the signs of these times as they appear upon the political horizon, irrespective of whether those signs reveal the attempted manipulation of men and nations in the name of political parties, religious bodies, or individuals. To do less than this would be for the* Monitor *to fail to fulfill its responsibility to its Founder and to the world.*[16]

The Directors didn't necessarily support Dixon's

incendiary attempts to drag Christian Science, and Christian Scientists, into the political arena, let alone into inter-religious feuding. But they did support the idea that the *Monitor* had an obligation to address problems that had alarmed the world and brought tragedy to millions. Dixon felt he had the backing he needed.

On November 11, 1918, Germany finally agreed to a cease-fire. Dixon felt he could not let down his guard. The next day, in an editorial titled "Kicking Against the Pricks," he wrote:

> *But there is another stage of Armageddon behind the curtain, if mankind does not learn its lesson. . . . Not until all those traits of animality, of greed, of selfishness, and of vainglory, have been eradicated from [human] consciousness, until, in other words, the old man has been put off and the new man has been put on, will a world have been found that is safe for democracy."* [17]

Dixon's theology was fearless. He was getting to the bottom of things, the sin that was behind the war. Unfortunately, he left his readers there. The rock on which his concept of church was based was still hard and unforgiving.

Taking sides

Dixon left for England after the Armistice, unaware of the precipice on which he stood. When he got back on February 11, he found that the situation had changed dramatically:

> *Flinn, whom I had always looked to as one of my great helps, was silent and morose. . . . In addition to this Warner, who had always kept up a warm correspondence with me from Washington, had become perfectly silent. In such conditions a child could have seen that something strange had happened.* [18]

He soon learned more from Cora Rigby, a staffer in the Washington office. She described how Warner had made a trip to Boston while Dixon was gone and had become alarmed at what he had discovered about the dispute between the boards. He talked with Flinn and others, and found that the concern was widespread. The Directors asked both of them, along with others on the *Monitor* staff, to meet with them, and Warner leveled a number of sensational criticisms at Dixon, including the charge that he had aspired to be "Pope of the movement." Some staffers, including Paul Deland, insisted that keeping the *Monitor* moving forward was more important and refused to criticize Dixon.

Dixon was shocked at what he heard. He met with Flinn, who, according to Dixon, poured out a complaint that, in the years he had worked with Dixon, his opinion had never been asked about the conduct of the paper. The complaints all sounded flimsy to Dixon, but they reflected the general sense of desperation that was building in the church.

Dixon, meanwhile, took public issue with a decision made by the Directors—something unusual, if not intolerable, in the church, especially for a senior official. In the fall of 1918, there had been an outbreak of influenza in Boston, and the city government had asked that places of public gathering, including churches, be shut. The Directors complied by cancelling a Christian Science lecture. Two days later, Dixon wrote a scathing *Monitor* editorial, called "A Mad World," which directly contradicted the Directors' decision:

> . . . *at the very moment when the churches should be filling the minds of the people with peace, and reassuring them of the impotency of evil, it is proposed that these churches shall be shut, and that the admission shall be made that it is dangerous for men and women to congregate to worship God, for fear the Lord's arm is so shortened that He cannot contend with microbes.* [19]

The Trustees backed Dixon, but the Directors finally had had enough. Issuing a private summary of problems to the Trustees, they criticized the *Monitor*'s "anti-Roman Catholic editorial policy" and the belief that "A Mad World" had "created a feeling that Scientists defy the law." [20]

The issue of who controlled the church's publishing activities was boiling over, and the Directors responded by trying to force the Trustees out. In response, the Trustees filed a bill of equity in the Massachusetts Supreme Court in March of 1919. The court issued an injunction, restraining the Directors from taking action, and the case was given to a court Master to decide.

Rumors were now circulating wildly that Dixon and the Trustees were disloyal to the church and Mrs. Eddy. *Monitor* circulation, supported mainly by Christian Scientists, plummeted below twenty-one thousand, and Dixon was distraught. In May, he wrote Algernon Bathurst, his London bureau chief:

> *Ever since this row began I have been the go-between, if you like a word I rather dislike, between the two boards. I have worked like a horse to prevent the ruction, and I am still endeavoring to prevent it, though it seems to grow harder every day. . . .*
>
> *The Trustees asked me to keep out of the row if I could, and keep the Monitor from getting into deep water. I have done that religiously, and I intend to go on doing it, for the safety of the Monitor is my consideration, whatever other people may have for theirs.* [21]

Bathurst, however, was also beginning to believe the worst about his boss. He began producing fewer and fewer articles, causing Dixon to object that the paper was becoming less international. When nothing changed, Dixon decided to shift the oversight of most of the foreign bureaus from London to Boston. For Bathurst, who had been with Dixon from the beginning, it was painful, but Dixon was determined to put business first. The *Monitor* had to get faster and more efficient:

> *It is essential that the least possible time should be wasted in the transmission of news. This is the only way, as you know, to make a really live paper. The London office thus becomes what it really should have been all the time, if the paper had been properly planned from the beginning, and that is an English office.* [22]

Bathurst refused to implement the changes his editor wanted. Dixon suspected what was going on. "Think twice before it is too late," [23] he cabled his bureau chief.

> *. . . you allowed the row between the two boards to enter into your soul, and your work went more or less to pieces. . . . I want the paper, at the end of the trouble, to be greater than it was before. That is my only wish for it, and a wish that is being daily fulfilled.* [24]

But Bathurst had turned against Dixon, and there was no going back. Bathurst was soon fired.

Meanwhile, Dixon found himself in the middle of the Trustee-Director dispute. Some people criticized him for disloyalty to the Directors, others for disloyalty to the Trustees. Few were neutral. *Monitor* advertising representatives even began criticizing Dixon and the paper to advertisers, who began withdrawing their ads.

Calls intensified for Dixon's removal; the environment in Boston was becoming treacherous. William McKenzie, who had become editor of the *Sentinel* and *Journal* when McLellan died, in 1917, and whom Dixon considered a friend, rejected an article by Dixon for the religious periodicals. Dixon suspected that McKenzie had been asked to do so by the Directors merely because the Trustees had requested that Dixon write it. Dixon asked for the truth. McKenzie refused to answer.

It was turning into the kind of crisis that splits churches.

The irony was that both Dixon and McKenzie, as well as all the Directors and Trustees and the others caught up in the passion of the period, were deeply sincere Christian Scientists and followers of Mrs. Eddy. They were committed to the reformist agenda of a church that wanted to alter radically the religious landscape. Dixon himself had taken a newspaper that was grudgingly acknowledged as decent and transformed it into something more: a widely respected international news medium, which could handle with assurance the deepest controversies in the world. In his view, it was doing the work Mrs. Eddy had laid out for it—transforming human thinking by spreading Science into the realm of public affairs. How could things fall apart so quickly?

War

In early March 1920, the court Master ruled in favor of the Trustees, but the Directors were not done. Both boards issued letters to church members explaining the situation from their points of view. On the 13th, Dixon wrote to a member of the business staff in London, one of those sticking by him:

What is unquestionably a plan for breaking up the periodicals went into effect yesterday. McKenzie having previously agreed to print the Directors' and Trustees' letters on the case, which had already appeared in the Monitor, in the Sentinel and Journal, and having been at one with everybody else in so doing, was apparently got at during the night. On Friday morning he came to the office and stopped the presses, which had already printed 9000 Journals, and ordered them to take out the letter of the Trustees and print the Directors' only. Of course this was an outrage and when Ogden as the Trustee on duty overruled him, [a number of employees, including McKenzie] . . . all marched out without notice in grossest breach of their engagements, and left the periodicals to their fate, without a word of explanation or help to guide those who had to pick up the pieces. [25]

The *Sentinel* was due to go to press the following Wednesday, and the Directors refused to appoint a new editor, apparently believing it was better for all the publications not to come out than to be published by a team they deemed disloyal. Finally, the Trustees appointed Dixon editor of the *Sentinel* and *Journal* as well as of the *Monitor*. He would now be writing editorials for all three as well as managing them. Only three staff members remained to help. Nearly two hundred people had resigned from the Publishing Society.

For a year and a half, Dixon struggled on until, in November 1921, the Supreme Court of Massachusetts overturned the earlier decision of the court Master and ruled that the Directors were indeed the ultimate authority in the church. Then came the news that, nearly a year earlier, the Directors had secretly appointed a new editor, Willis Abbot, a longtime writer and editor for William Randolph Hearst and a press operative for several political candidates. All the pieces were in place for a change.

There was no point in continuing the agony. With his fate sealed, Dixon resigned, as did all the Trustees. The last edition of the *Monitor* that Dixon edited was January 30, 1922. The lead articles that day offered news from Italy, Austria, France, India, Japan, and the United States. The *Monitor* was now a truly international newspaper.

To the Gentiles

The Directors were not done with Dixon. The Trustees had given him three-months severance pay when he resigned, but the Directors asked for it back. They had made the same request of others but backed off when the others threatened legal action. Dixon decided that valor required him to return his, and he did so.

In his final editorial for the *Sentinel,* called "Turning to the Gentiles," which appeared on February 4, Dixon's disappointment and wounded pride came pouring out:

> *From the time of the earliest records down to the records of today, [history] is a history of human drifting. Here and there a stronger swimmer reaches out from the drifters, but the drifters, as a rule, immediately bend their so-called energies to overwhelming him. They have one common objurgation: Why art thou come hither to disturb us before our time?* [26]

In clear reference to his own experience, Dixon spoke of the Apostle Paul, who initially drew public support but was persecuted by the Jewish rulers until the people turned against him. Dixon quoted the Bible:

> *". . . when the Jews saw the multitudes, they were filled with envy, and spake against those things which were spoken by Paul, contradicting and blaspheming. Then Paul and Barnabas waxed bold, and said, It was necessary that the word of God should first have been spoken to you: but seeing ye put it from you, and judge yourselves unworthy of everlasting life, lo, we turn to the Gentiles."* [27]

Dixon concluded the editorial with a flourish, which, in its triumphant kiss-off of the Directors and the church, contained a bald statement of Christian Science metaphysics that was not only wrong but destructive. It revealed, in part, what bothered the Directors about Dixon and what led to his incessantly unforgiving worldview; it also revealed what bothered them about the Trustees, who approved the publication of the statement:

> *What Mrs. Eddy wrote of herself applies to every man before her who bore the torch of Truth, and will apply to every man after her until the human mind is*

exterminated by the vision of the Christ. [28]

Mrs. Eddy never taught that Christ destroys the human mind. She constantly wrote of the Christ, or Truth, as uplifting the human mind, making it stronger, more perceptive, more loving. The only things Mrs. Eddy talked of destroying were sin, sickness, death, and the belief that man is separated from God. The goal was to demonstrate, through healing, that man shines with the light of God; he does not disappear. In Dixon's statement, there was no room for growth or healing, no compassion. Self-denial was everything. Love was a waste of time. Hope was only a distant possibility. "A single mistake in metaphysics, or in ethics," Mrs. Eddy had written, "is more fatal than a mistake in physics." [29]

For Dixon, hope was nearly gone. He had been pushed out of the job he felt that he had been preparing for all his life. In November, he moved to New York City to start a publication called the *International Interpreter.* He wrote, "I am endeavoring to tell the exact truth about public affairs to the world through the Interpreter, and this seems to me a scientific position."[30] But he knew a "scientific position" did not hold the same weight with a publication that did not have the Christian Science church to back it up. The stated purpose of the *Interpreter* was "To foster amity among nations; cooperation between Capital and Labor; equal opportunity for all, and liberty under law and order." [31] It was *The Christian Science Monitor* without the Christian Science.

Then, in March 1923, Dixon wrote an extraordinary letter to the Directors in which he spelled out where he thought he stood. He was not answerable to them; he had been appointed personally as chief editor by Mrs. Eddy, and any opposition to him was, essentially, disloyalty to her.

In the year 1908, in the face of an extraordinary opposition, Mrs. Eddy insisted on my being made an editor of the Monitor, and in my name being placed on the paper. Up to that time no names had appeared on the paper. In placing my name on the paper as associate editor, the names of the editor-in-chief and the managing editor were also placed on it, though Mrs. Eddy had never asked for this. The simple fact is that Mrs. Eddy did not intend me to be made an associate editor, but something entirely different . . . .

When Mrs. Eddy found she could not apparently get her way, she asked me to return to England, and to carry on my work there. In doing this, she did not consult with the Board of Trustees or the Board of Directors. She dealt with me personally and alone, and her decision came as a considerable surprise to the trustees and to the directors. I returned to England to resume the publication work and to edit the Monitor in the eastern hemisphere, and I remained in control of the whole of the eastern hemisphere work and of the publication office until I was asked to come to Boston and assume the editorship of the entire paper. . . . It is possible that I made a mistake in resigning. Having been originally appointed by Mrs. Eddy, I should, perhaps, have insisted on being dismissed. [32]

The Directors would have none of it and wrote coldly that they regarded his service as editor to have ceased even before they appointed Abbot. [33]

Dixon was deeply hurt. In his eyes, he had been a hero, keeping Mrs. Eddy's paper alive while undergoing "the most frantic abuse, the most villainous slander, the most abominable treachery." [34] Finally, he felt he had no choice. On November 5, 1923, his life in shambles, he resigned from The Mother Church.

In less than three weeks he was dead.

Many Christian Scientists did not miss him, but President Wilson's former assistant, Colonel House, wrote a generous remembrance for the *Interpreter*:

Had [Dixon] been a mariner, he would have

scorned to seek latitudes where one might find gentle winds and summer seas. He would have sailed rather into stormy regions where violent gales and turbulent waters would have called forth all his skill as a navigator. He would have done this not in the spirit of adventure, but in the spirit of service.

Therefore he was to be found wherever perplexing and difficult problems were in process of solution, . . . He could draw from an unlimited reservoir of knowledge as could no other man I know, and he could clothe his thoughts in luminous phrases and masterly English. He was an authority on foreign affairs, and was held in such esteem by public men of his day that every door was open to him and intimate policies discussed. . . .

He has crossed the Great Divide but he leaves us under the spell of his radiant spirit which will ever be an inspiration and benediction to those who had the honor and privilege to call him friend. [35]

Dixon was brilliant, articulate, indefatigable, and devoted to the *Monitor* and his church. Professionally, he was at the top of his game, understanding what a newspaper needed in his era to be competitive. He was not afraid to make hard decisions. The times needed someone who could point up the foolishness manifested daily during World War I, and Dixon answered the call. His tenure planted the *Monitor* in the minds of public figures and average readers around the world as an authority that couldn't be ignored.

As a writer and editor, Dixon addressed the public with the intellectual respect he expected others to give him. He gave insight, loyalty, and—above all—honesty. For all it cost him, he took Mrs. Eddy's words to heart:

It requires the spirit of our blessed Master to tell a man his faults, and so risk human displeasure for the sake of doing right and benefiting our race. Who is telling mankind of the foe in ambush? Is the informer one who sees the foe? If so, listen and be wise. Escape from evil, and designate those as unfaithful stewards who have seen the danger and yet have given no warning. [36]

For years afterward, the paper seemed cowed by the events and took a conservative route, trying more often to be respectable than to be a reformer. Editors, writers, and boards worked for a long time in Dixon's shadow, struggling to take the paper where he intended in terms of spiritual depth, but cowed by his fate from taking the bold steps that would enable them to do so.

The *Monitor*, though, had built a legacy of international coverage that could not be denied. Dixon missed half of Christianity with his emphasis on truth, not mercy, on insight, not love. The tone of genial persuasion that Mrs. Eddy had wanted seemed beyond his reach. But he did immense good for the paper and got it headed in the right direction.

5

Watching the World Go By

One could almost hear the sighs of relief across the Christian Science movement when the first editorial under new editor Willis Abbot, called "Christianity in Business," came out:

> *Some of these times it will be generally recognized among business men and institutions that the most practical, profitable way of conducting their business is on a generally Christian basis.* [1]

It was like advocating that people be nice to each other. Disputes between capital and labor were the topic, and the editorial maintained that they were solvable:

> *A few short months ago one would scarcely have believed that the great accomplishments of the arms conference at Washington could possibly have been achieved in view of the supposedly selfish interests of the nations concerned. And yet in the brief space of a few weeks international understandings have been reached that will at least help to make war improbable, and establish peace as the normal state of the world.*
> *To bring about a lasting peace between Capital and Labor the question of wages and hours of work must be approached in a true Christianly manner by both sides. Suspicion and greed must give way to a desire to do the right thing regardless of the immediate outcome.* [2]

If your taste was for wishful thinking about peace, here

was the perfect meal.

For all intents and purposes, "Let sleeping dogs lie" was the paper's new motto. If Dixon got it only half right, rousing the dogs but failing to calm them down, Abbot and the Directors seemed happy just to step over them. The result was an editorial that appeased readers' worst problem-solving tendencies. There was no recognition of underlying errors in the world that did not, in fact, make war improbable and capital-labor disputes susceptible to easy moralizing. There was no attempt to probe festering evils and to identify ways to eliminate them. And there was no effort to alert readers to the mental dangers all around, which they had power to handle through precise prayer.

No harm done? Not as far as the *Monitor* was concerned. Other papers may have been able to coexist with passive readers as long as the readers showed up. For the *Monitor* to be successful, readers had to be active participants in the work. The paper had to engage them at a level few other papers even dreamed of reaching. Ignoring the duty to inspire them constituted, in a fundamental way, the severing of the paper from a vital source of its own strength. For the *Monitor*, to have an inert but happy readership—looking on the bright side, gathering information only about the things that pleased, avoiding the difficult challenges facing humanity—was for the *Monitor* to have no readership at all.

Watching the world go by

The *Monitor* drifted along under Abbot. In his aptly titled autobiography, *Watching the World Go By*, he tells the story of his career as a newspaper reporter, editor, and owner, punctuated with periods as a political operative. He was at the elbow of William Jennings Bryan during his famous "Cross of Gold" speech, in 1896. He knew personally every president from Cleveland to Hoover. But perhaps the most telling period of his pre-*Monitor* career was as chief of the editorial page of the *New York Journal* under publisher William Randolph

Hearst. Abbot helped Hearst drag the United States into the Spanish-American war with distortion, hearsay, and outright fabrication.

"Much of—indeed most of—the fanning [of the war's flames] was done in the office of the *Journal*," he admits, "and it was my privilege to observe and to some extent share in this activity, though at no time wholly sympathetic with it." [3]

The *New York Journal* took simple incidents and twisted their facts to make it appear that the Spanish were brutal and despicable governors of Cuba. "Indeed, it soon became the fixed policy of the paper to exaggerate and misconstrue every military act of the Spanish commander, . . ." [4] Abbot wrote. He tells how a young Cuban girl who had been quietly searched by a female official aboard a Spanish ship was turned by the *Journal* into a victim who was stripped naked in front of lascivious male officers. At another time, the *Journal* doctored a photograph of a beach in Cuba, painting in Spanish soldiers supposedly forcing Cubans into the sea to drown.

It all added to the weight of "evidence" that the United States had to act. Yet Abbot was so gentle afterwards in his treatment of Hearst and of everyone else he ever came across in journalism and politics that one wonders not if he disagreed with Hearst's policies, which he apparently did, but why he never took a stand against them. Only later, after he became a Christian Scientist, did he make a break with Hearst, and even then, it was more for political than moral reasons.

Abbot started his career as a young reporter for the *New Orleans Times-Democrat*. He was taken with the gaudy and literary show that was old New Orleans, where editors and reporters seemed to work with a pen in one hand and a gun in the other. His own editor "walked with a slight limp, the cause of which I found out to be a bullet in his groin, deposited there by a rifle in the hands of the editor of the rival morning paper, whom he had challenged to a duel." [5]

Abbot was an entertaining and articulate observer of the human scene, an approach that is attractive in an essayist but problematic for the editor of a reformist newspaper. His attitude toward the masses was odd for someone who led a paper whose purpose was to bless mankind. At the end of his career, he still called the audience for yellow journalism "the moronic class" [6] and said he preferred papers like the New York *Sun*, which was "never written down to their intellectual capacity." [7] He liked the New York City of the 1880s, he said, which was "idyllic compared with the present maelstrom of races. . . ." [8]

Like Abbot, Dixon had elitist tendencies, but he did not disdain the masses. He may have treated them roughly, but his purpose was to uplift them. He tried to appeal to their deepest moral instincts, even if what he told them wasn't what they wanted to hear. Abbot seemed satisfied if his readers were simply content.

Part of his gentle treatment of Hearst may stem from the fact that Hearst's son had been healed by Christian Science. The boy was born with a blocked intestinal tube, and by the time he was ten days old, he had shriveled to almost a skeleton. Finding no help from doctors, Hearst listened when one of his editors, who was a Christian Scientist, recommended he try her religion. He did, and the boy was healed. After that, Hearst instructed his editors never to disparage Mrs. Eddy in his newspapers.

In 1912, when Abbot himself was sick with symptoms of extreme stress, he remembered the Hearst family experience, turned to Christian Science, and was healed. His parting from Hearst came three years later over a *New York Journal* editorial justifying the sinking of the Lusitania, a position that made the paper too pro-German for Abbot. He left and joined the New York *Sun* as an editorial writer.

After a few years, an intriguing opportunity presented itself. "In 1921, much to my amazement and joy," he wrote later, "I was called to Boston and told by the Christian Science Board of Directors that they would appoint me editor of the *Christian Science Monitor* as soon as the control of that paper had been definitely awarded them by the court." [9]

Abbot was aware of the inharmony between the two boards, but he was happy to have a new challenge. In the first issues he edited, he changed the paper in dramatic, if sometimes superficial, ways. Photographs and illustrations returned to the front page. Headlines were larger. American news resumed its prominence, and local (Boston and New England) news began to reappear. On his second day, the lead story was the departure of Senator William Kenyon of Iowa from the U.S. Senate to take a federal judgeship, something Dixon would have been unlikely to feature. On the third day, the editorial page included a large political cartoon. On the fourth, only one lead article carried a foreign dateline. The international coverage didn't disappear, but it came more into balance with American coverage.

More important for the harmony of the church, the voice of the paper was softer and less challenging to tightly held views. Where Dixon in an editorial had called Japan "selfish" in its behavior toward China, Abbot's *Monitor*, more forgiving in its outlook toward nations as well as people, noted, in an editorial called "World Peace and Good-Will," that the presence of French Marshall Joseph Joffre in Japan in 1922 was "glowing demonstration of an amity between races that cannot be thought to be superficial." [10]

On the surface, there was little to object to. But Abbot seemed oddly unaware of some of the *Monitor*'s basic elements. For one thing, throughout his autobiography he got the paper's name wrong. Mrs. Eddy insisted that the name be *The Christian Science Monitor*, with an uppercase T. Yet Abbot continually referred to it without the capitalized article. More fundamentally, he seemed not to understand the paper's objective, even getting its wording wrong:

> *Its founder, Mary Baker Eddy, left no specific directions of policy for the guidance of editors other than the declaration "The purpose of the* Monitor *is to injure no one, but to bless all mankind." . . . Of course it cannot be taken too literally—particularly the last phrase. Not everything in even the most restrained newspaper can be made to "bless all mankind."* [11]

Abbot did not have the depth of understanding of Christian Science that Dixon did, but perhaps he didn't need to. The Directors seemed to have chosen him, not because he was an experienced Christian Scientist, but because he would not make waves and would keep the standard of journalism acceptable. Abbot's view of the *Monitor* harked back to the days of McLellan and Dodds, with articles tending toward a pie-in-the-sky hopefulness. A lead article on July 22, 1925, featuring coverage of an education conference in Scotland, was headlined "Educators Hail Plan for Finer World Citizens." The May 12, 1926, front page included "Scouts Pledge World Unity at Campfire." The *Monitor* seemed at times to be a caricature of itself.

Big disasters were not ignored, such as the explosion, in 1922, of the Army dirigible Roma in Virginia, which killed thirty-four (although the *Monitor* only hinted at the deaths).[12] Foreign news was featured when it was important enough. Editorials gently suggested that governments could make better decisions, as when the British, in response to unrest in India, arrested Mahatma Gandhi, whose movement for nonviolence was in full swing.

The paper was busy trying to persuade readers that all was well again at a time, however, when the world was headed for much bigger disasters than a dirigible accident; when it could have used a sober and perceptive newspaper with the mandate to go beneath the surface of the news to address the greed, complacency, and fear that were growing by the day; and when, in a word, the world needed a means of getting at *sin* more effectively than had Dixon.

Roscoe Drummond, who started as a reporter at the *Monitor* in 1924 and later became one of its star correspondents and columnists, complained of a "tendency to concentrate so much on . . . constructive news that in those days we concealed from *Monitor* readers a faithful and authentic knowledge of problems and conditions. . . ."[13]

Fittingly, the paper's largest sustained effort was put into covering the struggle to fight off moves to repeal

Prohibition—an amendment to the U.S. Constitution prohibiting the manufacture, transportation, and sale of alcoholic beverages. Christian Scientists don't drink, so it was a subject of interest among readers.

Abbot inherited a few staffers, including Paul Deland, who became city editor. But most major posts had to be filled again, from heads of the Washington and London bureaus to head of advertising. Cora Rigby, who had alerted Dixon to the subterfuge in Washington and Boston, and was not a Christian Scientist, became the new head of the Washington bureau, making her the first woman to hold such a role at a major paper. She was an outstanding journalist, but her appointment was a signal that church membership was no longer a prerequisite for a senior position at the *Monitor*. Those who helped run the paper needed only to be sympathetic with the religion.

Meanwhile, new writers had to be trained in the *Monitor*'s approach to journalism, and Deland took on the task. For all his loyalty, modesty, hard work, understanding of journalism, and sincerity about Christian Science, Deland, like Abbot, was not the kind of thinker who would help take the *Monitor* down new paths. He continued to preach Dodds' idea that the *Monitor* needed to "turn the news right side up," telling new reporters to forget conflict, passion, and the like. Social importance and lasting meaning were key.

In keeping with his concept of the *Monitor*'s mandate "to injure no man," Deland tried to protect public figures from themselves. A rash statement may not reflect their true meaning, he said, and could safely be ignored. He would not hesitate to tell a young reporter who had included a grating quote, "I expect the man said what you have quoted, but that isn't what he meant." [14] The reporter would have to go back to the interviewee to get another quote or put what was supposedly his real meaning into indirect discourse.

The approach gained the appreciation of many an interviewee. The *Monitor* earned a reputation for fairness and accuracy, and in the sense that the paper was scrupulous in reflecting what public figures really wanted to say, this was true. But by letting public figures revise what they said before publication, the paper was also misleading. Their quotations may have been what they preferred to see in print, but they were not necessarily what the interviewees thought, and what they thought was the source of what they did.

Young reporters mastered the *Monitor* formulas quickly. Drummond and his colleagues discovered how to get their articles into a prominent position on the front page:

> *The magic formula was bound up in the words "Peace, Prosperity, and Prohibition." We found that if we could get one of these words in the lead, we were on page one; if we could get two of these words in the lead, we were above the fold; and if we struck the jackpot and got all three words in the lead, we led the paper.* [15]

Reporters start to chafe

Given the Directors' determination to keep the church together after the litigation, it is not surprising that the *Monitor* began taking positions that more closely tracked members' interests. In 1928, for the first time, and again in 1932, the Directors decided to make a political endorsement and had the paper support Herbert Hoover for president. The issue was largely Prohibition, which Hoover favored. The *Monitor* published an eighteen-part series leading up to the 1928 election, which showed, in the description introducing the series, "the fallacy of some criticisms of prohibition, presenting some of its latest moral, social and economic aspects, recording instances of its proven worth and giving reasons why it should be strengthened rather than modified." [16]

Abbot wrote later, "I am proud that the *Monitor* during all my editorial association with it ranked as the leading and most uncompromising Dry daily in the nation." [17]

Some reporters on the paper were of a different mind. Drummond later referred to the campaign for Prohibition as "this wishful, unscientific news policy."

> *What I look back on and feel that therein we offended true Monitor journalism is the extent to which we misguided, misinformed, and misled the Monitor's whole readership by failing to report, by deliberately refusing to report the grievous shortcomings in the enforcement of the law and the widespread public resistance to the law. We just refused to give our readers a true picture of what was going on, . . .*[18]

Abbot's tenure had its successes. The circulation numbers returned to their former high, reaching 129,000 in 1927. Some excellent writers got their start, including Drummond and Canham. Other writers took the *Monitor*'s coverage in unique directions. The English novelist and short-story writer V. S. Pritchett, whose father was a Christian Scientist (although the son was not), began his career, in 1923, as a reporter and book reviewer with the *Monitor*, sending graceful prose from Ireland and Spain. Bylined simply V.S.P, his pieces rose above the pedestrian nature of daily journalism to describe a world of lyrical beauty:

> *Since rainy skies are Ireland's lot, and the air of Dublin is oftener gray with wet than white with sunshine, I would have you go to the Abbey theater in the rain. These rainy evenings have the night glare of melodrama about them—the indigo of wet nights and histrionic passion, the fierce yellow of electric light and dramatic crisis.*[19]

Pritchett knew how to record things the eye could not see.

The *Monitor* needed a better leader than Abbot, and in 1927, the Directors made a change, one, in fact, that they had been contemplating since Dixon's time. With the turmoil of the litigation now past and Abbot, the anti-Dixon, having served his purpose, they appointed an editorial board of four members to run the paper. One was Abbot, who took a drop in title to contributing editor. The others included the managing editor, chief editorial writer, and manager (head business executive) of the Publishing Society.

Crash

The editorial board had little time to settle in before facing a troubling issue in the country and the world. A potentially dangerous financial bubble was growing. An editorial on May 18, 1928, cautioned readers on the exuberance in the markets, asking rhetorically what it all meant. The *Monitor*'s answer: "Experts differ" and "Lambs, beware!"

It is to the *Monitor*'s credit that it did not join those who saw nothing but blue sky ahead. But the question is not, Did the *Monitor* issue warnings, which any responsible paper could have done, as the signs of potential trouble were everywhere. The question is, Did the *Monitor* give its readers a new and useful way to think about the issue? Did it go beyond the material picture of easy wealth and easy moralizing to help readers both identify the mental tendencies that needed to be corrected in themselves and society and become inspired to make sure all would be well?

Unfortunately, the *Monitor* was mostly absent.

On October 25, 1929—Black Thursday—the market fell fast, and the next day, the paper published an editorial called "The Mirage of Easy Wealth":

> *A month ago there were thousands of people scattered throughout the United States who referred with pride to their handsome profits in the stock market. Today a large proportion of them look back with regret that they ever joined that army, numbering in the millions, who believe there are easy profits to be had from security speculation.* [20]

Wagging a finger and chiding, "You should have known better," was not particularly helpful.

Then on October 29 came the big crash. Looking desperately to find the bright side, the *Monitor* called the day "exciting" and focused on the positive news that the market didn't drop even further.

The next day's editorial, "Clearing the Speculative Mists," clarified the *Monitor*'s view of the debacle:

> *Clearly the American public has gone about the business of setting its speculative house in order, not so much grimly as savagely, and in the slashing process is throwing values out of the window which later, in chastened and calmer mood, it will be quietly ushering in again through the door. . . .*
>
> *When this historic stock exchange fray is seen in calm perspective, it will be found that actual values are unchanged and that merely the speculative mist has been blown away.* [21]

The editorial board apparently either did not grasp or did not want to admit the seriousness of the situation, preferring simply to imagine a future when all problems were past. An editorial the following day continued in the same vein: "The crash in stock market prices in the United States, like most disasters, is not without its value to that part of the public which learns from catastrophes rather than from experience."

Canham later wrote of the period: "The Monitor's editorial and news policies were precise and positive during the years when preventive measures might have averted or mitigated world depression, and might have preserved peace. . . . Had its proposals for constructive and remedial action been followed in time, the world might have been a very different place." [22] But was the *Monitor*'s purpose, like that of most other newspapers, to get governments, business, and others to act? Or was it to help readers take their own action, beginning with their own thinking and prayers?

By 1933, when the Depression had taken its toll and the paper's circulation as well as its earnings had suffered, the

Directors finally decided that everything should be re-examined at the *Monitor*. They set up a Fact-Finding Committee consisting of Abbot and other insiders, as well as two outsiders who wrote for the *Monitor*: columnist and magazine writer Rufus Steele, and Philip Kerr, the Marquis of Lothian, a sometime British government official who had written for the *Monitor* since the early 1920s.

The committee came up with three recommendations, all of which were accepted by the editorial board and the Directors:

1. Local coverage should be strengthened, with a larger and stronger dedicated staff.

2. The paper should have a more modern style. The suggestion referred to the inhibitions that hurt the *Monitor*'s image, such as a ban on mentioning jazz bands and the continued queasiness about dealing with crime, disaster, and the like.

3. There should be a weekly magazine section, with material from well-known authorities and one interpretive article seeking to apply Christian Science thinking explicitly to the news. This interpretive article turned into a sort of laboratory for experimentation, which soon began opening new possibilities for *Monitor* journalism.

It seemed a new day was finally dawning. On November 25, 1933, the *Monitor* published the last of a week-long series of articles to commemorate the twenty-fifth anniversary of the paper. It was called the Progress Edition and examined humanity's progress over the last quarter century:

> *Every day men are laying the foundation of the future. The man who builds a bridge across a stream, the man who puts a road across a state, the man who drops a seed into the soil is performing a service which will count in the days that are to come.* [23]

Articles rejoiced in advances in fields from aviation to

social-service work. With a new Publishing House being erected, even The Christian Science Publishing Society was making progress:

> *Fifty years ago a Publishing Society, the personnel of which consisted of three workers!*
>
> *Thirty years ago a Publishing Society with workers numbering 25, . . .*
>
> *Today a Publishing Society . . . employing 928 workers, and with branches and offices all over the world!* [24]

The positive news was gratifying. But did it help *Monitor* readers move beyond wishful thinking about the world? Did it help correct the dangerous tendency, afflicting millions of people in the 1930s, toward fear and complacency? Mammoth international problems were growing by the day, and alert citizens were needed everywhere.

The lead editorial, where the *Monitor* could focus some useful insight, didn't start out well. It praised an eighteenth-century writer, Antoine Nicolas Condorcet, for his "declaration of faith in the indefinite improvement of human faculties and social behavior." Other writers improved on the idea, the editorial said, until "today men merely take it for granted that they are moving toward an ever more desirable civilization." [25]

Later, the editorial came somewhat to its senses. Addressing Dixon's favorite reader, the moral thinker and metaphysical worker, it identified spiritual perception as the key to human progress, noting that the question of whether the signs of human advancement constitute progress or merely change "cannot be resolved by considering the outward material phases of living, but only by examining its spiritual content."

Then it stopped. There was no attempt to take the reader beyond the thought that a spiritual view is helpful to the world. Dixon had tried to lift his readers beyond parochial perspectives and abstract metaphysics to deal with fundamental moral issues. This editorial simply offered soothing views of life from a

Christian Science perspective.

The *Monitor* could be a good newspaper, as good as any in the world, with the writers it now had. But it was not intended just to be a good newspaper any more than it was intended to be a church propaganda organ. It had to bring healing and do it in its unique way. That could not be accomplished, given its mission, structure, and history, without an application of rigorous, practical Christian Science to every word that was written.

6

The Problem of Evil

Dear God,

> *I am thankful for my nice home. I love you God. I am thankful for my father and mother. They are dear. . . . I wish to make my father and mother happy. She is very good to me. I am thankful for everything I have. I love God.*

J. Roscoe Drummond
Third Grade [1]

When he was two years old, Roscoe would sit in the lap of Ernest G. Cook, the superintendent of the Methodist Sunday school he attended, telling stories based on the picture books in front of him. Later, Roscoe asked to be put to work as a reporter for the Sunday school newsletter Cook had started. He not only gathered stories about the church and its members but also discussed the make-up of the newsletter with Cook, who worked at the *Watertown Daily Times* in New York. "Again and again, as a youngster," Cook wrote later, "he asked about this and that problem in editing a paper. It was plain to see he was to be a newspaper man." [2]

As a student at Syracuse University, Drummond became editor of the campus newspaper, *The Daily Orange*. On a trip to Boston near graduation time, in 1924, he stopped in at the *Monitor*. By then he was a Christian Scientist. ". . . I thought that you had to have at least 20 years experience before the *Monitor* would hire you," he said. "But I found out that things were different, and that they would rather take you before you've been 'mistrained' elsewhere."

Drummond quickly found a home in the *Monitor*'s approach to the news. It wasn't the objective facts he learned from his investigations that were important, he discovered. It was what he intuited based on his understanding of people and circumstances. "Excellent reporting does not stem from exclusive information but from exclusive insight," he once said. "The most important capacity of a newspaperman is the capacity to think." [3]

Writing on topics ranging from Prohibition to disarmament, Drummond moved steadily up the ranks in the paper from reporter to assistant city editor to chief editorial writer to European editorial manager. In the process, he developed a style that laid out issues in bold terms. "Peace is a dangerous, adventurous, risky business," he wrote in a 1931 article. "It can hardly be expected to entice the faint-hearted or the skittish. Treaties may explode in your hands. Dangers lurk in the diplomatic trenches." [4]

In November that year, he wrote about a disarmament conference that seemed to be going nowhere. The article put the onus for action on the governmental participants; but with an emphasis on the work that still needed to be done, it did not exempt *Monitor* readers from their supporting roles. "Success or failure?" he asked. "What the peoples say between now and February 2 will dictate the verdict." [5]

By 1933, he felt that he had a good sense of what the *Monitor* was about, and he wrote an article for the *Christian Science Sentinel* that set out his view of the paper after twenty-five years of its existence. The paper, to him, had a clear religious mission:

> . . . Monitor *journalism has proved itself to be something different from both the worst and the best journalism of its contemporaries. The reason is that it is seeking to express the ideals of Christian Science;* . . .[6]

In 1934, Drummond joined the *Monitor* editorial board as executive editor, the top editorial position on the paper. He had a vision for the paper that included finding more creative and meaningful ways to bring a Christian Science perspective to daily news reporting and commentary, and he helped nurture other writers who thought as he did. One of them was Rufus Steele.

The March of the Nations

The son of a Southern Methodist minister, Steele had started his career, in 1896, as a reporter for the *Chronicle-Record* of Chico, California. A little over a decade later, he had become the Sunday editor of one of the San Francisco newspapers. Things were not going well, and he was at war with his staff and his boss. As a new student of Christian Science, he turned to the religion and concluded that, as much as he wanted to escape to a new job, he had to stay and, through prayer, work the situation through to a positive conclusion.

He labored to replace his irritation with patience and humility. After a few weeks, his general manager came to his office and shut the door. "'. . . [Y]ou've changed so that I hardly know you,' he told Steele. 'You're not the same person you were. You've got hold of something that is being reflected in your men and in everything about you. I don't know what it is, but I do know that I'm in terrible need of it, and that I'm not going to leave this room until I've learned what it is and how to acquire it.'" [7]

He felt, at that point, that his job was done at the newspaper, and he left to become a freelance magazine journalist. But he was burning to bring his religion more explicitly into writing on current events, and, in September 1931, he joined the *Monitor* full-time to produce a daily column called "The March of the Nations." It reviewed the daily news with prose that tried to capture the churning and hope of desperate times.

The first column began:

> *Tramp, tramp, tramp. The nations are moving. Marching. Not in recent times—perhaps not ever—has their striding been so engrossing. It never meant so much. He who keeps up with these unprecedented motions rates as an educated man. He who omits to keep up tugs uncertainly behind his great times.* [8]

Each day, the column tried to pull threads of hope from the tapestry of the news. That first day, Steele noted the ideas of an emerging Indian leader:

> *London looks at Mr. Gandhi. In wonder. And respect. Streets jam, ears strain. The haughty radio waits. The Indian question rages. But the Mahatma is more interesting even than his question. . . . Millions of lesser thinkers follow him because materialism cannot hide the diamond light of devotion to conviction from men's famished eyes.* [9]

It wasn't Pritchett, but in his attempt to give the *Monitor* an identity as the teller of the nations' mental dramas, Steele was breaking new ground. The attempt to find novel ways to apply the compassion and insight of Christian Science to news writing was invigorating, even if Steele's style was somewhat tortured.

Steele did not write only his column. Having worked as a magazine writer, he was one of the biggest proponents of the new *Monitor* magazine section. On August 22, 1934, his article "Clipping the Wings of Fear" was published in the weekly magazine section, and the article became instantly popular among *Monitor* readers. It profiled naturalist Charles Kellogg, who believed that not only animals but also humans could smell fear. He claimed to have proved that, if you mastered your own fear, you could walk fearlessly among dangerous animals, and also understand and deal with confusing and dangerous human beings and institutions.

The article got to the heart of one of the key points of Christian Science—that one has to master fear in order to heal—and extended the lesson to a world preparing for war:

> *Fear is a false thing, a shadow men will come presently to understand. Kellogg's discoveries make it a little easier to let in the light where the shadow hides. Among men, as among animals, love is the antithesis and antidote of fear.*
>
> *Drawing our own conclusions, we begin to see that much of prevalent, disastrous thinking may have spread on these fear wings. A man may send apprehension through a neighborhood, the neighborhood through a state, and a state through the nation. Perhaps the unchecked fear of a few nations drove the present pall across the world. And as we see how the thing was done, we shall know how better to go about its undoing.* [10]

With the overwhelmingly positive reaction from *Monitor* readers, the article helped set the stage for future pieces in the magazine to bring Christian Science into the coverage of public affairs.

In June 1935, Steele joined Drummond on the Monitor's editorial board and continued to write his column. He began developing the theme that, in desperately trying to avoid drowning in the Depression, humanity was sinking deeper into the mesmerism of war.

But on the day before Christmas that year, hope was his theme. Noting the world's fear that war was coming again, he expressed confidence that statesmen would "feel the Christ touch that is upon them in these times." He ended his column with a heartfelt prayer called "Just a Thought," which began:

> *At Christmastide men's hearts grow kind,*
> *The Bethlehem babe restrains their pride,*

> *The whole world feels the Christ-child's mind*
> *At Christmastide.* [11]

Two days later, *Monitor* readers learned that Steele had died on Christmas Day.

In a long appreciation, the *Monitor* noted that his ". . . highest contribution was when he poured into his column a sense of vision which enabled his readers to look beyond the mundane news and glimpse the workings of a higher plan, a nobler purpose, an unfolding prophecy." [12]

> *Rufus Steele took the side of progress. Others might see obstacles in the path, might laboriously weigh the chances of defeat; this son of California pioneers saw always the promised land.* [13]

"God will show you"

Steele and Drummond were not the only *Monitor* writers to venture beyond conventional news writing and to explore the possibilities of the *Monitor*'s mandate "to spread undivided [Christian] Science." [14] Ironically, one of the most visionary was never on the staff.

Philip Kerr had wanted to be a Catholic priest, but by the time the British youngster entered Oxford University, he had come to the conclusion that having a divine calling did not necessarily mean holding a position in the church. He wrote his father: "I wish either to be a priest or to go into the army. I want to serve God in the way he has chosen for me, but I can't quite tell what it is yet."[15] His father's advice: "Let it be your constant intention that God will shew you what is His will for you." [16]

Upon graduation, he chose the service of the Queen and took a job in South Africa, helping create "responsible government" in the new colonies of the British Empire. In 1907, he became editor of a monthly South African magazine called *The State*, which aimed to prepare the way for unification of the country after the Boer War and to promote British protection as the best option for South Africans.

Meanwhile, his religious ideas kept churning. "In religion he was still a practicing Catholic," his official biographer later wrote, "but the practice was now, apparently, a duty rather than a source of happiness." [17] He admired the British Empire but had matured in his appreciation of it. "It is a noble thing," he said, "but not fit to be a God." [18] Later, he wrote to a friend: ". . . religion in its wider sense is just what I want myself. The seed is there all right but it wants the waters of tribulation and the sun of adversity to bring it to a mature growth." [19]

In 1910, he became editor of an influential political journal in England, the *Round Table*, which published information and ideas about the "imperial problem." For all his reluctance to make the British Empire a god, he was clearly enamored with its possibilities as a force for good in the world.[20]

He was working and traveling incessantly, and in 1913, he had a breakdown. Prescribed rest from "brain work" by his doctor, he repaired to St. Moritz, Switzerland, where he met Waldorf Astor and his wife, Nancy, who was to become, six years later, the first woman to serve as a member of the British Parliament. They struck up a close friendship, and Philip's health improved. ". . . I no longer sympathize with suicides," he wrote his mother. [21]

Later that year, Mrs. Astor had her own spiritual crisis. She had gone through turmoil similar to Kerr's about his Catholic upbringing, and after an illness and surgery that convinced her that sickness was not God's will, she had read Mrs. Eddy's *Science and Health* and had taken up Christian Science with enthusiasm. She and Kerr kept in touch, and in December he wrote her:

> *It makes the whole difference to one's life when one realises that one's here to do God's will in some way he'll show us, if we give him a chance, not just to seek pleasure and happiness for ourselves. That's of*

course the whole meaning of the first half of the Lord's Prayer. We are all inclined to forget it in the rush and bustle of modern life. It's a jolly good thing, Nancy, that you and I have had our breakdowns and have had a lot of rest and some pain to help us to listen. We've both heard the voice too and now we've got to obey it—that's more difficult I fear. I wonder where it will lead us to. I have no idea yet. Have you? [22]

The following spring, she sent a copy of *Science and Health* to Kerr, after he had had an appendectomy, and he was as impressed as she had been. Faith, he now believed, came through "the experience of active love." He recovered rapidly and attributed his better health to reading the book. Later he wrote, ". . . I was able to undertake duties far more arduous than those which previously had broken me down and carry them through successfully." [23] He never turned to a doctor again.

Christian Science rapidly infused his work, and he found a spiritual nobility in his job as editor of the *Round Table*. "The only justification for staying out of the trenches [of the World War]," he wrote his mother in 1915, "is that one should write things which will help to put an end to the evils which have caused this war. And the only way to be able to do that is to pray about it." [24]

Respect for Kerr in the British government kept rising, and at the end of 1916, Prime Minister David Lloyd George asked him to serve as his private secretary, saying that Kerr had "a naturally hopeful disposition." [25]

Kerr was always open to more service to the Empire, but Christian Science was now at the center of his thought. After serving Lloyd George for six years, he resigned from the government and traveled to America to learn more about the religion. He wrote his mother, "I don't find C.S. negative! Just the reverse. It's the most positive thing in the world, to me. It just makes the whole of the gospels alive with meaning, . . ." [26]

Back home, his journalistic experience and political background and connections caught the interest of *The Times* of

London, and in 1923, he was offered the job of foreign editor. He declined. His heart just wasn't in conventional journalism, at least as a full-time job:

> *The more I think and look about the more do I become convinced that the only solution of our problems, economic and political, is in progress in morals and religion. Politics is really secondary. . . . All the great leaders and teachers of mankind have seen this, and have concentrated their efforts in the realm of ideas, rather than of practical politics.* [27]

Kerr wanted to spend more time with Christian Science. He tried to apply it to everything he touched, from personal affairs to political affairs to journalism. He would set aside time each day for quiet study. He once wrote of this time of prayer:

> *It's vital, otherwise one gets swept off one's feet with the rush and turmoil of modern life. It's the "still small voice" that matters, and, as Elias saw, nothing, neither earthquakes, nor fires, nor winds, nor movies, nor newspapers, nor wars and rumours of wars can hide it.* [28]

In 1922, he visited Boston, and the editors of the *Monitor* jumped at the opportunity to use his services. He began contributing editorials and articles on English politics, and in 1925, he began writing a regular column for the *Monitor* called "The Diary of a Political Pilgrim," under the byline "A London Correspondent." Drawing a portrait of governments and their actions from the perspective of a knowledgeable insider, he focused on mental states as much as physical events. In the first column of the series, he looked at Europe after the World War, particularly a conference in Paris to straighten out some post-war problems. ". . . [P]eople are watching these activities," he wrote, "not so much for the merits of the issues, for these have not been of great importance, but for the temper in which the conference has been going about its work." [29]

His first article for the *Monitor* under his own name appeared in October 1929. He traced Anglo-American naval relations from 1812, noting key points of controversy, and asserted that the Kellogg-Briand pact for the renunciation of war, supported by new leaders, Hoover in the United States and MacDonald in Great Britain, offered a basis for a fresh start between the countries. The agreement, however, was only the beginning:

> *The second [step] is clearly to work out the means by which the peace pact itself can be made effective all over the world. For if war is effectively outlawed the question of "the freedom of the seas" will never arise.* [30]

The article analyzed knowledgeably and succinctly a key international issue. Its ending, however—a blend of positive thinking and a call to duty, which aimed to touch the spiritual energies of readers—lost its mooring and drifted uncomfortably into vague hopefulness.

The danger of unmoored hopefulness also dogged Drummond and, eventually, Steele. As it turned out, it lurked beneath many attempts at spiritually perceptive news and feature writing in the *Monitor*.

The spiritual commonwealth

In March 1930, Kerr's column ended, except for a brief resumption eight years later. The survey of the world from a moral and spiritual perspective was soon taken up by Steele. But this did not end Kerr's relationship with the *Monitor*, although it did mark another change.

His cousin, the tenth Marquis of Lothian, died that month, and Kerr became the eleventh Marquis. He was not enthusiastic about it—"One cannot fail to be unpleasantly conspicuous," [31] he said of his new title—but he had inherited several large estates and felt obliged to manage them well. Thereafter, he took the Marquis of Lothian as his professional identity and byline.

By this time, Lothian had given much thought to the *Monitor* as an institution, and in 1933, he became a member of the Fact-Finding Committee and, with Steele, one of the strongest proponents of reform at the paper.

Lothian himself was now finding inspiration in an idea he had thought about for years: that not just a world pact outlawing war but a world government was the key to peace. It would start with a new commonwealth linking English-speaking peoples, particularly in the United States and Great Britain. He worked to connect the idea with his religious convictions, coming to the conclusion that a world union would be the logical expression of the kingdom of heaven on earth. ". . . [I]t is only Christianity which can create the true Commonwealth," he wrote a friend in 1933, "because it is only Christianity which rests its commonwealth on One God, the Father of all, and all men as brethren." [32]

In August 1933, he wrote an article for *The Christian Science Journal* called "Christian Science and Prosperity," which tried to bring the theme of world unity down to the level of individual lives, where it could be more than just a dream:

> *There is no limit to the possibilities of a world animated by spiritual love in place of the national egotisms and individual selfishness and greed which seem to dominate it today.* [33]

Two years later, he wrote an article on the *Monitor* itself, which made explicit the idea that individual spiritual progress and world progress are connected. He began by pointing out that Christian Science is meant to do more than just heal individual problems. It had a collective mission, too, and when that mission was accomplished, it would lead to "the eternal commonwealth of God." [34] For Lothian, the *Monitor* was an important tool for reaching that collective state of harmony.

Its main task, he wrote, was ". . . to help mankind in the great Armageddon between Spirit and materialism, which is now upon us, and so bring to light upon the earth the ideal—man governed by divine Principle. . . ." [35] It was an echo of Dixon, but in far gentler words.

The Christian Science reader, Lothian knew, was essential to making the *Monitor* work, but the reader needed to raise his sights beyond his own world. "Is it possible to think of a more effective way of enabling Christian Scientists to use their understanding of Science for healing world problems," he wrote, "than the intelligent perusal of *The Christian Science Monitor?*" [36]

But the reader alone could not do the job. He had to work in tandem with committed and perceptive *Monitor* writers and editors, who themselves understood Christian Science:

> *. . . how else can [readers] get to know and understand what is going on in all parts of the world unless they can daily obtain news, chosen, interpreted, and commented upon by those who can see what is significant because they both have the human machinery for journalism and live in the metaphysical watchtower of Science, and so are enabled to survey the field of human consciousness as a whole in the light of divine Principle?* [37]

In Lothian's view, the team—readers and journalists— would work together to help uplift the world. Conceptually, he was defining the *Monitor*'s mechanism for effectiveness more explicitly than anyone else had to date.

Was there a kind of journalism beyond what the *Monitor* had tried that could actually link journalists and readers seamlessly? Lothian took on the challenge of finding out. He had been asked by the Directors, in 1935, to become European contributing editor, and although he was still writing for *The Times* and the *Observer* as well as the *Round Table*, he began writing for the *Monitor*'s weekly magazine.

Not surprisingly, world government as the key to world

peace became his keynote. In a magazine piece called "'Butter' and 'Guns' in Europe," he surveyed the developing chaos on the Continent, so soon after the disaster of the Great War, and asked, ". . .[M]ay not the nations . . . be willing to consider how to overcome the fundamental evil of anarchy by beginning to create among themselves a true reign of law?" [38]

He saw the United States as a force for universal harmony. He had become a great fan of the country on his trips there and in his embrace of the American-born Christian Science, but he regarded America's approach to peace through arbitration and disarmament as "admirable as far as it goes, but . . . also negative."[39] He wanted Americans to embrace the positive goal of world union.

It was a noble idea, but the chasm between Lothian's dream and reality was huge. Mrs. Eddy once told a student, who seemed to understand her teachings but failed to grasp how to apply them to daily life, "Come down. Your head is way up there in the stars, while the enemy is filling your body with bullets." [40] Lothian seemed to have a problem identifying enemies.

Hitler

Lothian met Adolf Hitler twice in the 1930s and came away preaching forgiveness. Long after many people had concluded that Hitler had belligerent designs, Lothian sympathized with him and, in essence, blamed the Allies for his behavior. "Like most Liberals I loathe the Nazi regime," he wrote, "but I am sure that the first condition to reform it is that we should be willing to do justice to Germany." He believed that "there would be no peace in Europe until Germany was given effective equality." [41]

After his first meeting with Hitler, in January 1935, Lothian gave an interview to the *Monitor*:

Lord Lothian is just back from a visit to Berlin, where he had a long private talk with Adolf Hitler. He is convinced that Germany does not want war and that Chancellor Hitler is ready to sign a treaty absolutely renouncing war for 10 years, . . .

"You can't solve these mutual suspicions by a philosophy of hate," he said. Those who are trying to build a ring round Germany in order to gain security by an overwhelming preponderance of force are actuated by fear, Lord Lothian went on, adding: "It is love that is wanted, not fear and hate."

'I have not the slightest doubt that this attitude is perfectly sincere. Hitler's Germany does not want war. [42]

When Hitler invaded Czechoslovakia, in March 1939, Lothian acknowledged his error. "Up till then it was possible to believe that Germany was only concerned with recovery of what might be called the normal rights of a great power," he wrote, "but it now seems clear that Hitler is in effect a fanatical gangster who will stop at nothing to beat down all possibility of resistance anywhere to his will. . . ." [43]

But the problem for Lothian wasn't only Hitler. In his writing and thinking on world union, he had attempted to "bless mankind" with profound ideals; but healing, whether individual or collective, required more than ideals, no matter how deeply thought out. Healing also required a knowledge of how evil attempts to undermine those ideals. Mrs. Eddy had taught a relevant lesson:

Unless one's eyes are opened to the modes of mental malpractice, working so subtly that we mistake its suggestions for the impulses of our own thought, the victim will allow himself to drift in the wrong direction without knowing it. [44]

Lothian tried to take up the challenge of evil in December 1938, when he returned to his favorite theme in a *Monitor* column called "The Wide Horizon." Unfortunately, instead of a perceptive analysis of the forces that seemed to be moving masses to self-destruction, he edged uncomfortably close to Dixon's frustration with the moral progress of humanity, as if it were to blame for undermining world unity. He decried:

> . . . *the limitations of modern civilization, the idolatry of the nation state, the bitter racial and class selfishness and hatreds, the concentration on purely material values, which unless they can be overcome by spirituality, will destroy the civilization of today as certainly as their equivalent evils destroyed the civilizations of the past.*
>
> . . . *it is clear that growth in the moral stature of man has not kept pace with his increasing command over nature. The widespread frivolity, sensuality, selfishness and greed of our time, as compared with the Spartan virtues of an early Puritan age, and its consequences, international and party rivalry, fear, brutality, and wars and rumors of wars, bear eloquent testimony of this.* [45]

In the face of the mammoth evil now marching through Europe, Lothian's analysis was more depressing than helpful.

Ambassador Lothian

Then an opportunity to make his ideals tangible appeared. On April 24, 1939, it was announced that Lothian would become the new British ambassador to the United States. His misreading of Hitler seemed largely forgiven; Britain needed the Americans on its side in the war that was clearly coming, and Lothian understood them better than anyone else in the British government. The *Monitor* was ecstatic. "No other Englishman in public life has such close and wide knowledge of the United States," it said. [46]

Lothian worked hard as ambassador, helping resolve major differences between the United States and Britain.

Winston Churchill, the prime minister who appointed Lothian, later wrote, "'As the tension of events mounted, not only did Lothian develop a broad comprehension of the scene, but his eye penetrated deeply.' . . .under the same hammer that smote upon us all, I found an earnest deeply-stirred man." [47]

As the fall of 1940 progressed, Lothian frequently labored into the early morning hours on issues affecting the two governments. It was not uncommon for him to give a speech in New York City, then catch the 2:35 A.M. train back to Washington so he could handle urgent business in the morning. In many respects, the fate of the world seemed to depend on his work. Meanwhile, people were noticing that his physical condition was suffering. At inopportune times, he would fall asleep, sometimes even while speaking. [48]

In early December, he became seriously ill. Members of the embassy staff urged him to seek medical care, but Lothian declined. He called a Christian Science practitioner, who took a train down from Boston, and Lothian rallied. He could not give the speech he had been writing, however, and he asked an aide to make the delivery. It won praise from many quarters. *Time* magazine called it "in some respects Lord Lothian's best speech."

Late in the evening, Lothian's condition worsened. When Alistair Cooke, a correspondent from the *Times* of London called at the embassy the next morning to interview Lothian, the butler told the correspondent, "I'm terribly sorry, Sir, that will be quite impossible. The Ambassador died early this morning." [49]

The *Monitor* had lost a friend and a writer who braved convention by trying to bring Christian Science more to the forefront of public affairs, both in his government career and in his journalism.

The experiment continues

For a while, the paper continued the experiment with explicit Christian Science writing in the magazine. In 1944, two months before the U.S. presidential election, Drummond wrote an article for the magazine called "How Are You Going to Vote?" He elucidated "Eight Guides to a Thoughtful, Faithful, Prayerful Election"—including be fair, be wise, be intelligent, have integrity, be diligent. He spoke of the importance of having faith in democracy "in this hour and in this crisis of world chemicalization." [50]

But it was not much less vague than Lothian's call for world government. This experiment with explicit spirituality wasn't working. It was becoming clear that most writers simply did not have enough healing experience to break through readers' complacence, and deal compassionately and specifically with the evils that paralyze humanity. Without that healing experience, and the love and insight that accompanied it, bringing Christian Science terminology into the *Monitor*'s articles could simply paper over problems with soothing language.

One of those who objected to the way the articles brought Christian Science into the *Monitor* was Canham. He wrote in his history of the paper:

> *The articles themselves suffered from the defect of not being totally religious or totally secular. They were often neither one thing nor another, and they took on the disadvantages of compromise and mixture. It was seen that religious thinking can and should underlie anything and everything in the* Monitor. *Copy can be motivated, illuminated, and inspired by deep convictions and insights, but it must not be preachment or proselytizing.* [51]

Commenting earlier on a draft of Canham's book, Drummond objected to his friend's categorical dismissal of the experiment. Referring to the section of the book "in which you argue how wrong it was to try to find a way of appropriately including visible Christian Science thinking and some Christian Science terminology in those articles," Drummond said:

I would share your view that in the main they were not good enough. That may well have involved an unwise mixture, and all I am suggesting is that we do not conclusively assert that they were wrong in principle, because I can conceive the time coming when we will have growth, talent, and insight, and find ways to do this effectively and appropriately. [52]

Canham, however, did not change his text.

The *Monitor*'s work of not injuring, of blessing, and of spreading Science still had a long way to go. The world was at war, and hatred, violence, cruelty, and death were the stuff of the news. A paper that could handle the evil with confidence, exposing it without injuring people and without increasing the fear of readers, giving evidence that love was more powerful than all the bombs and bombast, could prove a valuable tool. The writing had to be vigorous and creative, and every word had to contribute to moral and spiritual progress in readers. It had to be practical as well as idealistic. If the writing could not always be great literature, it still could reflect the power, compassion, and fearlessness of Jesus' communication and the healing efficacy of Mrs. Eddy's. That, at least, was the aim.

Could the *Monitor* do that? Could it find writers and editors who could make Christianity more than just words and expose the dangerous subtleties of evil with healing insight?

7

A Prize and a Prophet

One man seemed to have the intelligence, temperament, journalistic skill, and commitment to Christian Science to finally pull things together at the top. He had come from the same rural New England stock as Mrs. Eddy.

Erwin Canham had grown up only 130 miles from Mrs. Eddy's birthplace of Bow, New Hampshire, but in quite a different environment. His family circle in southern Maine, though religious, had none of the thundering theology of Mrs. Eddy's father or the local preachers, and as a boy, he lacked the drive, spiritual or otherwise, that caused Mrs. Eddy to break early with the darker beliefs around her. In a short autobiography he wrote:

> . . . our lives moved along in a kind of overcast. Life had its joys and contentments. There were moments of resignation, and sometimes perhaps a touch of desperation. But there was little sparkle, little clarity, little direction in the things we did and felt. [1]

Already in the sixth grade by the time he was eight years old, in 1912, but with no appealing future visible from his one-room schoolhouse to fire his ambition, Erwin occupied himself by helping his father, who ran the newspaper in Sanford, Maine. The shy boy would check with the townspeople for the latest news about their livestock and families, then give his notes to his father to turn into copy. "I remember standing in back of the typewriter," he wrote, "resting my hand on the carriage, and letting it ride back and forth." [2] The family tried to live righteous lives, helping their neighbors and attending the

Methodist church regularly, sometimes three times on Sunday.

There wasn't much of a larger point to it all until moral uprightness met looming tragedy. When Erwin was ten, in 1914, his mother came down with such a severe throat infection that the family was told she couldn't live out the day. The doctor backed away, and Erwin's mother was left with the memory of a book she had once glanced at, Mrs. Eddy's *Science and Health*, given to the Canhams by a woman who had done some housework for them. Mrs. Canham got word to a Christian Science friend nearby, who then called a Christian Science practitioner in Boston and asked him to pray. "Within a few hours the growths broke and ran harmlessly away, . . ." Canham wrote. "It was as if sunlight had burst into our lives for the first time." [3]

The family began an intensive study of the religion. Mrs. Canham became a Christian Science practitioner, healing people professionally for the next forty years. Erwin's father continued for a while in newspaper publishing, then returned to his favorite subject, farming, as agricultural editor of the *Lewiston Sun*. The family moved to the small city of Auburn, and Erwin finally entered a school that could raise his sights. With high-school teachers trained in Latin, French, and English, he quietly absorbed the better environment; then, near the end of his senior year, he burst out with a play co-written with a friend, which was produced by the school and received delighted comment among his friends and teachers and in the local papers.

When he reached Bates College, a small school in Maine, Erwin immediately began earning A's. He spent all his college summers but one working for newspapers, first as a proofreader, then as an editor, and in the summer before his senior year, as Maine correspondent for two newspapers apiece in Boston, New York, Philadelphia, and Portland, Maine. In his senior year, he was nominated for a Rhodes scholarship, and when he graduated, he was offered a reporting job with the *Monitor*.

Canham was never good at small talk, but from the

beginning, he exuded an intellectual sincerity, which outshone his shyness and made people trust him. Advancing quickly and seemingly without effort, he was offered challenges such as covering the Boston State House after only a few months on the job. He had failed to receive the Rhodes scholarship, which he was nominated for at Bates, but he applied again and, this time, was accepted for three years of study at Oxford University in England. The *Monitor* gave him leave, and during breaks from school, he helped the paper cover the League of Nations in Geneva, Switzerland.

He learned to love the beautiful city between the Alps and Jura mountains at the tip of Lake Léman, a new world center full of history in the struggle for religious rights and humanitarian ideals. He also broadened his perspective on Christian Science:

> *I could see that my religion was not only the wonderful healing truth that had saved my mother in our little Maine town in 1914, thus opening our lives to rich personal fulfillments, but also a universal principle available everywhere and applicable to collective as well as to personal problems.* [4]

Where Lothian had soared majestically in his rhetoric about healing the collective problems of humanity, Canham took the more modest approach of an educated, but rooted, New Englander. He tried to practice Christian Science quietly in his immediate surroundings, whether in Oxford or Geneva. He had a generosity of spirit in what he called the "impersonal sense of God as the giver of all good," [5] and he developed a wide circle of contacts throughout Europe. His bosses noticed. Soon after his last term at Oxford ended, in 1928, he was put in charge of the *Monitor*'s bureau in Geneva.

His writing style, exuding intelligence and quiet confidence, was meticulous in its attention to accuracy. He made no pretension to detached or cynical reporting but put forth a touch of innocent hope that endeared him to *Monitor* readers.

In his first bylined article, written while accompanying British Prime Minister MacDonald on a trip to the United States in October 1929, Canham described MacDonald as "[e]xpressing confidence so inspired and breath-taking that even the studied language of diplomacy could not dim its radiance, . . ." [6] He was still trying to find his voice as a *Monitor* reporter, and the awestruck tone said more about Canham's inexperience than about MacDonald. Still, the language showed a self-assurance that made readers pay attention.

In 1932, he returned to the United States as chief of the *Monitor*'s Washington bureau and learned to navigate the treacherous waters of American politics. New president Franklin Roosevelt presented a particular challenge:

> *One had to avoid being carried away by that skillful charmer at biweekly press conferences and yet not lapse into negativism on the opposite side. The writing one had to do was apt to be criticized by conservatives as too sympathetic with the Roosevelt Administration, and by liberals as hopelessly reactionary.* [7]

Canham's idea of being neutral was getting the story right. In a speech he gave later in life, he discussed the importance of accurate reporting and told the audience, "I shall not use the word "objectivity" because I do not believe there is any such thing, but I believe accuracy is a standard which can be relatively if not absolutely sought, . . ." [8]

Spiritual values

Canham felt that one thing that made the *Monitor* valuable was the ability to go beneath the surface of the news. In a speech in 1935, he defined the work of the paper as twofold:

> *The first part of our daily task is to tell you what is going on. That can be relatively simple, almost mechanical. If that were all we had to do, our only problem would be to keep you from getting the idea that we were either knocking or boosting the events and policies which we were simply recording.* [9]

The *Monitor*'s second task, however, was more demanding:

> *. . . to take our fan in hand and winnow the chaff from the wheat.*
>
> *It is news when a group of four thousand farmers come to Washington to express enthusiastic support of the Administration's farm program. But you want to know more. You want to know what prompted the farmers to come, who paid the carfare, what their private opinions are, whether they are intelligent, reasonable, impartial men. In a word, you are entitled to know what is behind the news.* [10]

Canham believed that what lay behind the news was more than just the five w's of who, what, where, when, and why. There was also "which"—which sense of reality, the spiritual or the material, was driving the thoughts and actions of those involved.

Astute reporting uncovers motives and unseen influences. Any publication with clear-headed and courageous reporters and editors can do at least some of that. It takes a reporter with a metaphysical standpoint and a practical purpose to uncover the deeper moral and spiritual forces shaping mankind and then to share what he has discovered in ways that help readers respond constructively. Canham's idea of the *Monitor*'s role was to go boldly over the ground of moral and spiritual reality and define it in words that didn't just explain; they also healed.

His perspective influenced his choice of what to report.

Accompanying Roosevelt to London for the World Economic and Monetary Conference in 1933, he briefly quoted Prime Minister MacDonald's welcoming speech, then spent considerable time describing the "particularly impressive scene" as King George addressed the delegates "on a higher plane than mere economic and diplomatic debating grounds. . . . he effectively reminded the delegates that they were not simply an august assemblage, but actually the embodiment of the hopes and wishes of the whole world." [11] Then, having set his readers in the direction in which he wanted them to think, Canham described the challenge MacDonald put to the Americans—settling the issue of war debts—trusting that the fresh inspiration from the King's speech would enable readers to find their own inspiration for prayer from the rest of the story.

He was quickly gaining stature inside the church, and in 1939, he was asked to come to Boston as chief news editor, with Drummond taking Canham's place as Washington bureau chief. The move was widely seen as a demotion for Drummond, but he swallowed his pride and began the most productive period of his career, writing a column called "The State of the Nation," which was admired by readers around the world.

At the same time Canham came to Boston, the Directors finally decided to end the editorial board that had run the paper since 1927. They evidently felt that they now had the right person for the top position. For two years, a former manager of the Publishing Society, who had also served as executive editor on the editorial board, Roland Harrison, held the position of chief editorial executive with the title of administrative editor. When Harrison died, in early 1941, Canham took over as chief editor with the title of managing editor.

For the first time since Dixon, the Directors had a genuine star at the top of the paper. And this time, they were confident that their choice not only would not embarrass them or the church but would represent well the thinking and living that Christian Science could bring to world affairs.

The dark days are not forever

Canham's immediate challenge as editor was to direct the *Monitor*'s coverage of World War II. The *Monitor*'s job, he believed, was not just to report but "to help lead the nations back to peace." [12] He saw no contradiction between the teaching of Christian Science that God does not make or condone war and the need to fight Nazi and Japanese aggression. He did not hesitate to take positions that seemed biased to some, but were in fact an effort to find constructive ground between the pro-Nazi views of certain readers, who saw Hitler as the savior of German pride and prosperity, and the misguided faith of others, who saw Christian Science wrongly as a pacifist religion.

Canham began writing a weekly column called "Down the Middle of the Road," making clear that he did not see a contradiction between moderation in public affairs and radical spiritual idealism. He was a skilled enough writer not to have to resort to religious jargon to make his points, although he resorted to the language and ideas of Christian Science at critical times.

And yet, with all Canham's spiritual confidence, a certain sadness, even Old Testament despair, started creeping into his writing. Toward the end of 1941, a few days after Japan attacked Pearl Harbor, Canham wrote a column that made clear where his sympathies lay:

> *The United States and Great Britain have suffered severe naval reverses. Yet it is not out of order to speak of the tragedies of Japan and Germany. For all the people of these two nations will be the great and final sufferers in this world situation, and the fate of the two nations for long decades to come will be darkened by the deeds of their leaders in these days.* [13]

Canham laid out what would become a major theme throughout his tenure at the *Monitor*. Materialism, he insisted, is the real problem. Referring to Japan's leaders, he wrote:

> *What they do not understand, fundamentally, is Man. Their suicide squads may blow up a few battleships. But by that very fact, they seal their own doom. Man is real, and will live on. Suicide squads do not. You cannot absorb western civilization by attacking it. And what Japan needs is ideas, not bombs. What individual Japanese need is a recognition of their true selfhood as sons of God. Had they ever entered the stream of world civilization, they would have had their chance of gaining their heritage. Now they are disinheriting themselves.* [14]

It was thrilling stuff to many *Monitor* readers, who rejoiced at Canham's spiritual insight and moral courage. But his approach was also dangerous. In the same way that Lothian had tried to spiritualize the British Commonwealth, essentially God's chosen model for world peace, and then blasted the sins that seemed to prevent the fulfillment of his dream, Canham was beginning to spiritualize the West, particularly America, and to condemn the ignorance he saw as undermining its influence.

As for daily coverage of the war, Canham had a team of talented writers, but they were of various religious backgrounds, and he could not ask them to see things as he did. The approach that worked was to ask them to find the underlying significance behind the headlines of any given day. "[The correspondents'] job was to give an authentic picture of war and its meaning, not solely its adventures," he wrote. "And so, the adventures as such tended to be played down, the significance was emphasized." [15]

Canham's *Monitor* was straightforward about the war without being sensational. After Pearl Harbor was bombed, the paper featured, in bold type, a headline across the top of page one that could have appeared in any newspaper:

Congress Declares War on Japan;
3,000 Casualties in Hawaii Air Raid [16]

Canham was even willing to put headlines such as "Nazi Bombs Kill 8,098" [17] on page one, albeit further down the page. The paper's queasiness in its early years about noticing the dead was gone.

But facts alone were not the *Monitor*'s main purpose. Conveying meaning was key, and correspondents generally were able to capture the flow of military movements or diplomatic efforts in terms that not only gave readers a sense of the news behind the news but also gave them hope that the dark days were not going to continue forever.

One of Canham's best correspondents in the Pacific was Gordon Walker. In June 1943, he embedded himself with the U.S. Marines as they landed in New Georgia. His interest was not the fighting so much as the thinking, and he wrote in the *Monitor*'s magazine section of the lessons the Marines learned about "The Art of War in the Jungle":

> *Number one on the lesson sheet is the overcoming of fear. Fear was one of the earliest and biggest obstacles in the jungle—a fear which surpasses the ordinary brand of "battle fright" experienced in other combat areas. Its promulgation was one of the most potent of enemy weapons. It is undoubtedly the key to Japanese tactics.* [18]

In Europe, Richard Strout led the way with dramatic prose. During the Normandy invasion, in 1944, he traveled on the U.S.S. Quincy:

> *Midnight. It is June 6, D-day.*
> *The breeze has freshened. France is off ahead. There is a spurt of distant tracer bullets and a falling meteor, that is really a falling airplane. . . .*
> *I keep thinking of home. It's 7 p.m. there now. The family is just finishing supper. It's the same in millions of American homes, children doing home work, mothers at dishes, fathers reading papers. And here we*

are on the dark sea moving at half speed toward history.[19]

There was no blood and guts in Strout's writing. Boats that hit landmines were simply silenced. But the lack of jarring details actually helped the *Monitor*'s message come through. "After seeing the things I have in the past 24 hours," Strout wrote, "I know one thing now—the road may be tough but we can't lose." [20]

Toughness and discipline

The *Monitor*'s foreign editor, Charles Gratke, had the most to do, after Canham, with how the paper conducted its war coverage. He was a tough editor, demanding discipline of himself and his staff, including two secretaries, one who would take dictation in German and the other in French.

Loving his no-nonsense attitude, many reporters became devoted to him as someone who could teach them not only how to write well but how to think clearly.

The importance of thought as the mover of action was a constant theme for Gratke in his own writing. On May 7, 1945, the day the German army finally surrendered, he wrote of the "Challenge to World Thinking" that had been presented by the Nazis:

> *A series of errors in thinking has led, with the inexorability of a Greek tragedy, to the fall of the Third Reich.*
>
> *How much of the unregenerate Nazi thought remains?*
>
> *The men of Germany have had their weapons struck from their hands. But the world is not yet freed from the distorted concepts which unleashed five stark years of tragedy.* [21]

The idea of a master race, Gratke wrote, seemed

invincible, but in the end "it robbed the German nation both of the will and the capacity to govern itself."

> *To the conventional Prussian thought, the highest qualities are those of discipline, of devotion to duty, of obedience, in a military sense. Without the leaven of a higher idealism, they became subject to misuse—culminating in the acceptance of the lie that war, in itself, is a moral and desirable end.*
>
> *Such concepts, of course, contain the seeds of their own destruction.* [22]

It was a useful hint of how a *Monitor* reporter could write about evil—as something impersonal that eventually destroys itself.

It was a blow to the paper when, a few years later, Gratke was killed, with a dozen other correspondents from other newspapers, in a plane crash in India.

War without and within

As Walker, Strout, Gratke, and other correspondents and editors tried to elucidate the meaning of the war for readers, Canham, as top editor, presented in his column what was essentially the *Monitor*'s perspective on the war, as well as his own. At the end of 1942, he had written:

> *We have done much toward winning that war which is the war within. Our fighting men have won it already, and the rest of us are on our way. Our moral victory already is immense, for we have shown that the lies the enemy told about us—which we half believed—were only lies.* [23]

But as the war dragged on, Canham became as exasperated with his countrymen as he had been with the Japanese and Germans. In his summary of the war's progress at the end of 1943, he had written:

> *We Americans at home are, most of us, farthest of all from winning the spiritual victory which is indispensable if we are to win our war. 1943 has revealed this weakness, this need, in our body politic and 1944 must be the occasion for a rising above it unless we are to have a postwar nation grievously divided between the sober and the frivolous, the wise men and the fools. All I can say in conclusion is: Let's rise in our conscious stature of manhood, declare our birthright, and . . . wake up.* [24]

When Paris was finally liberated, in August of 1944, Canham gave his readers permission to breathe, but he still could not relax. Who was going to wake America? "We are not sure that we can prevent some of these evils from recurring," he warned. "We do not quite know how deeply the poison has penetrated." He complained about selfishness and greed "among some of the apparent victors." [25]

Pessimism and optimism were constantly at war in Canham as he watched the drama of the war unfold and then the drama of peace. He tried to keep hope visible. "The disintegration of the enemy is proof to us at last that the forces of darkness are vulnerable," [26] he wrote. But when he found himself in the audience of the conference in San Francisco that created the new League of Nations, now called the United Nations, he wondered why there was no celebration. Maybe people were numb from the war, he mused. Nearly a decade of barbarity and harsh rhetoric, victory and setback, had drained the world of emotion. But he would not accept the surface explanation:

> *There is another reason why we do not celebrate. We all know it is not over. Hitler and Mussolini may be gone, their armies may be crushed. But the problems they have called into being are far*

from gone. Hate and fear are not gone. Hunger is not gone. Disorder is still here. Cruelty and arrogance may turn into civility and cringing. But behind are the same problems. . . . It is not time for dancing in the streets, or for blowing tin horns. The war to end wars is not over. It is just beginning. [27]

Through all his years, now nearly twenty, of writing for the *Monitor*, Canham had developed his voice. He was no longer the inexperienced Christian Scientist trying to keep his feet on the ground. He was the solemn realist with a mission of faith, an Old Testament prophet despairing of mankind's weakness but determined to thunder his message, hopeful that some of his listeners would awake. There were big problems coming, one of the most notable being the new Cold War with communism. Canham's call for alertness blended with the call of the times, not just for the paper and the church but for America and the world.

At the end of 1944, the Directors gave Canham the title of *Monitor* editor. It seemed inevitable. He was bringing the *Monitor* visibility it had not had for a long time, if ever, and his prophetic thundering was defining a moral condition that many Americans, deep down, suspected was true:

The United States is rapidly destroying many of the values for which it has just fought the costliest war in history. It is engaged in destroying its position in the world, its tangible strength, its capacity to help stabilize the world and help save mankind. It is sliding down a very slippery slope. There is time to stop, but there is no time to lose. [28]

A big problem, in Canham's view, was a lack of clarity about America's mission. Russia had a mission as embodied in the Soviet Union. Britain had one, too. But America's only goal seemed to him to be "selfish materialism." America should have only one interest, Canham wrote, the fulfillment of its destiny.

"That destiny is spiritual leadership, carried out in practical terms."[29]

The American public, or at least the part that read the *Monitor*, loved hearing that their country had such a noble purpose. The fight against communism was beginning to shape America's view of itself and the world, and Canham's was now a voice of strength in that fight. But Canham was responsible for a newspaper too, and he needed to make sure its stature was rising along with his. Ironically, he was helped in that regard by a former communist.

The *Monitor*'s first Pulitzer

Edmund Stevens's route to the *Monitor* was unusual. He was American but grew up in Rome, learning Italian, French, and German along with English. He developed an early fascination with Mussolini, and when he returned to the United States as a teenager, he eagerly joined a fascist organization. His commitment was as total as a young New Yorker could make it: he wore black shirts, carried a dagger, and got into street fights with anti-fascists.

When he entered Columbia University to study international law, he discovered a new outlet for his raging ideals: communism. After graduation, he headed to Moscow, where good jobs were reportedly available, arriving in the spring of 1934, with a letter of introduction from Earl Browder, the head of the American Communist Party, sewn into his jacket lining. [30] He promptly landed a job for three hundred rubles a month as an editor with the Publishing Cooperative for Foreign Workers, a division of the Communist International, or Comintern, the international organization of communist parties.

Stevens eventually settled himself into the English-language section, staffed largely by Jews from the Bronx. Most of them had already given up their passports and taken Soviet citizenship. Stevens saw no reason to rush the process. Life was good, foreigners were tolerated, Russians were friendly, and travel was cheap. He visited Leningrad and the Black Sea resort of Sochi, the latter in the company of his friend Leo, an Italian who would volunteer only his first name.

That fall, Stevens met Nina Bondarenko, a farm girl from the Urals, who had dropped out of university in Leningrad to look for a job in Moscow. She liked him because he was unlike most Americans—he hated baseball and was well traveled. He promised to show her Rome someday.

During the Moscow University evening classes they both attended, she pushed her views on the instructor, arguing over the recent collectivization that had resulted in famine and death for millions. Nina had seen frozen corpses in the streets of her town and was in no mood to rejoice over communism.

Stevens was happy to take her side. His ideals, it turned out, ran only so deep. Soon the local trade union, realizing that perhaps the young American was not as committed a convert as they had thought, gave Nina a "social assignment." Using the movie tickets and theater seats they provided, Nina warmed up the relationship until Stevens proposed marriage in December. The trade union told Nina she was overdoing it. She didn't listen.

The problems of marrying a foreigner in the Soviet Union were numerous, and Nina did not say yes right away. She once stood Stevens up for a date and, early the next morning, rushed to apply for a factory job, anything to get away from the relationship, which seemed doomed. But he wouldn't give up, and they continued to see each other despite their differences. One spring day, they were walking by the Moscow River opposite the Kremlin. Ed turned to her and said, without much passion, "I love you, Nina, and I wish we could get married." [31]

Surprising herself, she agreed, and a few days later they went to the Office of the Civil Registry and got their marriage license for three rubles. To celebrate the occasion, Ed took Nina to the nearest coffee shop, on Gorky street, ordered a bottle of champagne, and drank it all himself.

Stevens chafed at the practical details of home life. He had his dreams, and they did not involve family. One night Nina came home late from work:

"Is there anything to eat in the house?" I [Nina] asked Ed.
"I guess not. I ate what was left, which wasn't much," was his reply, as he stretched his long legs across the room.
"You could think of going out to get some groceries."
"How? I have no money."
My mother came and lent us a ruble for a loaf of bread and a pint of milk.
"How long can we go on borrowing from my poor mother? What is wrong with you? Tell me what you are good for?" I kept nagging him.
"I am a writer," he said.
"Then what are you waiting for? Go ahead and write!"
"I am waiting for inspiration!" [32]

His friend Leo sympathized. What kind of life was this, numbed day and night with petty office and family issues? Leo had already spent time in fascist prisons, and he convinced Stevens it was time to put their ideals to a real test. They prepared to head for Spain to fight Franco, but Stevens stalled. Leo threw up his hands and took off for the front. He was killed almost immediately. Nina was grateful now for her husband's passivity.

Stevens's precious inspiration finally came when he saw that the problems they faced were quite a bit larger than an empty refrigerator. Stalin's purges had reached Moscow, and Stevens couldn't help noticing that writers, intellectuals, and government leaders kept disappearing. When his colleagues and neighbors began dropping out of sight one by one, he realized that the naïve dreams of his youth had finally run their course. He soon lost his own job. His American passport, which his inertia had kept him from exchanging, was probably the only thing that saved his life.

He was now desperate. Taking his writing skill, along with the acute sense of sympathy with ordinary people that had drawn him to fascism and communism in the first place, he registered as a journalist. In 1938, he started freelancing for British news organizations, including Reuters and the *Manchester Guardian*. In 1939, he approached the *Monitor* and asked for a chance to write for the paper. Foreign editor Gratke agreed to let him file stories from the Baltic states of Latvia, Lithuania, and Estonia, which Stevens felt instinctively would be news-making spots in the coming months. After a drawn-out battle with the Soviet government, Stevens was able to get an exit visa for Nina and their son. He dropped his family off with his mother, in New York, before heading for the Baltics.

For the first time in his life, Stevens was looking at the world through fully open eyes, and the *Monitor* editors were impressed with what they read. Set against shockingly brutal events, his reports were informative and calming, historically aware, and full of compassion in their choice of detail. It was as if the tenderness Nina had longed for from him could finally come out, but only on the page.

The *Monitor*'s style of interpretive reporting suited him well, and he added his own narrative flair. In one of his first stories, he wrote of the hurried exodus of Germans from Latvia:

> *Yesterday prospective emigrants bought up every trunk and suitcase in Riga and also extensively purchased clothing, woolens and foodstuffs. I saw one woman buy five pairs of shoes of graduated sizes for a single child. She explained that Prime Minister Neville Chamberlain said the war would last a minimum of three years.* [33]

A short time later, Stevens moved north to cover the Russo-Finnish War and noted where the priorities lay for the Soviet government. He now held no love for the government, if he ever did. The Russian people and their suffering, though, was another story:

> *As the Finns during the past few days have driven the Russians back across the icy plains of*

Lapland, eyewitness reports disclose a tragic tale. For Russian soldiers captured in the Salla sector, just north of the Arctic Circle, have been found with thin, ragged clothing. Even in this sudden cold, which sent the mercury down to 20 degrees below zero, the majority of Soviet troops were gloveless. [34]

Later, Stevens turned his attention to the other side:

Under cover of darkness I visited the Finnish front-line positions. The road had been bombed during the day and for the last few miles our driver turned out his headlights and steered by the pale cold light of the aurora borealis. It was an eerie world of stunted trees against a snowy background where men in snow capes and cars painted white were invisible. Up ahead at intervals Russian artillery flashed blue and red against the sky. [35]

But always, Stevens returned to the plight of the people:

Returning from the front the other day I arrived in Lappeenranta, a small town 30 miles northwest of Viborg, 20 minutes after a bombing.

The sidewalks were piled with furniture, bedding, and household articles salvaged from the burning houses. I saw a housewife open her laundry drawer out on the sidewalk, and reach for a handkerchief, just as she had done for years in the privacy of her own home. [36]

He went on to cover events in Stockholm and Oslo, then moved to Romania. Gratke brought him home in 1941 to work for a time on the *Monitor*'s foreign desk—Nina and their son had moved to the Boston area—but Stevens proved too restless for office work and, in ten months, returned overseas, leaving Nina pregnant again. Gratke and the spouses of other *Monitor* writers watched over the family, and the Stevens family attended the Christian Science church in Concord, Massachusetts, regularly. But neither Stevens nor his family ever embraced the religion, nor did they experience any healings through Christian Science. Once he left the *Monitor,* in the 1950s, he never set foot in the church again. [37]

In 1943, Stevens moved again to Moscow to be the *Monitor*'s correspondent there, and after the war, his family joined him. He had one more surprise for Nina, though. She had shipped her nicest clothing ahead of her, having let it rest in a trunk for years because she did not want to appear immodest during the war. When she arrived in Moscow, ready to set up her new life, she discovered that her husband had sold all her clothes, thinking she didn't need them. The greatest indignity for her was walking around Moscow, seeing her dresses and hats on other women.

For three more years, he filed dispatches from Moscow and made extensive notes of post-war life. He understood as much of the Russian soul as a Westerner could. When he and his family left the Soviet Union in 1949, he wrote a forty-four-part series called "This is Russia—Uncensored," which caught the tone of the times and provided the practical counterweight to Canham's moral vision.

The attitude in Russia toward Americans, allies in the war but ideological opponents, was hardening. His first article in the series, on October 18, began:

> *An ever-widening gap divided us from Soviet soil as the good ship Byeloostrov cast off. While Leningrad slipped astern, our immediate feelings were of unrestrained relief.*
>
> *After years of hope and frustration, our final memory of the U.S.S.R. was a three-hour bout with customs officials that left us angry and exhausted. Every carefully packed article was dragged out and scrutinized. A dydee doll of daughter's that squeaked when squeezed roused special suspicion.* [38]

He described how the air had become thick with hate and suspicion, how correspondents were condemned as spies, how his children were taunted as "Amerikantsi." He had even caught the family's maid thumbing through his address book and realized she was a government plant.

As the series moved along, with sarcasm where it was deserved (the privileged lives of Soviet elites) and with an honest assessment of a system that sometimes worked and often didn't, Stevens showed how life was generally better than in the years immediately following the war but still uncomfortable for citizens near the bottom of the economic ladder:

> *Not many families in this category—which comprises the overwhelming majority of the Soviet urban population—can, at present writing, boast even a small set of matching dishes or cutlery. If a relative or friend drops in for dinner, more often than not an extra plate, cup, knife, fork, and spoon must be borrowed from the neighbors.* [39]

One article followed the day of a peasant woman named Dasha:

> *Ever since her husband went off to war, never to return, "Auntie" Dasha's whole economy revolved around her cow. Each morning at 4 she milked the patient animal, trudged two miles to the railway station with her two cans of milk, and caught the 5:30.*
>
> *Arriving in Moscow by 6:15, she delivered by streetcar to her five steady customers, caught the 7:15 back from town, hurried home with her empty cans, helped herself to some boiled-potato mash from a big black pot on the cold stove, and after some hasty instructions to son Grisha, age eight, was out of the house in time to report at 9 o'clock for the day's field work on the collective farm.* [40]

When the state raised her milk quotas, Dasha had to consider whether chickens would be a better investment than a cow. Stevens was not optimistic. "One day the government may unexpectedly relax the pressure on the peasantry," he concluded. "Till then there will be millions of Auntie Dashas pondering whether to trade their cows for chickens or vice versa." [41]

Other articles examined Soviet fashion and the people's rejection of the state-prescribed hemline level; the workings of the markets for goods both common (aquarium fish) and high-level (fine caviar); the ubiquity of petty graft despite state efforts to tamp it down; and the pressures on Soviet women who, like his own wife, had married foreigners and wanted to emigrate.

And then there was the secret police apparatus, "unfettered, omnipotent police power reduced to practical organizational form—the state in the full sense of Lenin's definition of the state as a "machine for suppression." [42]

Toward the end of the series, Stevens came to conclusions similar to Canham's about the nature of evil in the 1940s:

> *The common denominator of naziism and communism is in the appeal to materialism, in the conviction that violence and coercion can settle any issue, in the belief that power justifies any means. Above all, both inherit, from a common philosophic source, the rejection of fixed standards of right and wrong, true and false. Without these moral compass points to steer by, no nation can cleave to the course of progress. Technology and organizing efficiency, instead of benefitting mankind, then operate for evil.* [43]

He loved the people he had lived among for close to a decade. "The Russians as a race are neither domineering nor aggressive nor xenophobe," he wrote. "They are warmly human, gregarious, and endowed with an avid and friendly curiosity about other peoples." But he saw the Soviet state as a destroyer of their dreams, and he cautioned his readers to identify the right enemy:

> *It is essential that the West learn to distinguish between the police state and the Soviet people, for if the former are implacable foes, the latter, unless stupidly antagonized, are potential friends and allies.*
>
> *And it is they who eventually will decide their country's destiny.* [44]

The series was a masterful survey of a people about whom the West was now intensely curious, and it earned for Stevens and the *Monitor* the 1950 Pulitzer Prize for Distinguished Reporting on International Affairs. As journalist and Pulitzer winner Leland Stowe had said in his nominating letter for the series:

> *. . . I know of no reporting on the Soviet Union, over a period of at least the last ten years, which can compare with the Stevens' series for breadth and depth, for remarkable marshalling of pertinent facts, for intimate details of Soviet developments to the American people.* [45]

With American journalism's most emphatic stamp of approval, and with an editor who clearly felt the pulse of the times, the *Monitor* had officially arrived.

In 1949, Stevens and his family moved to Rome, where he could finally fulfill one of his first promises to his wife. He became the *Monitor*'s chief Mediterranean correspondent, until leaving the paper, in 1956, to return to Moscow once more, this time for *Look* magazine.

The prophet rises

Stevens had laid down the facts about America's new

threat. Canham now saw it as his task to define the vision of America's future. He began taking on a role that seemed, in some ways, larger than the *Monitor* itself. In a lecture presented at Yale University called "The Authentic Revolution," reprinted in the *Monitor* on July 15, 1950, Canham proposed a thesis:

> *. . . the struggle for the salvation of free society in our time will be lost unless we in the West—and particularly we in the United States—awaken to and project the fact that we are the great revolutionaries in world history, and that our revolution is basically a spiritual one which we have already proved in action.* [46]

He identified the fundamental problem in terms that anyone who read Canham's *Monitor* would be familiar with: "We have let most of the world think that the American achievement is primarily materialistic." But America for Canham was not a materialistic culture, and he called on America to speak up. "The basic need is to understand and to proclaim the truth," he said. "The West must find its voice."

> *Today we have the opportunity of knowing as never before that there is indeed a God, who is the loving Father of all mankind. We do not necessarily have to identify God merely with the single three-letter name, G-o-d. Perhaps it is useful to redefine God as the central Principle of the universe. Perhaps it helps to think of Him as eternal Truth and Life and Love.* [47]

For Canham, the truest defender of mankind's hopes was America, and the clearest voice of America was Christian Science. His goal was not to defeat a rival political system so much as to help construct a universal family based on an expansive sense of God. America was not only the principal carrier of the message, he believed, but also the bearer of the burden of humanity's progress. He told his audience at Yale:

> *We are on the march. . . . There is a hill up which we must climb. We will not decline in slothful ease. We will pit ourselves against the lies which in our time assault the deep foundations of truth. These lies cannot prevail, even to the extent of setting civilization into a relapse, if we are worthy of our heritage.* [48]

Canham's demeanor and tone may have been Old Testament, but the focus of his jeremiads and other pronouncements was thoroughly modern. In some ways, he was becoming America's prophet for the 1950s.

His audience, at least in the United States, loved it. Eugene G. Grace, chairman of Bethlehem Steel, called the Yale speech "truly a masterpiece," and Robert B. Stewart, Dean of the Fletcher School of Law and Diplomacy at Tufts University, said, "The Authentic Revolution ranks among the finest thinking and writing of our time, indeed, among the truly great messages of all time, spiritual as well as secular." [49]

Canham was on the pinnacle. With his growing fame, along with the paper's Pulitzer, the world was listening to the *Monitor* and to him. He intended to use the opportunity to goad people into higher moral duty, not just opposing communism but uprooting their own materialism and replacing it with more spiritual thinking and behavior.

In 1950 and 1951, Canham had the *Monitor* publish a series of twenty articles on "The World at Mid-Century," then gather them into a book, which added one significant word to the title—*Awakening: The World at Mid-Century.* The articles were more essays than reported news or features.

Canham wrote the first piece:

> *Cannot it be said . . . that the struggle of our time is the confrontation of spiritual reality and validity on the one hand and the assertion of all-powerful materialism on the other?* [50]

What can the average citizen do? he asked rhetorically.

> *. . . he can do his part in awakening himself and his fellow man to the real nature of the crisis. It is immediately and urgently needful for those who must preserve freedom to win the battle against materialism within themselves and within their own society.* [51]

Other *Monitor* writers in the series echoed Canham's theme. The woman's editor, Jessie Ash Arndt, wrote on "The Rise of Woman Power," asking:

> *What is stronger than the atom bomb? It is a race so morally and spiritually developed that such an instrument of destruction could never be used.* [52]

Education editor Millicent Taylor observed that "it is in our time that education has taken a step ahead that can only be described as approaching the spiritual.... The schools today, with varying degrees of success, are committed to helping students to perfect themselves." [53]

Dorothy Adlow, the *Monitor*'s art critic, noted the gray materialism of the postwar period:

> *Mid-century, the artist seems to have lost the former spiritedness, the dynamic vigor, the prismatic range of color. The palette of many a painter has become somber and neutral; . . .*

But she, too, wanted to inspire readers with a more uplifting vision:

> *While art at mid-century may still appear disparate, the artists seem to share a desire to say something cogent, something meaningful, something helpful.* [54]

Editorial writer Robert Peel looked at literature and saw turmoil coming out of a Europe still torn by the latest war. But he observed another trend:

> *Behind the anger and dogmatism, behind the groping and disillusionment of these and scores of lesser writers is a profound conviction of the essential oneness of humanity.* [55]

In a summary chapter he wrote when the articles were collected into the book, Canham listed his ideas on what humanity had to do to survive the 1950s, such as strengthening physical defenses against aggression and preserving the economic soundness of the free world. His last prescription was his most deeply felt:

> *. . . humbly seek to understand the viewpoints and the needs and the spiritual pride and hunger of other peoples and other races. . . .*
>
> *The world in our time will not be saved by a new messiah, whether political or economic or religious or social. It can be saved by awakening individual thinking. . .*
>
> *We must make the truth as simple, as persuasive, as impelling, and as interesting as the lie often seems to be.* [56]

The language was religious, but with the messianic mission to save the world from communism that Americans believed they had, it resonated far beyond the *Monitor*'s readership. And the *Monitor* and the church behind it were getting the credit. The editor of the *West Delaware Tribune* in New York wrote on the front page of his paper:

> *If it is true that an institution is but the shadow of man, it can certainly be said that the* Monitor *is the strong shadow of a faith . . . that man is a spiritual being, created in God's image . . . and the standard of perfection is no less than the likeness of God. This truth*

is exemplified in the editorials, features, and news columns of the paper. The Monitor *quickens our imagination, crystallizes our principles, restores our faith in journalism as a high profession and makes us proud to be the editor of a country weekly.* [57]

Leaders of American society started asking Canham to give service outside the *Monitor*. In 1954, he was appointed president of the United States Chamber of Commerce, the leading business trade association in Washington. He carefully explained in his autobiography, "Only after very prayerful thought was it decided that the service I might perform in helping articulate the role of private enterprise in a world where it is under the most severe attack, would justify the acceptance of the office." [58]

He also took on the chairmanship of the United States Advisory Committee on Information, which counseled the State Department on its global information program, and membership on President Eisenhower's Commission on National Goals. Increasingly, he became a member of boards, from the Boston Museum of Fine Arts to the Federal Reserve Bank of Boston. He resisted many offers of full-time government jobs, however, including assistant secretary of commerce. He was alert enough to recognize that the *Monitor* was his indispensable platform:

The battle for peace takes place initially and basically in the individual's own consciousness. The Monitor's *role is to inform and to awaken those who must move toward this awareness. Its service is not alone to Christian Scientists, but to awakening thought everywhere. There can be no greater individual fulfillment than to serve in such a cause.* [59]

In 1955, Canham faced a challenge that he later said was one of the most meaningful experiences of his life. Four inmates of the Massachusetts State Prison in Charlestown took several guards hostage and threatened to kill them unless their demands were met. After a tense standoff, they asked that Canham, along with six other men they respected, be allowed to talk with them and hear their story.

The prisoners took the visitors on a tour of the prison, particularly solitary confinement cells, where inmates had to sleep on the stone floor without bed, mattress, or blanket, receiving a loaf of bread and some water each day. As Canham wrote later in the *Monitor*:

> *Teddy Green [one of the convicts] asked me to step into one of these gloomy dungeons. He shut the barred door and turned out the lights in the corridor. Then, in his tense, hard voice he described life in these cells. That was at about 2 o'clock Friday morning, and I have rarely had a more intensely moving 2 a.m.* [60]

The prisoners promised a decision the next day.

> *Frankly, on our second visit, we could not discount the possibility of a negative decision by the convicts and the chance they might like to up their ante of hostages.*
>
> *But again, as we went breathlessly through the barred door, the tension eased when we shook hands with the men again and talked with them as fellow beings.* [61]

The hostages were released.

Everything Canham did was golden. The *Monitor*'s circulation had reached 164,000, its highest so far. [62] The paper was sent to some 4,500 newspaper offices every day, had a budget of $6.5 million, and employed about 150 people in the editorial department. About half its readers were not Christian Scientists, a sign that it was at last being appreciated outside the church.

Jenkin Lloyd-Jones, editor the Tulsa *Tribune*, whom Canham called "one of newspaperdom's most perceptive cynics," wrote:

> *The immense popularity of* The Christian Science Monitor *among non-Christian Scientists, including many godless newspapermen, springs from the fact that the publication is both factual and hopeful. The* Monitor *knows the score about as well as any American newspaper. It recognizes and decries the weak spots in the dike and the pitfalls in the path. It is capable both of alarm and righteous indignation. But it never gives up the ship. It never discounts its ultimate faith in the triumph of decency.* [63]

The business of salvation

Canham was proud that the paper's mission shone through every aspect of the paper, including both editorial and business operations. When Canham assumed control, in 1941, Norman S. Rose headed the advertising department. He had built it from a staff of thirty-six to 136 over twenty years. The "true function [of advertising] is," Rose wrote, "not to entrap the unwary, through craft and mesmeric appeal, into purchasing articles for which they have no real need, but to render, through the giving of helpful information, an important service and benefit to the public." [64] Historically, the *Monitor* had been instrumental in establishing the first "Truth in Advertising" campaign in the early part of the century.

The paper had a grassroots operation of advertising representatives around the world, including those in Christian Science churches, doing their work in the spirit of the *Monitor*. "The advertising salespeople and representatives are all Christian Scientists," Canham noted in his history of the *Monitor*. "They are deeply committed to the help and healing of human ills and problems." [65]

Circulation was a concern for Canham, as for any editor, but the problems for the *Monitor* were greater than for most papers. Readership was flung around the world in 120 different countries. Ninety percent of subscribers received their paper by mail. *Monitor* deadlines were necessarily earlier than for most papers, and issues sometimes reached subscribers several days later. "Stand-up journalism" was the goal—stories had to be worth reading long after they were written—hence the paper's focus on interpretation rather than breaking news.

But like Mrs. Eddy, Canham did not see circulation as just a business issue:

> *As mankind responds more intently to the grave problems of our time, as clearer and more responsible thinking deepens in the community, as education and enlightenment elevate thinking, the* Monitor *can confidently expect a growing response.* [66]

In 1958, at the *Monitor*'s fiftieth anniversary, he published his history of the paper. In it, he laid out the philosophy that had become the keynote of his career:

> *The* Monitor *ends its half century. The ferment of forces and ideas, some new and some very old, stirs the world. Under the silent whirl of the satellites, in the shadow of the mushroom cloud, mankind needs more than ever to awaken from the false dream of security in materialism. The time for spiritual solutions is at hand.*
>
> *Thus the mission of* The Christian Science Monitor *is more urgent than ever before. That mission is—with honesty, moderation, foresight and candor—to help give humankind the tools with which to work out its salvation.* [67]

As the 1960s dawned, Canham was busy trying to forward that mission both inside and outside the paper. Circulation had climbed still further to 175,000. After more than thirty years as a reporter and editor, he spoke confidently of what the founder had wanted the paper to be:

> *Mrs. Eddy did not establish a newspaper to advertise Christian Science or simply to edify the general public with clean journalism. She set it up so that Christian Scientists would know what was going on and do something about it.* [68]

What he himself saw, however, was beginning to weigh on him. On November 26, 1963, four days after President Kennedy was assassinated, and with Kennedy's assassin in turn having been killed, Canham wrote with undisguised disappointment at what his country had allowed to happen:

> *The United States now has two stains to expiate from its national honor. Manifestly they are different orders of magnitude. But each is grave. Each is murder. Each stems from the same roots of lawlessness. And of each the United States stands accused in the eyes of the world.* [69]

After all the years of faithful chiding he had given to America, Canham's hope was still there, but it was beginning to thin:

> *The sense of national shame is widespread. Unless the lesson is learned there will be other tragedies. But the well-springs of good, of spiritual commitment, which alone justify the American nation can restore its place in the ranks of mankind.* [70]

He voiced his frustration, too, at *Monitor* readers. Were they doing their jobs as vigilant actors in prayer? "The *Monitor* unopened," he would write two years later, "is the symbol of self-centeredness and apathy." [71]

He started a column called "Dialogue with Youth," in which he answered questions from young people about everything from social and political issues to the strange new fashions in clothing and hair. He had always loved teaching teenagers in Sunday School, where he was known for making issues clear and simple. Now, it almost seemed, he was turning to young people in the desperate hope that they could do what their elders could not—create a better world.

In May of 1964, he received the final blow. The Directors announced he would be given the title of editor in chief and "expand his activities in the field of public affairs and [become] responsible for broad outlines of editorial policy of the paper." [72] It was obvious he was being kicked upstairs.

His replacement, DeWitt John, had worked earlier in his career as a reporter and editor for the *Monitor* but had left the paper, in 1948, for the church's public affairs arm, the Committee on Publication, eventually becoming its head and then a Christian Science teacher.

Why Canham was moved out of his position was not explained. "The Directors never give you a reason to fire you," said one later editor, who asked not to be identified. "They trust that you put out the paper every day and won't do anything to violate standards. As long as they trust you, you're there. The moment they don't trust you or think you're not the best for the job, you're gone."

But it was obvious, at least to those on the paper, that Canham's attention had flagged. He had turned the *Monitor* into a topic of conversation among the most distinguished journalists in the world, not to mention business, government, and academic leaders. The church's prestige was higher than it had been in a long time. With the best of intentions, he had shifted his focus partly away from the paper, to outside interests, and the boards and committees and honors had begun piling up. But after peaking in the 1950s, the *Monitor*'s influence seemed to be dropping. Other newspapers, seeing the *Monitor*'s success, had begun imitating its in-depth journalism. Some of the writing was becoming stale. The newsroom was not getting the attention it needed.

Surprisingly, the *Monitor*'s announcement of the change included no hint of appreciation for Canham's years of service. It simply stated his and John's backgrounds, ending by mentioning that the two had published a book together about what Christian Science had meant to them, with John writing "the longer portion."

It was a quiet denouement to a very public career, which had helped America and the world come to grips with some of the great problems of the mid-twentieth century. Canham had shown, to a degree, how the *Monitor* can uncover evil without making it bigger or getting sucked into its vortex of fear. It had taken the paper more than fifty years to get there, but the foundation for a solid future seemed to be laid.

Canham never spoke openly of the change, nor did he mention it even to some of those he knew best. But one can't hide deep feelings. After the announcement, Budge Sperling, one of his reporters, met him in his office, and they shook hands. "Erwin's hand was wet," Sperling says. "It was the first time I ever felt that." [73]

8

More Love

Canham had called DeWitt John "the kingmaker."

In the run-up to the 1941 race for Boston mayor, John uncovered behind-the-scenes cooperation between campaign workers for former governor and mayor James Michael Curley, who was running for a fourth term as mayor after an absence of seven years, and popular School Committeeman Clement Norton, who was himself thinking of running. Curley's supporters were working with Norton's to help a minor candidate, Joseph M. Heffernan, amass enough petition signatures to get onto the ballot, a move each camp felt would play to its advantage in the race to unseat incumbent Mayor Maurice Tobin. [1]

When John reported the Shakespearean maneuverings, along with apparently unethical efforts to form a campaign committee for Heffernan, Norton immediately withdrew, paving the way for a Tobin win. [2]

It was a rare public demonstration of the effectiveness of a reporter who was willing to comb city files and trudge the dreariest streets of Boston to get a story for the *Monitor*. John wasn't the stereotypical tough-guy news reporter, but he was tenacious.

John had wanted to write for the *Monitor* since attending Principia College, a school for Christian Scientists in Illinois. The *Monitor* for him was a paper of deep thought and excellent writing. After he graduated from Principia, he earned master's degrees in political science from the University of Chicago and journalism from Columbia University. Then, in 1938, he became an editorial writer and sometime reporter for the *St.*

Petersburg Times in Florida. Learning to make the mundane stories of the local reporter not only interesting but useful to readers, he finally got the *Monitor* to notice him, and Roscoe Drummond brought him to Boston, in 1939. He was placed on the copy desk, proofreading articles and writing headlines.

He was eager to prove himself, and he began finding news in Boston that no one else was covering, at least in the same way. He tackled complicated projects, gathering information and then honing the story until it emerged from the clutter of disjointed facts. Every word and phrase had its task in building to a conclusion, while keeping the reader interested. The style was plodding at times, sacrificing art for clarity, but readers got what they needed.

Describing an improvement to Huntington Avenue in Boston, John detailed the likely effect:

> *An estimated 15,000 motorists will use the new thoroughfare each day, not counting Sundays. If each saves 10 minutes, the total time saved each year will be:*
> *45,000,000 minutes, or*
> *750,000 hours, or*
> *93,750 8-hour days.*
> *If a man worked 40 hours a week, it would take him 360 years to work that long. You can use your own imagination about the saving in gasoline, wear and tear, money and annoyance.* [3]

Like Canham, who became chief news editor the year John arrived, John worked hard to unite heart and mind in his writing. He tried not so much to get himself out of the way as to insert his best self—hard-working, earnest, practical, and compassionate. His sense of *Monitor* journalism was to help people solve their problems through useful and enlightening information. He avoided soaring rhetoric, and he saw no point in inserting metaphysical concepts where they didn't belong. He simply wanted to meet the needs of readers.

John shared one important factor in his life with

Canham: a dramatic healing of his mother, which made him a lifelong Christian Scientist. Soon after DeWitt was born, in the small desert town of Safford, Arizona, in 1917, his mother, Frances, contracted what her doctor called malignant blood poisoning and fell into a semi-coma. After seven weeks and five operations, the doctor said he could do no more for her.

For many years, his mother had been what DeWitt described as a militant atheist, having given up on religion as an answer to anything. But one strange episode punctured her certainty—a healing of a friend that she had witnessed. The friend had fallen violently ill during a train trip, and Frances, who had met a Christian Science practitioner a year earlier and had read a loaned copy of *Science and Health* out of curiosity, happened to have a copy of *The Christian Science Journal* in her suitcase. The *Journal* lists Christian Science practitioners around the world, and she called one who lived nearby. The practitioner came to the Hutchinson, Kansas, hotel room where they were staying and prayed until midnight. The girl woke the next morning, healed.

DeWitt's father, who had heard the story, wired the practitioner and asked for his help. The practitioner prayed from a thousand miles away, and in two days, Frances suddenly regained consciousness. In another two days, she was out walking with her new baby.

When the war started, John took a leave of absence from the *Monitor* and joined the Navy, where he earned a bronze star for his work as head of public relations on Guam for Admiral Chester Nimitz, commander in chief for the U.S. Pacific Fleet. He developed an interest in international reporting and was crushed when he returned to the *Monitor* and found himself again on the copy desk.

But John applied the same determination to his own career that he put into reporting stories, and with perceptive book reviews and more local reporting, he got the attention of Charles Gratke, who sent him on a trip to Europe to cover postwar developments.

There John wrote about the Berlin Airlift:

> *Operation Little Vittles has just completed its 95th air lift mission to Berlin. I rode the flight from Frankfort to the besieged German city.*
>
> *We parachuted our "cargo" to crowds of sweet-toothed German youngsters in the American sector which fringes the Templehof airdrome. The cargo consisted of some 500 chocolate bars tied to handkerchief parachutes.*
>
> *Lieutenant Halvorson flew our ship to Berlin. He is a "regular guy," with sandy hair, keen blue eyes, and a face that zips into a merry smile on the slightest provocation.*
>
> *His story, "Little Vittles," is, as he says, a little amazing. But it looks as though the explanation is the pulling power of a generous idea.* [4]

On another trip, he wrote about one of the thorniest problems in Germany and Austria:

> *Among all the displaced persons of central Europe, the problem of the homeless and the stateless is perhaps most fully epitomized by the plight of the Volksdeutsche in Austria.*
>
> *These people are the remnant of German-language minorities expelled from eastern Europe and returned to Germany and Austria, from which they and their forebears originally came. But now they are strangers. They are the DPs nobody wants.* [5]

John loved working under Gratke, and he continued to write on foreign affairs while he waited for an overseas job to open.

Learning to manage

Meanwhile, he got an invitation from the Committee on Publication office to write for it full-time. He turned it down.

The *Monitor* was an island of excitement and prestige in a sea of sometimes rote thinking at the church. For an aspiring journalist, who saw the possibilities of the *Monitor* for transforming world thought, working in some other area of the church seemed, at best, a waste of time and, at worst, a tangent that could destroy a promising career.

John, however, had a sharpened sense of duty to the religion that had healed his mother and that he felt could lift humanity out of the poverty of limited thinking, and six months later, when he was again offered the Committee job, he took a deep breath and said yes. It felt like the buildings were falling down on him. [6]

He feared that the stimulating conversations about politics and world events, the camaraderie of people whose horizons went far beyond Boston, would dissolve into religious talk and parochial interests. His writing skills would now be used mainly for church public relations, and it seemed almost like a squandering of talent. Then again, the cause was one he believed in and wanted with all his heart to support.

It proved to be a valuable move. He learned to think broadly about the church and its role in the world. He also learned to encourage people to excel in an environment, at church headquarters, if not in the Committee itself, where mediocrity was sometimes tolerated.

He rose to manager of the Committee and quickly hired editorial writer Robert Peel from the *Monitor*. Peel was a Harvard-trained intellectual star and brought a perspective on Christian Science that included historical and cultural context almost unheard of at the church. He would go on to write a three-volume history of Mrs. Eddy, which is still regarded as the most complete, perceptive, and accurate biography of her ever produced.

John's focus had been on his own writing. Now it was on how to get the most from other people and organize them for collective accomplishment. He worked closely with the staff, listened to their views even if he disagreed, and gave them the freedom they needed to pursue their projects. He expected his staff to pray as he did and to get inspiration to perform their jobs without relying on him.

John kept up his *Monitor* friendships, feeding his appetite for conversations about public affairs with Saturday-night dinner parties at his home. But it turned out that the environment at the Committee, especially with Peel and others around who enjoyed the intellectual challenge of defending Christian Science from the biases of the world, was more stimulating than he had expected. At the *Monitor*, the rush of the news often overwhelmed more serious reflection, and journalism, even there, did not always fit naturally with religious thinking. By contrast, at the Committee, John had to study the Bible and Mrs. Eddy's writings constantly, apply their lessons wherever he could, and bring out the results in work that was measured only by its effectiveness in changing minds.

Meanwhile, the Directors were wondering what to make of Canham and his activities. Was the *Monitor* gaining more from the visibility he brought than it was losing from his divided focus? They decided to move him gently out of the newsroom, if possible, without interrupting the good he was doing for the paper and the church. They began searching for a new editor who understood journalism and Christian Science but who was not going to turn the editorship into a platform for activities that were not germane to the paper's mission. They wanted someone, simply, who would pay more attention to managing the paper.

That they settled on John was a surprise to him as much as to anyone. At the *St. Petersburg Times* and the *Monitor,* his reporting and writing had been promising, but that was a long time ago. For more than a decade now, he had been laboring in relative obscurity inside the church.

But he had several advantages that made the choice logical. He had enough experience to know how a newsroom worked, but he was not so immersed in the field as to be tempted to ignore the religious mission of the *Monitor* for the sake of his own career. His writing was still sharp. His work at the Committee had forced him to keep current on how the world was thinking, and this knowledge could help him direct news coverage where it could be most effective.

And one thing more: That year—1964—he would become a teacher of Christian Science, which meant that he understood the religion enough, and had done enough healing work, to explain it to others in a way that would enable them, in turn, to become healers. Teaching Christian Science demanded a maturity, alertness, and self-control that could prove helpful in furthering the *Monitor*'s work of blessing humanity and spreading Science. It could help get the paper back on track.

Allison "Skip" Phinney, a younger colleague of John's at the Committee and later a teacher of Christian Science himself, is convinced that being a teacher helped John. "It made him more conscious of the purpose of the *Monitor*," he says, "that it was more than an excellent piece of journalism. Instead of asking, How do we compete with *The New York Times*, he would ask, How does *Monitor* journalism translate into something different, something more concerned with helping humanity?" [7]

Focus on healing

As soon as he took over, John had the paper redesigned to make it more readable. He also announced that reporters would be freed for more investigative reporting. "Our aim," he told *Newsweek* magazine, "is to provide the readers of the *Monitor* with a greater level of exclusive news . . . in an interesting and highly readable form." [8]

And more than just news: Reporters were to focus on people. "He insisted that reporting have a human element to it," says John Dillin, a new copy kid in 1964 and eventually a national and international correspondent and managing editor for the *Monitor*. "We had to get to the grocery stores, talk to people in the street. No sitting in the office and reading reports and then writing." [9]

For subject matter, they were to focus on things that needed improving—in a word, healing. John began hiring more editorial staff, beginning with the Washington bureau, and upgrading the writing. *Newsweek* made fun of him for using a "fog index" to measure how clear the writing on the paper was, but the magazine acknowledged that the writing had become noticeably obtuse under Canham. The magazine also mocked a memo John sent to the staff, in which he called for "an increased sense of love." [10] What place, the magazine asked, did love have in a newsroom? But *Newsweek* had little concept of what the word meant for John or of how he was planning to apply it at the *Monitor*. Divine Love, as Mrs. Eddy said many times, was the Principle of Christian Science.

Even before having the paper redesigned, John set about redesigning the relationship of editor to staff. He was determined to pay his reporters and editors better. He did not see the *Monitor* as some others, both inside and outside the church, did—as a secular activity not germane to the church's mission. His staff deserved full respect. But he was careful to put the money where it would do the most good.

One of his first hires was Frederic Hunter. Hunter had been working for the United States Information Service in Africa for six years and loved the continent. Two *Monitor* correspondents in Africa had recently died on the job, and the paper was having a hard time filling the post of Africa correspondent. John saw that Hunter was a good writer, if an inexperienced journalist, and he offered him a job and a salary that was above the norm at the paper. John was careful, though. "Don't talk about the money with others," he told Hunter. "There are people who have been here longer who are earning less." [11] Hunter went on to cover Africa for several years.

But John wanted to do more than just pay a few reporters better. Across his large desk at home and along the sofa, he spread comprehensive charts showing newsroom structure and pay rates, and where he felt the *Monitor* was failing its workers. He worked on the charts until he felt the picture was clear, then presented them to the Directors. They responded with enough money for across-the-board raises.

He then met with the staff, one at a time, to understand

their concerns and needs. When Canham had walked through the newsroom, as one writer put it, "I felt the floor thundering."[12] John's footstep was decidedly softer, and after the initial staff meetings, he conferred mostly with top editors, even adding a features editor between him and the education, arts, and other feature pages, which irritated some of the staff. It made him seem aloof. But his method of approaching problems made an impression. The same writer who said Canham thundered called John "the grappler," because he took on complex challenges like the pay problem and, gathering evidence and applying careful analysis, wrestled them into a solution. It was not unlike the way he approached reporting a story.

It was also not unlike the way he approached spiritual healing. "The prayer that heals goes so much deeper than words," he once wrote.[13] John would take a problem and patiently, mentally, reverse each claim of imperfection until all that stood out was man as the perfect creation of God, reflecting the ever-present divine Love. If he then needed to say something to the patient or, in his work as editor, to make a move to adjust things, it became obvious. Every challenge was an incentive to use prayer as a first remedy, not as a last resort.

John's approach invited the sort of cynicism *Newsweek* showed, and some on the staff expected the worst. But others liked the fact that John wasn't pushing himself but was supporting them. "DeWitt was an editor with a heart," one *Monitor* reporter said. [14] Another put it more bluntly: "DeWitt in many ways was more of a journalist, had more of a love for journalism, than Canham. Canham traveled a lot. He was sort of a roving ambassador. He was not the hands-on guy DeWitt was." [15]

Love in action

John started immediately to put his stamp on the *Monitor*'s content. Shortly after assuming the editorship, he put together a group of correspondents and asked them to produce a series on freedom. It covered some of the same ground that had been covered in Canham's own writing and by some of the articles in the series he had overseen, and it took a similar advocatory position. As the introduction to the series put it, "Individual freedom still remains a priceless heritage. It must be preserved."

But John's series approached the issue from a very different standpoint, reflecting in part the difference between the certainty of the 1950s and the complexity of the 1960s. In Canham's series on the world at mid-century, the writers wrote with large brushstrokes about the progress of human thought. Their articles were closer to essays than reports. Their conclusions were based on observation and broad familiarity with their subjects, but it was almost as if those conclusions were reached without leaving the office. "Let's write a series of articles that will keep the spirits of readers alive in these days of turmoil," seemed to be Canham's well-meaning assignment for his staff. But the result seemed closer to positive thinking than to Christian Science healing.

John took a very different approach. "The focus could have been wide," he wrote in the first article in the series. "But we have made it close-up. On the individual himself. This newspaper's deep concern is for the individual and his freedom." [16]

In keeping with the subject and his own method of reporting, he had his correspondents do "shoe-leather" research, and focus on what people were actually saying and thinking. He had learned from the Committee on Publication as well as his own healing practice that it was individual thought, not mass opinion, that needed to be worked with. Mass opinion was built from individual thought:

> *. . . progress is the outcome of ideas. And ideas come to individuals. They do not come to groups. Groups may accept them and act upon them. But they must first come to individuals—individuals who are free to think and to say what they think!* [17]

There was one more big difference from Canham. John believed, as did his predecessor, that the biggest enemy of freedom was materialism. But John did not draw the fatal conclusion that people were therefore the problem, whether at the individual, societal, or governmental level. The tendency to blame humanity for its own problems was the biggest obstacle to the tone of genial persuasion the *Monitor* needed to adopt to be effective. What the times demanded, John felt, was "a stronger sense of human brotherhood, a greater respect for one another, a more generous consideration for one's neighbor. They call for more love in action." [18]

As the series went on, it examined such issues as whether small business owners had freedom to grow in the face of increasing government regulation; whether the freedom that unions gained for workers outweighed the pressure to conform to union demands; and how children's freedom was stifled in some schools while others were opening windows to accomplishment. It looked at sports and considered whether trends such as coaches calling football plays from the sidelines constituted more or less freedom for players.

American news editor Robert Colby Nelson noted that the recent clashes in Birmingham, Alabama, and other cities were not just about the freedom of "blacks." They were about the freedom of everyone:

> *There is little room for doubt that in today's world progress in overcoming the barriers and restrictions of race prejudice is necessary if individual freedom is to prosper and grow.* [19]

It was all setting the table. The final article in the fifteen-part series, written by Roderick Nordell and called "What really makes men free," put the Christian Science brand on the reporting that went before:

> *. . . . mortal existence, taken on its own terms, is meaningless, absurd, as postwar philosophers and*

artists have vividly recognized. To make sense, a higher basis is required for the human struggle to improve both society and oneself.

This higher basis is the relationship of the individual and God, defined for what some have wryly called the post-Christian age.

In this relationship God is the source not only of freedom but of the strength and intelligence to use freedom well. . . .

This relationship stands above all the topical problems and opportunities for freedom discussed in the previous articles in this series. [20]

It was not the type of series to win a Pulitzer. There was no extraordinary bravery or doggedness involved, no government malfeasance uncovered. But the series showed some of what the *Monitor* at its best is about—perceptive of mental trends and unhesitating in judgment among them; pointedly reformist of the way people think; confident of the triumph of good but counseling alertness.

John had taken what Drummond and his contemporaries had tried to do—including explicit Christian Science teachings in their writing—and moved it to a level that didn't just apply the words and values of Christian Science. In many ways it *was* Christian Science. More precisely, it showed characteristics of Christian Science healing treatment in action. A deep familiarity with fundamental, practical Christian Science and how to heal with it had been lacking in the previous attempts at breakthrough *Monitor* journalism. Drummond had been right. A better way to produce distinctive journalism at the *Monitor* would come with time.

The power of simplicity

Less than a year after the last article in the series on freedom was published—on February 8, 1966—Budge Sperling, a reporter based in Washington, asked Charles Percy to lunch at the National Press Club. Percy was running for one of the U.S. Senate seats from Illinois, and Sperling, who had met Percy while covering the race, wanted Percy to meet some of his newspaper friends. Percy, like Sperling, was a Christian Scientist.

It was a chance for David Broder and Bob Novak of the *Washington Post*, Phil Potter of the *Baltimore Sun,* and nearly a dozen other correspondents to get to know an interesting political figure, and they asked Sperling to do it again. A meal was more intimate than a press conference, more relaxed than a formal interview, and it allowed for at least the semblance of a friendly chat.

Sperling also knew John Lindsay, who was running for mayor of New York City. Lindsay agreed to meet with Sperling and his friends. When the National Press Club told Sperling there were no tables available on the day Lindsay would be there, Sperling switched to breakfast. Next came Governor George Romney from Michigan, and it was breakfast again. "I couldn't believe no one else was doing this kind of thing," Sperling says.

Breakfast turned out to be the perfect time. "Early in the morning, people are confident," he says. "They talk about what they really think." [21] The breakfasts soon became events on the Washington press calendar. After some trial and error, Sperling set the ground rules: everything on the record, meaning that what the guests said could be attributed to them; no electronic media or wire services, just newspapers; and civility. He believed that people would say what was on their minds if they were treated with respect—if not always gently. [22]

"This is worth $100,000 to you," Richard Strout, who was now a Washington correspondent for the *Monitor*, told Sperling. Sperling indeed had offers. At one point, *Newsweek* proposed giving him three times his *Monitor* salary to move. Sperling gathered his wife and children.

"I could get a new bike," his son said.

"We have always been a *Monitor* family," his daughter said.

Family won, and Sperling stayed with the *Monitor.*

Sperling's mother had abandoned her family when her son was eleven. As a teenager, Sperling read *Science and Health* "to keep it together." And he had healings: As a young teenager, he pushed an ice pick deep into his hand. He wrote about the experience later, in the third person:

> *Quickly he pulled the pick out and put his hand behind his back so that his thought would not be diverted from his effort to see the real man, made in the image of God. He repeated a few of the prayers he had learned as a child, including the Lord's Prayer. There was no pain. When he had occasion to look at his hand a few minutes later there was no sign of where the pick had entered.* [23]

In the best sense of the word, life became *simple* for Sperling. "Life that is God contains nothing that is complicated," he wrote, soon after joining the *Monitor.* [24]

He started in the circulation department, then moved to the copy desk. Ninety-five-year-old Arthur Stubbs, who had worked for the *Monitor* since the days of Frederick Dixon and had no other means of support than his *Monitor* job, sat near Sperling. He wrote a headline in the morning, then called it quits for the day. Sperling and his younger colleagues did the real work.

It was taxing, caring for the details—the headlines, the grammar, the spelling, and the clarity—that encourage a reader to trust a paper. For Sperling, though, the demand for perfection was invigorating. By the late 1950s, he was bureau chief in Chicago, covering twenty-three states and loving the demand for "stand-up journalism," which forced him to dig deep into stories to make sure readers were satisfied even days after the paper was published, when many would receive it.

He kept working hard on simplicity. He tried to make his writing as clear as possible so readers could understand it easily. He taped a piece of paper with the admonition "Try to be fair" to the front of his typewriter. He liked being part of a paper that was interested in truth. Through his contagious decency, he built a family of political contacts, which served him well in Washington. The contacts were as loyal to him as he was fair to them. The breakfasts did not just happen to be successful. They were built on Sperling's legwork and heart. Ultimately, one couldn't say no to Budge Sperling, whether he was asking you to be a guest at a breakfast or to comment on a news development.

Without the profound modesty of people like Sperling, Canham and John would not have been able to turn the *Monitor* into a vehicle "to bless all mankind." Sperling helped give structure to the inherent simplicity of the *Monitor*'s purpose.

Freedom to go with the story

If it took hard work for Sperling to create the decency and you-have-to-be-there status his breakfasts represented—after his retirement they continued as "Monitor breakfasts"—it took the same, with an added measure of insight and fearlessness, for John Hughes to get the story of the Indonesian leadership crisis for the *Monitor* in the mid-1960s.

Hughes was a naturalized American who had been born in Wales and educated in England. He started his career at age sixteen, in 1946, as a junior reporter with the *Durban Natal Mercury* in South Africa, where his family had moved; then he returned to England to work for the *London Daily Mirror* and a London news agency. "Head down to Piccadilly Circus tonight and see if you can find a story," his editor would tell him. It's often the best training a young journalist can get, to dig up his own leads and turn them into compelling news. [25]

After two years, the *Mercury* wanted him back to head its state capital bureau. It wasn't a hard choice—Hughes loved Africa—but his ambition was bigger, and while at the *Mercury,* he started free-lancing for several other papers, including the *Monitor*. He knew the paper from his home. When Hughes was nine, his father had picked up a copy of *Science and Health* and started reading. "This is what I've been looking for all my life," he told his wife and son.

After a few more years in Africa, Hughes took a trip to Boston, where he met Canham. The editor offered him a copyboy job, running errands and sharpening pencils. "My humility was tested," Hughes admits.

Having to find his own stories again, he scoured Boston and came up with enough material with an African slant that the overseas news department got interested. In a short time, he was abroad again as the *Monitor*'s Africa correspondent, covering the painful birth of independence in nation after nation.

After six years in Africa, Hughes returned to Boston, where he spent a year as a Nieman Fellow at Harvard and then a short time as assistant overseas news editor. He was soon headed overseas again, this time for Hong Kong. His beat stretched from Burma to Okinawa.

By this time, Hughes was one of the best writers at the *Monitor* as well as a superb reporter. He knew where to get the information he needed and how to present it so that the reader felt well informed without having to wade through mountains of extraneous material.

DeWitt John realized what he had in Hughes, and he was convinced that the way to create more interesting and effective journalism in the *Monitor* was to make sure correspondents like him had the freedom to pursue the stories that seemed most promising to them. The big stories, he was sure, were the ones that dealt with the big problems of humanity, and he wanted his writers to stake their claims to them.

In 1964, Hughes, now the paper's Hong-Kong-based Far East correspondent, was watching Indonesia closely. President Sukarno had held onto power since declaring independence for his nation from the Netherlands, in 1945, but he had to balance carefully the three main forces that provided his power base—the Army, Islamic groups, and the Communist Party, all of which distrusted each other deeply.

On a trip to Jakarta, the Indonesian capital, in early

1965, he watched a speech by Sukarno—President for Life, Prime Minister, Supreme Commander of the Armed Forces, Great Leader of the Revolution, Mouthpiece of the Indonesian People:

> *The huge stadium is packed.*
>
> *Down the stairs to the dais on the floor of the arena pads a stocky little man, dressed in a chocolate-colored uniform. On his head is the traditional black kopiah.*
>
> *With a roar, the thousands surge to their feet. The bright revolutionary banners hanging from the walls flutter a little in the breeze. The air crackles with electric excitement. . . .*
>
> *The man begins to speak. Slowly, in a hoarse, caressing, mesmeric whisper. Then faster. And louder. And faster and louder still. Until he has the crowd in an ecstatic fervor.* [26]

But Sukarno had enemies, and on September 30, the top blew off the government. Six senior army generals were killed by a group called the "30 September Movement," and Major General Suharto took control of the army. He claimed that the Communist Party had engineered a coup attempt, and he began cracking down on communist newspapers. The army was now in an open fight with its chief rival for power, and Sukarno was more and more isolated.

From Manila, Hughes reported the first stories of the attempted coup—whether it was engineered by the communists or the army has never been determined—but in a few days he was able to get to Jakarta. His visa had expired and the government wasn't issuing more, especially to journalists. But the army was busy minding the crisis and wasn't paying close attention to the airport. All the better for an astute correspondent. "There was enough confusion you could talk your way into the country," Hughes says.

It turned out he was the only American who got in.

Rumors flew that Sukarno was a virtual prisoner of the army. To demonstrate his independence, or at least that he was alive, his staff organized a photo opportunity for journalists. Hughes stood a few feet away from the president and struck up a conversation:

> *Sukarno: "You are from?"*
> *Hughes: "The Christian Science Monitor."*
> *Hughes: "Have you some words for the foreign press?"*
> *Sukarno: "Just a smile."*
> *Hughes: "We note the smile but would prefer some words."*
> *At this the President and Cabinet broke into laughter.* [27]

They continued bantering for a while until an official broke in.

It was this kind of ease with power—a self-confidence that wouldn't be sidetracked—that enabled Hughes to blend quickly into the story and become a close witness to unfolding events. He reported as the communists fought back and the army unearthed forty-two mutilated bodies in Central Java. He wrote about how the army took revenge by training young people to go after its enemies, which soon stretched beyond communists to members of the Chinese immigrant community, long resented for their wealth, and even to personal enemies. Deaths eventually numbered in the hundreds of thousands.

As the crisis rushed toward a climax, protesting students seized the Indonesian foreign ministry, and other demonstrators stormed the American embassy. Hughes was inside the embassy when he heard that a communist mob in Merdeka Square was setting the library on fire. "I've got to get down there," he told his interpreter. The embassy was locked down, but Hughes and the interpreter climbed the fence and were soon sprinting down alleyways toward the library.

Then they came to an abrupt halt. Moving toward them

was a crowd of young Indonesians clearly set on mayhem. Hughes's interpreter was white with fear. Hughes himself, however, felt "an amazing sense of calm." What came to him, he says, was this: "I am about God's work. I am a child of God. They can't kill me."

The crowd saw the two men and stopped.

"There's an American. Let's kill him!" someone shouted.

"No, wait," a leader of the group shouted back. "We're not going to kill him. He might be Russian." The mob continued down the street.

"I've never felt the presence of God more than I did then," Hughes says. "I just knew they weren't going to kill me."

By September the finale was near:

> *During the year which has elapsed, President Sukarno's power has been steadily whittled away. Until a year ago he dominated the Indonesian scene and few dared challenge him. Now, however, he is an object for scorn among many younger Indonesians. He is openly criticized, and anti-Sukarno cartoons which would have sent their originators hurtling into jail a year ago today flourish.* [28]

Sukarno was finally stripped of his presidential title, on March 12, 1967, and died under house arrest, in 1970.

Hughes's series of articles constituted superb on-the-spot reporting of a major crisis in an important country, and it earned him the 1967 Pulitzer Prize for international reporting.

The prize was not without controversy. The journalism jury panel had voted to award it to Harrison Salisbury of *The New York Times* for dispatches from North Vietnam. The Pulitzer advisory board, however, overruled the panel and voted six to five against Salisbury because he failed to give the source of casualty figures he had obtained from Hanoi. Hughes was the second choice of the panel and received the prize.

Hughes's reporting showed not only the calm, insight,

and faithfulness to the story expected of *Monitor* correspondents but also a certain raw instinct for the news. DeWitt John's determination to create a newsroom where journalists felt supported was also indispensable. He refused to let artificial roadblocks stand in the way of a story that needed telling, and he made sure reporters such as Hughes had the resources they needed. After the Pulitzers were announced, Hughes gave the Associated Press a reason for his success: "The *Monitor* has given me freedom to go where and when the Asia story dictates. It is a tremendous advantage and one for which I am most grateful." [29]

The "love" that *Newsweek* had mocked was paying off. The successes for John and the *Monitor* were just beginning. He was determined that the paper make bold and practical contributions to the world, not only by reporting on major events with insight and patience, as Hughes had done, but also by reporting on the broader and deeper ills that plagued society, and helping to engineer reforms.

Seat-of-the-pants reporting

One of those societal ills was the dysfunctional state and local court system in the United States. John had talked with some judges he knew and realized that incompetence and even corruption stretched across the country. The public was suffering. Here was a subject that needed the *Monitor*'s attention.

One of John's new hires was a brash young man from Chicago, Howard James. James had made a name for himself as an investigative reporter for the *Chicago Tribune*. He was relentless in his pursuit of a story, even following Attorney General Robert Kennedy into a bathroom when he visited the city and interviewing him while Kennedy sat on the toilet.

James had always loved journalism, but when a finicky high-school English teacher told him that he would never be a writer because his punctuation and spelling were poor, he turned to electronic media. At Michigan State University, he majored in radio, TV, and film, and worked his way through college as a correspondent for several radio and TV stations. His senior year, he borrowed money from a bank to buy a TV camera and started a news service that covered the state capital, feeding reports to Michigan stations and eventually landing an office next to the lieutenant governor's. The legislators were thrilled to have television pay such close attention to them.

Upon graduation, he became a TV news anchor in Marquette, Michigan, and when he was asked by the station's owner to write occasionally for the local paper, which was owned by the station, James finally stopped hearing the voice of his high-school English teacher. Writing was where he belonged.

The *Chicago Tribune* liked his spirit and eventually hired him for its city desk. He learned to follow his instincts and not let a story go until it bore fruit. The *Tribune* knew it had a budding star, but James would not let himself be cornered. When he was asked to move to Washington, D.C., to cover national politics, he quit the paper—"I didn't like the environment in Washington," he says[30]—and took a brief job as a city editor in Iowa. He hated the desk job and quit again, this time buying a pickup truck and traveling the West for six months. When his father died, he came home to Indiana to help his mother, then returned to Chicago, where he worked for a public-relations firm for a while and then opened several new stores for Montgomery Ward. He heard that the *Monitor*'s Chicago bureau chief was moving to Boston and contacted new editor DeWitt John to inquire about the job.

The *Monitor* was not just another paper for James. When he was young, he was troubled by a severe case of eczema. His grandfather was a doctor and his grandmother a nurse, and they took him to the local university medical school to get help. When he was not cured, another relative, who had just taken up Christian Science, suggested that Howard's mother take him to a practitioner. He was healed completely, and from that day, Howard, his parents, and his brothers and sisters all became Christian Scientists.

John met James in Chicago and was so impressed that he asked him to come to Boston to interview further. As far as he knows, James says, he was the only reporter ever to be interviewed by all five of the church's Directors. They asked about his background and philosophy of journalism and experience in Christian Science, and were satisfied enough that John hired him and flew him back to Chicago. He trained for six months and then became bureau chief.

James watched how work was getting done at the *Monitor*, especially on the big series, and he didn't like what he saw. The series were traditionally split among the various bureaus, with Los Angeles taking one part, Chicago another, Washington another, then the whole thing merged into some kind of whole. It's not the way to do it, James told John. It creates internal arguments, with different concepts of the story clashing. The whole couldn't possibly have a clear identity. You have to assign a series to one person, give him time and an expense account, and let him loose, he said. The personal investment of a good reporter is where the power will come from.

It was, of course, how James liked to work.

All right, John said, the state and local courts in this country are in trouble. Take your *Monitor* credit card. You have ninety days.

James didn't know a lot about the courts. He had a few conversations with law groups in Chicago, then hopped on a plane and headed out. He started each day, he says, asking God, "Father, what am I supposed to do today? I need some help." In city after city, he found extraordinarily helpful people and places, from which he slowly built a mountain of information.

He spent most of the ninety days on the road, interviewing judges, court officials, prison inmates, crime victims, politicians—anyone who could help round out the picture. Then he returned home and set up an office in his basement, where he wrote furiously to meet his deadline. Roughing out the series based on what he remembered from the trip—the material that stood out in his memory was, he believed, the material that was important—he then checked the facts with his notes and polished the articles. One by one, he sent them to be reviewed by the church lawyer, then to be polished further by the copy desk. Even after the series began running in the paper, James was completing later parts.

The series started with a focus on judges. In many cases, James had just sat down in courtrooms and listened. He told of a judge in Louisville, Kentucky, who did crossword puzzles while listening to testimony, another in New York who read a law bulletin, "lowering a corner to listen now and then." A judge in San Francisco made sarcastic comments to defendants in traffic courts. Courtroom regulars said the judge was "'a brilliant criminal lawyer who thinks he is above hearing traffic cases' but must, under the system, take a turn at it." [31]

After further research, James concluded that roughly half the judges in the United States were unfit for their jobs. He carefully noted extenuating circumstances and examples of good judges to counter the bad. He did not want to stack the deck. But the damaging evidence was far too heavy to miss. In the end, he gathered the problem judges he found into eleven categories, ranging from hacks, who got their jobs because they knew a politician, and retirees, who were relaxing after a grueling career as trial lawyers, to bored, lazy, prejudiced, or failed lawyers.

That was just the first article.

As week followed week, readers learned of inexperienced and poorly trained prosecutors, corrupt court staffers, and brutal jail guards. The juvenile court system came off as shockingly uncaring, both for young defendants who needed help and for the public, which had to cope with those young people who were truly criminal but were released because the system did not support careful jurisprudence.

James's series was full of stories, stories, and more stories. Like the *Monitor*'s earlier series on freedom, it was built on solid reporting, the kind that takes time, resources, and not a little patience after the information gathering is done to sort through the memories and material, and separate the inconsequential from the meaningful. The point was to paint a picture so convincing—and accurate—that those in society who cared would act to make reforms.

James devoted the final article entirely to ideas for reform—105 of them—ranging from what citizens could do, to where legislators, educators, and lawyers could get involved. James concluded that "there is still a long, tough trail ahead."[32] But the impact of the series was immediate. As the Associated Press noted later in an article published by the *Monitor*, "bail-bonding practices were changed in Pittsburgh. In Miami, a boy wrongly jailed was released. In Anderson, S.C., public—but actually restricted—jail records were opened as a result of the investigative reporting for the series. . . . A California judge said the articles helped him recognize his failings and launch reform in his courtroom." [33]

There was no magic in James's accomplishment. It was hard, seat-of-the-pants (many hours on courtroom benches!) reporting. His months on the road cost him a marriage—"I would be gone a month at a time, trying to save the *Monitor* money. I didn't want to fly back." And he did some things of debatable wisdom, such as suing the sheriff of Greenville, South Carolina, on behalf of the *Monitor* to get information on a case—without the *Monitor*'s knowledge.

But in the end, he got the job done, and his work made people's lives better. The *Monitor* was putting itself back in the national picture again, this time as a place to find tough investigative reporting.

The next spring, the Pulitzer awards were handed out, and James's series won (jointly with the *Des Moines Register*) for national reporting. Doubts that John belonged in the editor's chair no longer had traction. Like Hughes, James had been given the freedom to pursue the story where and when he needed to. The priority was to get at the truth, whatever the cost.

"DeWitt was the best editor I ever worked for," James says. "As long as I produced the kind of stuff to make the *Monitor* successful and win awards, DeWitt would let me have my own way with things. He trusted me totally, and I never let him down."

Getting the story, telling it well

Growing up in Arizona, John had always loved the West and its wide-open spaces. His home town of Safford was only three hundred miles from the Grand Canyon. He gravitated toward the big themes, in journalism, in music (he was a fan of Mahler), and in nature.

The national parks in the United States were becoming highly popular—forty million people had visited them in the past year—and some experts were afraid the parks were facing ruin. John asked reporter Robert Cahn to investigate. Cahn, a former reporter and writer for several publications, including *Life* magazine and the *Saturday Evening Post*, had joined the *Monitor*'s Washington bureau in 1965.

John let Cahn alone to work out his series. Over nine months, the reporter traveled twenty thousand miles and visited twenty parks. He wrote up his findings and gave them to John, who read the articles along with his wife. They both agreed: The series was flat. Cahn had got the facts in abundance. But there was little freshness, little of the narrative arc that keeps readers moving along.

John set to work. It was a cool springtime in New England, and as he sat in a chair by the fire at home, he started pruning. Slowly, the story began to shine. The series was no longer just reported. It was written.

The series was titled "Will success spoil the national parks?" and it began with the big theme in full view. One park in Colorado required admission tickets because crowds were so large. Then, in North Carolina:

> . . . *I braked to a stop behind a line of cars winding along a tree-shrouded hillside road in the Great Smoky Mountains National Park.*
>
> *Ahead—the red glow of a traffic signal.*
>
> *Admission tickets? A traffic signal? In America's*

national parks?

Yes. And more such curbs are on the way. The era of almost unrestricted use of the parks is coming to an end. [34]

Cahn discovered overcrowded campgrounds in Yosemite, "bear jams" (cars stopped to view the wildlife, endangering themselves and causing traffic jams), in Yellowstone, and recklessly speeding logging trucks. He was careful, as James had been, to note the positives along with the negatives: the families ecstatic at the breathtaking views, the enthusiastic park naturalists, the officials who cracked down on huge house trailers, which clogged the narrow roads.

But because of the mounting problems of crowding, the number of restrictions was also climbing. Campgrounds were charging fees or cutting their sizes, and plans for new roads were being canceled or re-examined. Some members of the public fought back, claiming a right to drive and camp where they pleased, when they pleased. It only added to the growing tensions.

Would future generations be able to enjoy the parks?

Article after article in the series started with an incident, the better to bring the reader into the story and make the point stick:

"Please keep your voices down. We are coming to an area where some bald eagles nest in a cottonwood tree."

Frank Ewing, our guide on this float trip at dawn on the Snake River, skillfully poled the small rubber raft around a bend, avoiding the protruding gnawed logs of a beaver dam on the bank. . . .

The current swept us around another bend. Frank put a finger to his lips and pointed to a high cottonwood snag. Sitting on a jagged top, perfectly still, was a baby eagle, gazing into the sunrise.

It was a moment to frame forever in memory. . . .

And then . . . people.

Almost with a shock, after seeing nothing but scenic beauty and wildlife for three hours, we heard the sound of cars and looked up to see the 20-foot high garish Indian-tepee facade of a highway chuck-wagon restaurant. The float trip was over and we were back to the sights and noise of civilization. [35]

Through style as well as content, Cahn and John built the tension between making the parks more accessible to the public and saving them in their natural state; between private ownership and access to resources, and public ownership and preservation. The *Monitor*'s view came through clearly. Not to preserve the parks was to deprive everyone of something deeply nourishing.

Again, the journalistic community was impressed, and again, the *Monitor* walked away with a Pulitzer, the 1969 award for national reporting. It was beginning to seem that John's approach—finding a problem of major proportions; digging into the causes by talking with many people on different sides of the issue; proposing practical solutions; being willing to spend the time and resources on both reporting and editing to do the job thoroughly; and turning it all into a compelling story—could bear abundant fruit. Given the problems the world faced and the *Monitor*'s objective of blessing mankind, the possibilities were rich. The only roadblock would be if church officials changed priorities and decided to focus resources elsewhere. After all, it was expensive to produce these series.

The church builds

It was not an idle concern. In the mid-1960s, the church's Board of Directors had decided to undertake a major expansion and renovation of the church grounds and buildings, and they contracted with the firm of famed architect I. M. Pei to design the project. Construction began in 1968. "In this second century of its existence [since Mrs. Eddy's discovery of

Christian Science]," the Directors told church members, in 1969, "the Christian Science movement is becoming more aware than ever of what a greater outreach to humanity can mean to the world." [36] Church officials were confident the combination of cash reserves and future contributions would cover the cost—estimated at fifteen million dollars—and would not affect operations, including the *Monitor*.

The reaction, however, from some of the church membership was not expected. Despite the insistence of the Directors that the new Christian Science Center would be a jewel of the Back Bay area of Boston, welcoming the neighborhood to a spacious plaza and reflecting pool, and providing space for expected expansion of church offices, some members felt that the project smacked of arrogance and self-promotion, and anger not seen since the end of the Dixon era began building in the membership. Some people believed—how many was not clear—that the church was headed in the wrong direction. It didn't help that the costs of building the new Church Center were multiplying.

Noble behavior, or creepy?

The mood echoed that of the nation as a whole. A revolt against traditional authority and a resistance to lockstep thinking on the one hand, a determination to reach out to the world and a refusal to change under pressure on the other, all made the United States a volatile nation in the late 1960s and early 1970s. At the center was the Vietnam War, raging on the battlefield and in public opinion.

DeWitt John, who had supported the war from the beginning, had undergone a change of heart when he joined a group of editors at the exclusive World Newspapers Conference in Kyoto, Japan, in 1966. Only one other American newspaper, *The New York Times*, was represented. Discussing with his colleagues the big issue at the time—the bombing of North Vietnam by the United States—John had come to the conclusion that American policy was wrong. "The United States is playing with dynamite,"[37] he told *Monitor* readers. It did not sit well with the large conservative readership of the *Monitor*, but John could not hide his views when he had concluded that speaking out would do more good.

The *Monitor* also tried to bring its healing perspective to the war through coverage from several correspondents. One was Elizabeth Pond, who was writing from Vietnam and then took a year-long leave of absence from the *Monitor,* in 1969, to do research in Southeast Asia on an Alicia Patterson Foundation fellowship.

On May 7, 1970, she was traveling in a jeep in eastern Cambodia with two other journalists when they were stopped and abducted by Khmer Rouge anti-government forces. Their capture brought to thirteen the number of missing journalists, at the time, in Cambodia.

Pond and her colleagues were told that if investigation proved they were truly journalists, not CIA agents, they would be released. They were brought in a truck, at gunpoint, to several villages, where they were displayed as American captives. Pond tried her best to calm the situation:

> *As I looked at the people I tried to convey to them that I bore them no ill will, that I loathe war and the passions of war, destruction and hatred and enmity between men—and that if any of them had lost loved ones my heart went out to them.* [38]

The group was finally walked blindfolded through a crowd of jeering Cambodians and then taken to a schoolroom, where a guard tried to attack Pond and took her rings. "I said aloud that this was not necessary," she wrote later, "that he was my brother and I was his sister. Nothing happened for a few minutes and then he replaced the rings on my fingers." [39]

A higher officer had heard of the arrest and intervened, and the captives received better treatment and even an apology for what they had been through. Over time, everyone relaxed, and the soldiers even left weapons in the journalists' presence.

Pond said she and her colleagues never contemplated escape and were treated almost like guests after the first week. In all, they stayed in the homes of ten different families, often moving at night. They played chess and drank tea with their guards. Toward the end of their captivity, one soldier told them, "I want you to live. I want to see you safely back with your families. . . . I just want them to see you face to face again. . . . Sooner or later you will be released." [40]

Five and a half weeks later, word came that they were to be given their freedom. Pond thanked the regional commander for the hospitality and good treatment they had received. At a gala good-bye dinner, almost every officer they had met showed up. Then they were taken to a village schoolyard where a celebration was starting:

> *There was a gathering of about 1,000 villagers; there was an honor guard of Cambodian irregulars; and there were new banners that were translated for us as thanking American people who oppose aggression by the Nixon administration in Cambodia. We were shown places at a small table in front of the podium.* [41]

They were finally set free and hitched rides to Saigon, Vietnam, in an empty South Vietnamese convoy.

After their release, Pond wondered why they had been freed when, by this time, some twenty other correspondents were still held in Cambodia. She was concerned that her behavior toward the captors would be construed as appeasing the enemy. She acknowledged that she and her colleagues could have remained silent or challenged their captors directly, on the basis that the soldiers who held them were enemies of the United States:

> *As it turned out, we made a choice that was not one of confrontation. We expected to be treated as journalists once it was ascertained that we were not spies, and we acted this way.* [42]

Readers wrote from both sides of the political divide, some thanking Pond for her story and "nobility of character," some decrying the "creepiness" of three Americans developing "too much rapport with the other side." [43] The *Monitor* itself, in an editorial, expressed gratitude for the release of Pond and her colleagues and noted the irony of the treatment they had received for honest reporting:

> *There has never been a war in which American correspondents, and those associated with them, have sought harder to do a competent, factual, straightforward job of reporting than has been the case during the current conflict. Indeed, so successful have they been in this effort to be accurate and factual that they have often come under attack at home.* [44]

The *Monitor*'s position on Pond's experience and against the war in Vietnam continued to bring plenty of vocal opposition from conservative readers. But John was not about to compromise his integrity to appease critics. For him, this was part of love: honesty with oneself and others, and willingness to speak the truth no matter the consequences.

But fairness and tolerance were less and less the standard for discourse in the United States. Combativeness was seeping into every part of society, including the church. It would take extraordinary patience, love, and spiritual strength to steer the *Monitor* through the turbulence.

Unfortunately, the paper would soon not have DeWitt John to help.

9

Defenseless

On August 24, 1970, the Directors announced that DeWitt John would become a member of their board. The job was a full-time responsibility, so he would have to leave the *Monitor*. In contrast to his earlier move to the Committee on Publication, he didn't resist. He realized that the new position was of immense importance to the church, and he felt that he could help the *Monitor* as a director.

John Hughes, who had been the paper's managing editor since the previous year, would become the new editor. With his Pulitzer fame and sterling qualities as a journalist, he seemed a logical choice.

When John had invited him to take the managing editor job, Hughes had balked. He loved reporting from Asia. "There wasn't a country I disliked and didn't feel warmly toward," he says. "But duty calls." When he accepted John's request to come to Boston, he told his wife, "After what I've been through, managing editor must be a cushy job."

It didn't turn out that way. There were personnel as well as journalistic issues. There were relationships with two boards that had to be nurtured. And then there was the matter of working at church headquarters. Any position at The Mother Church, especially one as senior as *Monitor* editor, carried with it a need for constant alertness to where one's thought was going. Fighting the urge to slip into comfortable habits of thinking could be exhausting. Mrs. Eddy had expected her workers to be always "on one's game," and the demand took its toll on many of her officials. Those who came out ahead found that they had to pray constantly. The demand hadn't changed in the decades since.

Maybe it gets easier as you go higher, Hughes thought. When he accepted the new job, he told his wife, "After managing editor, editor has to be a piece of cake."

Wrong again.

Hughes had big shoes to fill. DeWitt John had taken the *Monitor* even higher than Canham in terms of circulation, reaching more than 218,000 by 1970. He had created an environment in which reporters felt that they had the freedom and support to produce great journalism.

One of Hughes's first moves was to place a call to Howard James, who was in Iowa gathering information for a series called "The American Family." James and Hughes recall the conversation somewhat differently—Hughes says it occurred in person—but they agree the result was an unhappy one. It happened roughly like this.

Hughes, who, according to James, felt the reporter was "dawdling," asked if he had finished the series:

> *James: "No, I have more work to do."*
> *Hughes: "How many pieces will it be?"*
> *James: "I can't tell you that."*
> *Hughes: "How much longer will you be on the story?"*
> *James: "I can't tell you that either."*
> *Hughes: "You have to understand, Howard, there is a cost to what you are doing. We have to know."*
> *James: "John, you don't understand. Judges and lawyers are waiting to see what Howard James writes. I can't be tied down."*
> *Hughes: "We have to put out a paper."*
> *James: "I can't work like that."*
> *Hughes: "Then we've got to straighten you out."*
> *James: "No, you are not going to straighten me out, because this is my last day on the* Monitor.*"* [1]

And with that, one of the *Monitor*'s star reporters was gone. Hughes asked him to turn in his notes, which James refused to do, and his series on the family never appeared.

"I had admired John from afar," James says. "He was a great reporter. He probably had very good reason to want to straighten me out. But I would not let him curb my ability to get things done."

Hughes was hit hard. "It was not an easy thing for a new editor to lose one of his best reporters," he says. But he was not about to go soft.

His management tactics began to be watched closely by the staff. Judith Frutig, who was a reporter in the Chicago bureau, didn't spend much time in Boston, but when she visited, she saw something she had been hearing about. "The newsroom was focused on [Hughes'] ability to reduce to tears the paper's most highly respected men from all parts of the world," she says. "His tactics were apparently so well known that when people in the newsroom saw correspondents enter his office, they watched to see their emotional conditions as they exited. Then [managing editor] Earl [Foell] would take them to his desk and tell them what they were doing well." [2]

It was a classic good cop/bad cop routine, but it didn't seem to be a scheme. "I think Earl watched what John was doing and did what he could to right it," Frutig says.

Hughes was trying to create what he called "healthy tension" in the newsroom. He had spent considerable time professionally in the rough-and-tumble of Fleet Street, London, and he believed that pressure brought out the best work in people. "He was tough," says David Winder, a young reporter from South Africa, who had just been transferred to Boston from the London office. "He was an excellent correspondent. But he was very poor in reading people." [3]

Some people saw things differently. "[Hughes] was upbeat and full of energy," says Paul van Slambrouck, who was hired by Hughes as a New England reporter. "He was a very clear thinker and very straightforward. That might have been tough on some people." [4]

Everyone agreed he could be charming, at least outside the newsroom. "People found him articulate, fun, very intelligent, and relevant," says David Morse, who came to the *Monitor* as national advertising manager from the *Los Angeles Times*. "He was profoundly thoughtful and a delight to work with." [5]

With his firm hand, Hughes began to give a different shape to the paper's content. "There's nothing we can't cover," he reaffirmed in an announcement to the staff. The important thing was how the story was handled:

> *Mrs. Eddy had a clear concept for her newspaper. It was to be a healing and constructive force. This didn't mean we had to see the world through rose-tinted glasses. It did mean that even when shining a spotlight on difficult problems, even ones offensive to some readers, we could not leave the reader wallowing in despair. Somewhere, some professor or expert was thinking about it and offering up solutions, and we had to find him or her and integrate positive conclusions with the negative.*

The same went for the editorial page:

> *We had to write editorials explanatory and exhortatory. Sometimes we would offer up solutions and campaign for them. Sometimes we would just shine light on a problem to encourage readers to take action themselves, either by prayer or human involvement.* [6]

Finding an expert with a solution and encouraging readers to act was positive and even noble. It differed, however, from John's approach, which was not to encourage so much as to inspire. One was an external motivation, the other an internal. Ultimately, the internal was more powerful, but it had to be stirred by the writer, not just by an expert, and come out of the writer's own spiritual breakthroughs and insight. It was a tall demand that not many journalists, even under John, were able or willing to meet.

Hughes wanted to focus on the most current news, where his own interest lay. "I wanted [reporters] to be so steeped in the news," Hughes says, "that they could write the second-day story on day one."

To John Dillin, who became Atlanta bureau chief in 1971, the approach led to superficiality:

> *[Hughes] wanted to bring more of a punchy style to the paper, more headline stuff, shorter stories. He had this sense we had to be on top of things. We would sometimes run after spot news stories we wouldn't normally cover, stories that were transient in nature.*
>
> *One of the stories was in New Orleans. I think it was a hostage taking. I made some phone calls from Atlanta and did a quick story, but thought at the time that this was not where the* Monitor *should be going.*

For Dillin, it took just as much time to write shorter articles as longer ones. He and other *Monitor* correspondents had been going in depth on their pieces, trying to produce something lasting. They still went after depth—this, they felt, was what made *Monitor* writing stand out—even if the article ultimately contained fewer words.

After a while Hughes backed off. "He just stopped pushing it," Dillin says. "Then we went back to more in-depth stories." [7]

"I've got them"

Hughes wanted to make sure the *Monitor* was as much on top of the Vietnam story as any other paper. In mid-1971, *The Washington Post* and *The New York Times* began publishing excerpts from the Pentagon Papers, a top-secret study, which the Nixon Administration tried to suppress, that revealed embarrassing details about decision-making during the Vietnam War. Hughes was eager to publish something as well, but he didn't have a copy.

One day Canham walked into Hughes's office.

"I've got them," Canham said.

"Where did you get them?"

"Can't say."

He presented Hughes with a package in a plain brown wrapper. Canham never said where they came from. Hughes pulled several writers off stories they were working on, and they read through the papers that night. Then Hughes sat down with the Directors and convinced them that publishing the Papers was the right thing to do. [8] An excerpt appeared in the June 29, 1971, edition.

Some readers thanked the paper for its integrity. Others decried the paper's decision to break the law by printing the Papers.

One of the *Monitor*'s readers was a Christian Scientist, John Ehrlichman, who was Nixon's assistant for domestic affairs and one of his most vocal defenders. Intent on closing leaks of sensitive information, he came to Boston on November 8, 1971, and gave a closed talk to church employees. According to those who attended, he was irate at the *Monitor*'s decision to publish the Pentagon Papers and accused the paper of being full of communists. DeWitt John later admitted that the Board was embarrassed to have invited Ehrlichman, and he apologized to Hughes.

Hughes was not about to be intimidated by the government, but he and others at the *Monitor* were cautious. Republican support ran deep in the church. Then in June 1972, burglars were caught breaking into Democratic Party headquarters in the Watergate office complex in Washington. It was soon revealed that the burglars were connected to the Republican Party, to which Nixon belonged. As the scandal moved closer and closer to the White House, implicating Ehrlichman and eventually Nixon himself, the country fell into angry recriminations about treason and lying.

Hughes refused to back off, and DeWitt John and the rest of the Board supported him. It didn't sit well with many readers. Years before, the paper had supported Hoover and

Prohibition, which were popular with Christian Scientists, and readers felt an affinity with the paper. Now the *Monitor* was breaking with the political views of its core constituency, and for some, it would be a signal that the paper was no longer theirs.

Cynthia Parsons had been education editor on the paper from 1962 to 1969. She had left the *Monitor* to work at the World Bank as education editor, then at the U.S. Office of Education. In 1970, Hughes offered her a freelance column called "Parent and Child," which was eventually syndicated, and in 1972, she returned as education editor. She was struck immediately with the change in environment:

> *Generally, in my earlier seven years as education editor, when you got a letter from a reader, they talked about what the article covered. Or they talked about what the article included or left out. When I returned, 90 percent of the letters attacked you [personally] as the writer. It caused the editors to begin dealing with things at that level. It made exchanges more difficult. People were annoyed. The Directors were pushing to do some things they hadn't done before, like building the new plaza. People didn't like what was happening at the church level, and they decided to let loose on the newspaper level as well.* [9]

The concern of Christian Scientists, however, was not just about the building project and the *Monitor*'s coverage. Along with other Americans, many of them were also lashing out at what they saw as creeping immorality in society. Roscoe Drummond, writing an opinion column called "Point of View" in the summer of 1974, gave voice to many of these readers:

> *There is little doubt that as a people we are witnessing and participating in an inner moral and political decline comparable to that which brought the downfall of the Roman Empire.* [10]

The fundamental struggle between those who saw the Roman Empire collapsing around them and those who could look at the times with more confidence, based on a willingness to see the best in people despite their failings, became more and more apparent in the church. Once Nixon resigned, the tension did not disappear but seemed to plant its roots deeper.

The love and dominion DeWitt John had brought to the paper seemed to be disappearing. On Sunday morning, September 8, 1974, Gerald Ford announced he would pardon former President Nixon for "all offenses against the United States which he . . . has committed or may have committed." The extraordinary act of forgiveness inspired some Americans to hope that the country could finally put Watergate behind it. But millions of others found the pardon disturbing and dismissed Ford's action as politically motivated or just wrongly timed.

The *Monitor* sided with the skeptics. In an editorial a day later, the paper laid out its case:

> *In granting former President Nixon a 'full, free, and absolute pardon,' President Ford responds to the need for compassion urged by many voices, including this newspaper's, as an accompaniment to the workings of justice.*
>
> *But unless it becomes clear that the workings of justice have also been served, compassion for Mr. Nixon and his family will not serve Mr. Ford's intent 'to firmly shut and seal this book.'* [11]

The editorial was well reasoned and fully in line with what most other major newspapers were saying. It did not, however, illuminate any particular way for *Monitor* readers to cut through the lingering bitterness to reach their own level of compassion. The editorial was disappointing, particularly for those looking for something distinctive and hopeful from the *Monitor,* something to challenge conventional thinking and help them find a sense of peace and healing that could, in turn, help the country and the church cope.

Besieged

Meanwhile, the most explosive question of all was beginning to be asked in Boston: Were there more efficient ways than an expensive-to-produce newspaper of reaching out to the world?

In an address to the members back in 1970, Trustee Howard Palfrey Jones had laid out the facts and the challenge:

> . . . *The* Monitor*'s prestige has never been higher; its circulation level is at an all-time high. But even this level isn't high enough to attract the amount of advertising required to put the paper on a paying basis. Inflation, higher costs, inadequate revenue, present us with the kind of challenge Christian Scientists have always met.* [12]

The paper, it turned out, was in the red and had been since 1962. Jones praised the prizewinning work of Howard James and Robert Cahn and insisted, "The *Monitor* will continue to focus on the problems of our society and hammer out solutions to those problems." [13] It was a formulation of the *Monitor*'s purpose that was as combative as the times.

At the 1972 annual meeting, the treasurer, Roy Garrett Watson, admitted that the cost of the church center construction was higher than expected. "It is necessary at this point to use reserve funds to pay for construction costs and to equip and furnish the buildings," [14] he said. The cost, in fact, had more than quintupled, from the original estimate of $15 million to close to $88 million.

At the same meeting, the Trustees announced proudly that The Christian Science Monitor News Service, created and syndicated through the *Des Moines Register Tribune*, was growing, about to reach more than a hundred newspapers with more than twelve million readers. [15] But tensions were mounting, and the Trustees asked for the continued prayers of the members. With the vastly more expensive church building project, along with the recession and inflation in the United States, arising from the oil embargo imposed by the OPEC nations of the Middle East, with prices of everything from transportation to postage to energy soaring for the *Monitor*, money was becoming tighter and tighter.

The Saturday edition was soon eliminated. Budgets were cut and people were laid off. The dynamic, award-winning *Monitor* of the 1960s, not hammering out solutions so much as inspiring them, seemed to be fading, and a besieged, resource-deficient paper seemed to be taking its place.

Roominess of the spirit

On June 18, 1974, a timely series called "The World's Struggle for Resources" started running in the *Monitor*. The author was the paper's Paris correspondent, Takashi Oka, a Japanese-born writer who, except for a three-year stint at *The New York Times*, had spent his career with the *Monitor* in Boston, Hong Kong, Saigon, Moscow, and Tokyo.

The immediate issue was the oil embargo, with Arab nations capping their production until the price of oil exploded. The embargo was cutting deeply everywhere. It raised the specter of copycat embargoes on other commodities and of diminishing supplies of everything from minerals and food to capital and even human skills.

With a resource deficit weighing heavily on the minds of the church, the significance of the series for the *Monitor* went beyond an oil embargo.

Oka clearly didn't have the means to copy Howard James and Robert Cahn and jet himself to every corner of the globe to get the story. So he resolved the problem in a way unique to the *Monitor*—he wrote the series from the standpoint of a thinking and working Christian Scientist.

He decided to focus on only two countries, Japan and India, as representatives of the problems faced by everyone.

Oka headed first to Japan, the country where he had grown up. Despite the fact that they lived on just a few islands, with almost no natural resources, the Japanese had been able to achieve an economy of sufficiency through cleverness and energy. Now, though, they faced a different challenge, one depending more on collaboration with the world:

> *. . . to shed their island mentality and to take on some of the characteristics of a continental or global people— that is the challenge confronting the Japanese. They have broken the scarcity barrier—for themselves. They are just beginning to find they cannot reach abundance without a certain roominess of the spirit.* [16]

Here was something the Monitor's core readers—Christian Scientists—could grab onto. If there was one need any of them would not only grasp immediately and identify with but also be inspired to pray about on behalf of Japan and the world, it was roominess of spirit. Besides Love and Truth, Mind and Principle, God, to a Christian Scientist, is Spirit.

Oka ended the article on Japan with a quote from Eljiro Machida, managing director of the trading company Mitsui:

> *"It's already out of date . . . for a company employee to think he is working for the company, or even for Japan. In our business, we have got to think in terms of working for the world. This is not idealistic fluff, it's hard common sense. In this day and age, we are not serving the interests of our own company unless we are working for the interest of mankind."* [17]

India's situation was different. The country desperately needed a steady supply of food, and the oil crisis wasn't helping. Oka told of his visit to a family:

> *"Shall we cook an egg?" said a girl to her older sister as a welcome but unexpected guest arrived.*

"Well . . ."

"Oh, come on, let's cook an egg!"

And so on, for half an hour, the discussion went on, the unspoken assumption being that if the egg was cooked now, what would happen tomorrow? [18]

India had taken great strides in making its agricultural production more efficient. But food production had wavered with the dramatic surge in energy prices and fertilizer shortages. With less fertilizer, less diesel oil, less electricity, we seem to be going back to the age of bullocks and Persian wheels, one farmer told Oka.

The United States and Western Europe, far more prosperous than India, had turned inward and left the developing world to fend for itself. In the long run, it was a self-destructive approach, Oka warned:

. . . the economic defense of any single Western country is impossible except in an international context. In that context, India's plight and that of others in the same boat—Bangladesh, Sri Lanka, Ethiopia, Sudan, Mali, Bolivia—cannot be ignored. The well-fed nations do have a responsibility toward their ill-fed brethren—a responsibility that goes beyond charity. [19]

It was a responsibility that started with helping countries like India develop the capacity to sustain themselves. But in Oka's world, responsibility also included what readers had to do: pray scientifically for humanity.

Scientific prayer—a term Christian Scientists use to mean prayer that is specific, thorough, persistent, and consistent with the teachings of the religion—would join people in a universal welfare system, generating ideas to forward the common good and leaving no stone unturned in rooting out the causes of instability and poverty.

Oka's method was a kind of metaphysical reportage, based not only on reporting what he saw and heard but also on what he perceived to be spiritually true in a universe where one Mind, or God, rules.

It was an approach to journalism that could work for the *Monitor* in any economic environment. It wasn't a replacement for the investigative journalism of James, Cahn, and others, which had its own value. But when times were tight, as they were in the 1970s, Oka's style of perceptive and healing journalism could help the *Monitor* fulfill its role in a powerful way. It could help lift *Monitor* readers out of vulnerability to shallow and prejudicial thinking and give them courage to do something about mankind's problems.

"Never lose your joy"

Oka had never adopted the traditionally narrow Japanese view of the world, what he called "the mental straitjacket imposed by centuries of feudal rule." [20] His parents had enrolled him at an early age in the Nishimachi School, in Tokyo, started by a woman named Miyo Matsukata, a friend of his mother's who had lived in America. It was designed originally to give Japanese children a bilingual education and prepare them to be international citizens, but by the time Takashi entered, its reach was considerably broader.

Takashi developed friendships with children of diplomats and businessmen from Russia, Mexico, Great Britain, Argentina, and other countries. He spoke English at home with his mother, who, with her diplomat parents, had lived in—and loved—Canada and the United States as a teenager. She made sure Takashi understood what the Western concepts of freedom, equality, democracy, and individuality meant. The school backed up what she taught him, laying much more emphasis on the individual than had the Japanese school he had attended for a few years before coming to Nishimachi:

> *Nobody told me, in so many words, but I soon worked out for myself that in almost everything I did or learned, there were two distinct aspects: the Western*

and the Japanese. The two aspects coexisted in consciousness, but never merged. At school I spoke English and thought in English. I learned Longfellow's "Hiawatha" and Whittier's "Snowbound." I learned about the Civil War and how Lincoln freed the slaves.

Outside school, and partially at home, I spoke Japanese and did much of my thinking in that language. On New Year's Day I woke up early to worship at the Meiji Shrine with my father and thousands of others. [21]

Openness to the world made life difficult at times for the Okas. In the Japan of the 1930s, militarism and anti-Western attitudes were fast taking hold. As a sensitive young boy, Takashi hated the isolation from his fellow Japanese, which his family's stance imposed on him. But it gradually made him at ease wherever he found himself.

Besides Western cultural ideas, Oka's mother brought something else back from her time in the United States: Christian Science. Takashi had been in and out of hospitals as a small child, and the family had moved for a time to Hawaii, for the warmer weather. One day, his mother had shared a taxi in Honolulu with Miyo Matsukata's brother, and Mrs. Oka had poured out her heart about her family's health problems. The man told her that his family members "never went to doctors and never got sick" [22] and described their religion. Mrs. Oka was able to get a copy of *Science and Health*, and after Christian Science came into the family, Takashi remembers, "I wasn't going to the hospital anymore." He recalls being healed of an ear infection at the age of seven and recovering quickly from a fall from a horse.

Takashi attended a small Christian Science Sunday School in Tokyo, and when he began fifth grade at the Nishimachi school, he discovered that his Sunday School teacher was also his new teacher at Nishimachi. Florence Boynton, an American, had come to Japan in 1905, as a governess for an American family.

The Bible was a focus in her life, and she would often

point out to the Nishimachi class that the Japanese, like the Greeks, worshipped the holiness of beauty, whereas the Jews in the Bible worshipped the beauty of holiness. It was a concept that would remain with Takashi.

Boynton encouraged her students to read the *Monitor,* even though it would often come to Japan a month late. Through the *Monitor,* Takashi learned of things that weren't covered in the Japanese press. Boynton, he said, "shook with anger when she told of Stalin's concentration camps or of Nazi torture of the Jews." He learned about things that were especially troubling to him, such as the Rape of Nanking, when Japanese soldiers raped and massacred hundreds of thousands of Chinese after the Japanese capture of the city, in December 1937.

Takashi had become close to Boynton, and when, in the summer of 1940, relations with the United States deteriorated and she had to leave the country, he was devastated. Later, he wrote her as he mourned the deaths of his grandfather and a cousin, and he lamented the likelihood that he would never be able to fulfill his dream of going to college in the United States. He felt that his life had become pointless.

Boynton wrote back a short note that did not mention Takashi's frustrations but gave him a simple message: Never lose your joy. Oka called her words "the bright light beckoning to me from beyond the miasma of shattered hopes." [23]

Oka's family moved to the small mountain village of Karuizawa during World War II, where foreigners had gathered to escape the bombing of Tokyo. In 1942, he started college in Tokyo. With the help of a sympathetic Japanese professor, he kept up his study of American literature, devouring Walt Whitman's *Leaves of Grass* and Carl Sandburg's *Lincoln.*

When the war ended, Oka's family was still living in Karuizawa. One day on a trip to Tokyo, Takashi overheard a woman describing to a friend how, in the middle of the war, she had run out of her house when it caught fire during an air raid. As she reached safety at a riverbank, she looked back and saw her neighborhood in flames. But then she looked higher and caught her breath. There, in quiet splendor, shone the full moon.

"'It was so beautiful,' the woman said. 'I almost cried.'" [24]

It was the kind of incident Oka would notice many times in his career—the detail that told, not just what happened or why, but where, in the midst of suffering or just plain life, hope lay resplendent.

Melody of Mind

One day, two American men arrived on the train to Karuizawa to visit the Matsukatas, who were also living there. The Matsukatas had sent their children to Principia College during the war, and one of the men, Robert Peel, a professor of English at the college, had letters for Mrs. Matsukata from the children. He was accompanied by *Monitor* correspondent Gordon Walker. Walker carried a pistol, as he didn't know what kind of reception to expect from the Japanese so soon after the war. Peel, although he was in the Army, did not believe in carrying guns.

Oka met them at the train station and talked nonstop with the visitors as they walked the mile back to the village. They were the first adult male Christian Scientists Takashi had met. While they were there, Peel got a stomach virus and asked Mrs. Matsukata to pray for him. He was fine the next morning and said that now he was sure Christian Science had survived intact in Japan. [25]

Walker asked Oka to be his translator on a trip through Japan, and Takashi jumped at the opportunity. Walker had "the tense energy of a coiled spring," [26] he says, not stopping until he got a story. Oka liked the idea of being a journalist.

After three years as an interpreter for Japan's War Crimes Tribunal, he was finally able to fulfill his dream and come to America. He graduated after two years at Principia College, then taught at Principia for a year before heading to Harvard for graduate study in the school's China and Japan program. He had been writing occasional book reviews and other articles on Japanese politics for the *Monitor* and continued doing so at Harvard. In 1953, he started a Ph.D. program at Harvard, but he was tired of living on scholarships and approached Canham for a job. Canham hired him, in 1954, as Asian news editor.

The next year, he took his first trip through Asia as a reporter. One of the countries he visited was Burma, where he had scheduled official interviews but wanted to get closer to the people. He found a merchant who was willing to show him around, but they seemed to be talking in circles, Oka saying he wanted to visit schools and farms, the merchant countering with monuments and pagodas. Oka was frustrated, but instead of reacting in anger, he prayed. How he described the situation gives a view into how many *Monitor* correspondents approach problems during reporting trips:

> *There could not be two minds clashing with each other—my friend's and mine—but only one, the Mind that is God. Both of us were actually reflections of that Mind. Gradually, my frustration subsided as I began to hear in my own thinking a new strain, what I would call "the melody of Mind."* . . . *I thought of a point in* Science and Health: *"The intercommunication is always from God to His idea, man." "That's it,"* I said to *myself. Although it seemed that there was conversation between my friend and me, the truth was that Mind, God, was communicating His thoughts to His idea. There really weren't two tunes."* [27]

At the next break in the man's monologue, Oka repeated his requests, and this time, the man responded exactly as Oka had hoped. He supplied Oka with a car and driver, and let him tour Burmese villages on his own. "I had a marvelous couple of days . . . and came away with lasting memories of a wonderful people in a beautiful land," he wrote. [28]

Strong and wholesome faces

Oka was far from the first newspaper reporter to turn to prayer on the job, but his experience in Burma illustrates how important religion is to many people who work for the *Monitor*.

One such reporter was Charlotte Saikowski, who had a long and award-winning career writing from Moscow, Tokyo, Boston, and Washington. She once faced a severe case of food poisoning. Puzzled that it did not yield to her prayers after a week, she prayed more earnestly, asking God what she needed to deal with. The answer came to her—pollution. She remembered reading an article about the suffering that people and cattle had faced in Michigan as a result of the agricultural application of the chemical PBB:

> *Now, I had been nowhere near Michigan, and there was no apparent link with my physical difficulty. But I did realize how subtly the belief of pollution had crept into my thought. I began praying again. But this time, instead of focusing on my own distress, I addressed the collective belief of pollution, vigorously affirming the existence of only one universal consciousness, the one divine Mind, which could never be contaminated by evil. I declared man's spiritual—not chemical—makeup, and denied the power of mortal mind to victimize mankind.*
>
> *Within the hour all symptoms of the malady disappeared.* [29]

Healing one's own illness by handling the world's thought about it—it's a process and result that both reporters and readers of the *Monitor* have experienced, and it is one reason why the *Monitor* can't be separated from the church that publishes it.

Then there was Geoffrey Godsell, a boisterous Englishman and former BBC correspondent, who was likened by colleagues to Winnie the Pooh. In 1956, Godsell found himself in Cairo as the *Monitor*'s Mediterranean correspondent, where the Suez War had just exploded. He had been labeled an "enemy alien" by the Egyptian government, his car was declared war booty, and his bank account was seized. After two weeks of virtual imprisonment in the Semiramis Hotel, with other foreign correspondents, he was kicked out of the country.

He wanted to return as quickly as possible, but he faced obstacle after obstacle. He kept insisting silently that the law of God is superior to any human law. The confidence his prayer inspired kept his spirits high.

In a few weeks, he was able to get a flight back to Egypt, even as other correspondents were still being forced to leave. And convinced that his prayer had been effective in his personal life as well as in his professional, he found that the Egyptian authorities had never seized his car, the only exception he was aware of to the war booty order. He also got his money back. [30]

None of the details about his prayer appeared in the *Monitor*. But Godsell was convinced that a demonstration of the power of God's law over human law had enabled him to get back on the story more quickly.

This practical religious perspective has been part of the paper's character since the beginning. It is carried not only by many reporters, who search for the right words to convey meaning about the world's news, but also by those who work in visual media.

One of those was Gordon Converse. The *Monitor* has had a history of fine photography, and Converse was one of the best photographers. Early in his career, he found himself in an unnamed East European country and decided to get up early to photograph a small-town outdoor market.

As he entered the market, he faced a wall of suspicious faces.

> *For a few moments I hesitated but moved in slowly, keeping my camera well hidden. As is so often the case, I refused to accept what seemed to be before*

me. As I walked around the market, I thought to myself, "Why, each of these people is 'the noblest work of God.'"

Eventually, their eyes began to soften. The atmosphere took on a new warmth. Before long, I took out my camera and started to work, recording faces like I had never seen before. [31]

The spirit with which Converse approached his work has often infused visuals at the paper. Fulfilling the *Monitor*'s purpose through photography meant, to him, pursuing ". . . photographs which are timeless; photographs which capture some universal truth; those precious moments in time worthy of preserving forever, pictures which inform, yet fulfill Mrs. Eddy's purpose for the *Monitor* 'to injure no man, but to bless all mankind.'" [32]

The religion of people like Saikowski, Godsell, Converse, and Oka help set the *Monitor* apart from other newspapers. The words journalists write and the pictures they publish make a difference, but so does the thought behind the work.

Neglect and deficits

In 1966, Oka was appointed the *Monitor*'s Moscow correspondent. As he flew into the Soviet Union for the first time, accompanied by his wife and two small daughters, he panicked. How would foreigners from an American paper be treated? His first impression was of "one huge concentration camp."

As he had after the war in Japan, when he overheard two women talking about the beautiful full moon, he started looking for what was good around him. He had never seen such richness of culture, he says. The Pushkin Museum, the Bolshoi Theater, the Moscow Circus made the time there one of joy for his family. He was frustrated, though, with what he saw as a lack of appreciation from Boston. "I wanted a Gratke-like relationship," he says. In the 1960s, he had been based in Vietnam and felt neglected when he wrote an article every day for a month and got no reaction. Curious, he had written only two articles the next month and got the same reaction. The feeling had now returned, and he bolted to *The New York Times*, where he served as the paper's Tokyo correspondent for three years, until 1971.

Work at the *Times* was more strenuous: He wrote seven days a week. "The upside was, everyone read you," he says. "The downside was, you had little life outside work." It was the life outside work, including religion, that fed him and helped make his writing sing. "[Working at the *Times*] was a good experience," he concluded, "but not amazing."

Hughes hired Oka back, in 1971, and placed him in Paris, where he wrote the series on "The World's Struggle for Resources."

Meanwhile, Hughes struggled with the growing financial problems at the paper. In the 1960s, deficits were seen as a cost of doing business for the *Monitor*. Mrs. Eddy had instructed that profits from the Publishing Society be paid over to the church, and no one liked the fact that there were no profits. On the other hand, until it was clear how to eliminate the deficits, everyone believed that the *Monitor* had to keep performing at a high level.

Once the church building project started, however, and money was needed there, the cost of the *Monitor* became an issue. Were there ways to increase revenue? Could the *Monitor*'s cost be reduced without reducing its effectiveness? Soon after he became editor, Hughes was told to cut more than a dozen jobs.

The budget cuts forced reporters to do more with less, which, ironically, sometimes resulted in even better reporting. By 1973, David Winder had become United Nations correspondent, the *Monitor*'s only one. His office, shared with the *Chicago Tribune*, was next door to that of *The New York Times*. The *Times* had four permanent United Nations correspondents and a staff that swelled to twelve when the General Assembly met each fall.

During General Assembly time, Winder would get frustrating messages from Geoffrey Godsell, now overseas news editor, telling him to cover this and cover that, and giving him assignments that meant being in more than one place at once. Godsell would irritate Winder with questions on why the editors hadn't seen stories from him that they had read in the *Times*.

There were rumblings of trouble in the Middle East, and the pressure on Winder was acute. "I couldn't cope with the situation," he says. "I was getting sandbagged by all these demands, and I had to turn to prayer."

As he usually did when he was in trouble, he opened *Science and Health*. His eye fell on a section where Mrs. Eddy talks about the foresight Bible prophets gained by seeing reality from a spiritual basis. "It is the prerogative of the ever-present, divine Mind," she writes, "and of thought which is in rapport with this Mind, to know the past, the present, and the future." [33]

Winder studied the sentence for several weeks, when he had free time, and thought about it at home and at work. As the meaning of the passage took root in his thought, he began to understand what it meant to be an expression of a divine Mind that not only knows all but created all and made it spiritual and good. He went to sleep one night with a sense of calm he had not known in a long time. In the middle of the night, he opened his eyes and sat up.

There's going to be war in the Middle East, he thought.

On the surface, it made no sense. Egypt's United Nations ambassador was pushing very publically for peace. But it occurred to Winder that Egypt's strategy was more subtle than it appeared, that Egypt had in fact adopted a two-pronged policy: First, invite the international community to align with it in the pursuit of peace. Second, if the effort failed, Egypt would say it had no recourse but war to reclaim captured lands from Israel.

Illogical as the idea was—Israel was far superior militarily, and no one else was reporting a move toward war—Winder spent the next day sounding out several Arab ambassadors. Amazingly, the lights were green. He then approached Egyptian Ambassador Mohamed Hazem El-Zayat.

"I've been following your situation," Winder told him, "and I've noticed Israel isn't handing back any territories since the 1967 war. I'm sensing you think the international community isn't taking action, and you feel you have no other recourse than to go to war."

El-Zayat smiled. "You got it," he said.

The Yom Kippur War broke out a week after Winder anticipated it. El-Zayat had been promoted to foreign minister of Egypt by that time, and he came back to the United Nations and spoke to the press. When he got up, he lashed the media for not realizing the frustration Arabs were experiencing. Then he saw Winder. "There is only one correspondent who understood what was happening," he told the group, "and he's sitting over there, David Winder of *The Christian Science Monitor*."

Winder won the Special Achievement Award of the journalism fraternity, Sigma Delta Chi, for predicting the outbreak of the war. To Winder, the award wasn't just for his journalism. It was also a confirmation of his breakthrough on dealing with stress. "I could not have dissolved the pressure humanly," he says.

Compact format

As the 1970s moved along, the church's financial problems kept growing, and officials decided they had to take more action. The Directors and Trustees reviewed everything Mrs. Eddy had said about the *Monitor* and set up a task force of managers and editors "to examine, challenge, and analyze every facet of the *Monitor*'s operations." [34]

Out of the task force came one dramatic change: The *Monitor* would be reduced to a "compact format," better known as a tabloid, saving the paper some two million dollars each year in newsprint costs. The news hit some of the staffers hard. Even though the *Monitor*'s approach to the news would not change, its new appearance, they felt, would have the effect of diminishing the paper's stature in the eyes of many readers.

"They cut our stories from about a thousand to six hundred words," says Judith Frutig, who was now Chicago bureau chief. "The information that made it the *Monitor* was being cut, and it was more and more like other papers." When she went to Boston to complain, she says, pointing out that no other respected paper was published as a tabloid "and there's a reason for it," she was told that "within a few years the elite papers would all become tabloids."

The Trustees tried to be optimistic. Chairman Robert G. Walker reported on the changes at the 1975 annual meeting and told the members that "[m]any are saying this new compact format is just great." He noted that the Publishing Society had "reduced by nearly 50 percent its budgeted deficit for the coming year. It is the first time in years that we can report a reduction in our operating losses!" [35]

The circulation numbers, though, tell another story about what was happening at the paper. By 1976, subscriptions had plummeted to 168,000. Glenn A. Evans, the Trustees' chairman that year (the position rotated annually), read a carefully worded statement from Hughes:

> *As we enter a new year, I believe the* Monitor*'s role is to uncover, underline, and reaffirm the good in our society, while constructively pinpointing its deficiencies and abuses. The* Monitor *is a newspaper committed to healing, but that healing can only come about as a result of action spiritually motivated and humanly expressed."* [36]

With a role for the *Monitor* of mainly pointing out what was good or bad in the world, it was almost as if the new compact size reflected the narrower thinking of a publication that was careful not to offend.

The satisfaction that writers like Oka felt in producing a newspaper of depth, breadth, and healing spirit was being squeezed. Evans called publishing the paper and the other periodicals not a joy but a "solemn obligation." For the first time, church members were told the actual size of the annual deficit of the Publishing Society: more than ten million dollars, most of that coming from the *Monitor*. The Trustees also announced that the Publishing Society staff had been reduced thirty percent. This brought the deficit down, but there were many more problems to solve. The *Monitor* was still largely delivered by mail, for example, and mail service was deteriorating around the world.

That same year, for the first time, the church treasurer laid out exact numbers for the funds that The Mother Church had on hand and felt that it was necessary to tell the members, "As you can see, The Mother Church is not bankrupt." [37]

Then rumors began circulating that the Directors saw the *Monitor* as a burden dropped on them by Mrs. Eddy, that they would do anything to take its weight off their shoulders. *Monitor* staffers felt that the paper was no longer getting the respect it deserved from church officials. Oka says one Director, holding a tabloid edition, told him that "the *Monitor* is such a little paper. It's so cute." Another, he says, spoke of the *Monitor* as being the crippled man at the temple gate called "Beautiful," described in the Bible, who was eventually healed by the apostles Peter and John. "I thought it was all wrong," Oka says. "The *Monitor* wasn't the patient. The world was the patient."

DeWitt John was now in his last year as a director. He reminded members in a speech:

> The Christian Science Monitor *is inseparable from our Church. It is just as much an integral activity of our Church as any other activity. Our Leader did not found a Church and a newspaper. She founded a Church* including *a newspaper as one of its vital, fundamental, major activities. Why? Because the work of the Church is to uplift society as well as the individual—to bless all mankind.* [38]

Like Oka, John saw the need as more than just solving a

newspaper's challenges. The greater need was to help heal the troubles of humanity. That the two needs were linked was obvious to both men. They saw the challenge of the times as helping the world right itself through prayer. If that was done well, they were sure, the *Monitor* and the church would be secure.

As evidence of the Directors' continued commitment to the paper, John announced the opening of an Endowment Fund for The Christian Science Monitor and invited the contributions of members. [39] The Fund would accumulate capital and use the interest to help fund the paper.

Another Pulitzer

In 1978, the *Monitor* got some good news. Richard Strout was awarded a special citation by the Pulitzer Prize committee "for distinguished commentary from Washington over many years as staff correspondent for *The Christian Science Monitor* and contributor to *The New Republic*." Strout had started with the *Monitor* in 1923, after working as a reporter for the Sheffield, England, *Independent* and the *Boston Post* and earning a master's degree in economics from Harvard. Driving his Model T Ford down from Boston, he had taken up residence in Washington and, except for World War II, had spent his whole career there covering Presidents from Harding onward.

In 1943, Canham had given Strout permission to write a regular column for *The New Republic* called "TRB from Washington," which was widely read as an articulate representation of the liberal perspective on American politics. The column sometimes diverged from the *Monitor*'s tone, but he was seen by many as the best writer in Washington, and Canham and future editors felt that the *Monitor* gained from the association. Strout went on to win a number of reporting awards in addition to the Pulitzer.

"Gird up your loins"

The Pulitzer celebration was short-lived. A report to the Directors by the manager of the Publishing Society in 1978 laid out a stark financial conclusion: If nothing was done about the deficit, the deficit would eventually bankrupt the church. [40]

The Directors felt that the time for gentleness had passed. Harvey Wood, a Christian Science practitioner and teacher from Chicago, had joined the Board in 1977, and in 1979, he became chairman. That year, at the annual meeting, he told church members, quoting the Bible, "Gird up [your] loins." [41] A more activist Board was coming.

In keeping with past approaches that described the problems of church and society as stemming from the moral problems of their members—and got those who pushed these approaches, such as Dixon and Canham, into trouble—Wood began insisting that Christian Scientists were talking more to themselves than the world, and he encouraged them "to rid themselves of whatever would hinder free and purposeful use of all that is necessary for moving the Cause of Christian Science forward." [42]

The primary bringer of the bad news, at least in financial terms, was the *Monitor*, and that was Wood's first target. In what he described as fulfillment of the Directors' responsibility to see that the church's "periodicals are ably edited and kept abreast of the times," as Mrs. Eddy had instructed them, he announced at the meeting that "the Directors have reassumed direct responsibility for the editorial content of *The Christian Science Monitor*" [43] as well as the other periodicals.

What this would mean for the paper remained to be seen, but one move had already been announced six months before: Hughes would be replaced by his managing editor, Earl Foell. Foell had started at the *Monitor* as a copyboy, in 1949, a mathematics major fresh from Principia College, and worked his way up to editorial writer and United Nations correspondent. He had won the Sigma Delta Chi Deadline Club Award for the best United Nations coverage of 1963.

Foell was sincere and articulate, a nurturer, as Hughes had found out when he tried to impose his "healthy tension" on the shocked staff at the *Monitor*. He was also a "renaissance man with broad interests and depth in the arts as well as news," according to Cynthia Parsons, who was still education editor. From Budge Sperling came one of the highest compliments a reporter can give: "He had a light touch as an editor."

One of his sub-editors, Rod Nordell, wrote later of him, "Like Antaeus touching the earth, he used common humanity to connect needed knowledge of the world to people where they are." [44] *The New York Times* was less flourishing in its description, describing him as an editor "with a romantic attachment to precision and clarity." [45]

Foell brought in John Dillin as his managing editor, and together, they tried to shape a newspaper that could function well in tight times. They soon realized, however, that the Directors had their own ideas. The Board was "keeping close tabs" on the paper, Dillin says, and assigned a member of their staff to watch for and report on items of interest to them.

"I remember one day we had run a story which we thought was quite good on the Cambodian famine," Dillin says, "and we had a picture on page one that showed someone obviously suffering. Mrs. Eddy says not to depict suffering, so we heard about that." He was referring to her requirement that testimonials of healing published in church periodicals or given during testimony meetings should "not include a description of symptoms or of suffering, though the generic name of the disease may be indicated." [46] Mrs. Eddy's intention was to avoid implanting fear in the minds of readers and listeners, but whether the same logic applied to photographs of news events in the *Monitor* was open to interpretation.

Judith Frutig didn't like what she was seeing. "The *Monitor* was tumbling into something I didn't recognize," she says. In 1980, she took a leave of absence and never returned.

Lifting the blanket of fear

In October of 1979, a few months after Foell assumed the editorship, Takashi Oka took up residence in the People's Republic of China to become the *Monitor*'s first correspondent there. In its dramatic emergence from the Cultural Revolution, its vigorous pursuit of economic growth, and sheer size, China was fast becoming one of the most important nations in the world.

Oka's presence promised a fresh perspective on a country still partly in turmoil but looking to demonstrate a powerful new economic model for the world. As when he first entered the Soviet Union, Oka approached his new assignment with trepidation. He prayed. What came to him was the need to become clearer about the *Monitor*'s purpose in the world. The *Monitor* itself, he decided, was a prophet:

> *Any world condition that requires healing needs to be healed first in individual consciousness. On a day when the news seems particularly alarming, the greatest contribution a person could make might be to refuse to be overwhelmed by the horror or the enormity of the problem. . . . To the extent that one prays in this spiritually assertive way, one can help lift a little corner of the blanket of fear that often seems to smother the world in regard to many situations.* [47]

The *Monitor*, Oka maintained, brought this spiritual vision to the major events and trends in the world. As he pursued his assignment in China over the next several years, he saw himself as a representative of a deeply prophetic voice.

He had to maintain his vision, however, largely alone. "It's difficult to say this to *Monitor* staffers who aren't Christian Scientists, or even to most Christian Science staffers," he says. "They think you are trying to foist an idiosyncratic view of things on the world. I've always thought it would be interesting for *Monitor* staffers to discuss how to prophecy, see things from a spiritual perspective that would apply to the material scene."

New media

It was now 1982, and the *Monitor*'s yearly loss was hovering around $8 million on revenues of around $17 million, or $30 million if all circulation, advertising, and syndication income were included. [48] The big question was, How could the Directors increase revenue and control costs for the paper, especially in the face of inflation?

The Monitor Endowment Fund was growing at $250,000 a month and stood at $3.2 million. The church could use only the interest, but it helped. The paper raised subscription prices and centralized advertising sales in Boston, enabling the closure of offices in Los Angeles and Chicago. Circulation of the weekly international edition, started a few years earlier, was up, but the goal was to widen circulation for the daily. "The *Monitor* has so much to offer the world," Chairman of the Board of Trustees Michael A. West insisted, "—a world athirst for refreshing spiritual insights and constructive, encouraging news." [49]

"Constructive, encouraging news" was a formulation for *Monitor* content that meant something. In an address to members in 1982, Hal M. Friesen, outgoing chairman of the Board of Directors, described the Board's efforts to "strengthen the utility" of the paper:

> *We hope you've noticed that [the* Monitor] *is giving increased attention to those areas of human activity that were of special interest to our Leader—to trends of thought affecting the family, business, education, religion, and the physical sciences, including certain aspects of medicine.* [50]

These subjects were more easily positioned as being constructive and encouraging than the more painful news of the day. The problem was, the subjects were not what the *Monitor* was known for. From the days of Dixon, the paper had risen to world stature because of its attention to the news, especially international news. Oka himself had been quietly practicing the genially persuasive style of Christian Science reporting, trying through his boldly calm writing style to bring inspiration to major issues. It seemed, however, that the Directors were returning to the days of McLellan and Dodds, assuming that safe subjects and clean journalism were all that Mrs. Eddy had expected of the paper and all that the paper's Christian Science readers needed. The issue was again coming down to a deceptively simple one: What was it that made the *Monitor* distinctive? Why would people feel they had to read it?

Monitor subscriptions continued heading down, and the Publishing Society reported a loss of $9.5 million. On the upside, *Monitor* journalism was now syndicated to 206 newspapers and 311 radio stations, raising the number of potential readers or listeners by an additional 15 million. [51]

Those alternative formats and means of distribution, especially broadcasting, began catching the Directors' interest. Back at the 1979 annual meeting, Wood had told church members that the Directors would "redefine the role of broadcasting in the promotion and extension of Christian Science." [52] They could begin thinking in terms of broadcasting, in part, because, despite the troubles of the *Monitor*, the church had now amassed $120 million in reserve funds, $70.6 million of that unrestricted. With only $35.9 million in expenses the previous year, the church was well into the black. [53] Even while the *Monitor* was narrowing its scope to deal with hard times and conform to the Directors' vision of the paper, the financial picture of the church organization as a whole was looking better.

Circulation figures for the paper in 1983 showed a further drop to 144,000. The *Monitor* had now lost more than a third of its subscriptions since John left the editorship. The Directors decided it was time for another change. They granted Foell the editor-in-chief title—Canham had retired in 1974—with a portfolio similar to Canham's, "to represent the *Monitor* on the world scene." [54] Replacing Foell was the paper's first woman editor, a respected editor and publisher from Alaska, Katherine "Kay" Fanning. Her paper, the *Anchorage Daily News*, had won a Pulitzer Prize for public service in 1976.

Journalism of redemption

Far from Boston, Takashi Oka thought about what more he could do for his struggling paper. Again, he examined the *Monitor*'s role in the world, trying to get some deeper insight. He decided there was one group of readers that was key. "Newspaper experts say that the health of a newspaper depends on the extent to which it is considered essential or indispensable by its core readers," he wrote in *The Christian Science Journal*. The *Monitor*'s core readers are Christian Scientists, he noted. "Without this vital core of dedicated Christian Scientist readers, the *Monitor* would find much more difficult the accomplishment of its mission to heal mankind and to help in rescuing humanity from the worldly miasma of danger and violence." [55]

As he had before, he noted the importance of the individual prayers of readers, the kind that transforms the readers themselves. "Individual redemption is inseparable from world redemption," he wrote. By including the world in our prayers, he was convinced, we help ourselves. Helping ourselves, we help the world.

He saw the challenge facing the *Monitor* and its family—readers, staffers, and church officials alike—as not financial or political but spiritual, requiring greater depths of love:

> *. . . when the way seems humanly closed, as it does in so many intractable situations around the world, let us know that divine Love is at work, that it will remove every barrier, dissolve every obstruction—gently, surely, effectively, leaving nothing festering, no unhealed hurts or wounds.* [56]

Ironically, and perhaps unwittingly, Oka provided the counterweight to Canham's reprimand to church members from years before: "The *Monitor* unopened is the symbol of self-centeredness and apathy." Oka wrote:

> *If a pile of unread* Monitors *stares accusingly at the busy housewife or office worker, there is no need to lose heart. Not self-condemnation, but self-examination, may lead one to discover anew the* Monitor*'s essential role in promoting individual and world salvation.* [57]

The gentleness and insight with which Oka approached his reporting and his relationship to readers were possibly the very qualities needed to solve the broader problems of his church and his newspaper. But few people were listening.

Sound and fury

In Boston, the Directors, led by the energetic and determined Harvey Wood, hired a Boston consulting firm to evaluate operations in the church and to come up with recommendations for improvements.

One of the firm's principals and the leader on the project was church member John H. "Jack" Hoagland, Jr. His father, John, Sr., had been manager of the Publishing Society from 1944 to 1962, and Jack had seen his father struggle to maintain *Monitor* profitability. No matter what the elder Hoagland had tried—speedier presses, remote printing, heavy marketing, discounted subscriptions—the paper's small profits had gradually disappeared. In 1962, the *Monitor* had moved into the red, from which it had not returned, and in the same year, Jack's father, still on the job, had died.

Jack and his consulting firm submitted a series of reports between 1980 and 1982, asserting that *Monitor* expenses were far above historical levels and also above those of other American papers. But it was not just a financial problem, he said. It was also a management problem. His final report, a five-year plan for the Publishing Society to regain profitability, said bluntly that The Christian Science Publishing Society was not well run, at least by the standards of most organizations. Among other things, he recommended that there be more business oversight of *Monitor* editorial operations to help reign in expenses.

The Directors were so impressed with Hoagland's work that they asked him to take on the Publishing Society manager's position himself. After some hesitation, he said yes, and by December 1982, he was installed in his father's old office.

Immediately, he set about trying to change what he saw as a tired and inefficient culture. He brought in professionals who had been successful in businesses and publishing, people who would understand and support his and Wood's determination to create a new day for the church's publishing operation, especially the *Monitor*. Hoagland and his new team were described as being ". . . hard-driving people who found no contradiction between the demands of their faith and the pleasures of excelling in the secular world. Honored and excited, they answered the call to come to Boston and put their shoulders to the wheel, almost always, like Hoagland himself, accepting significant pay cuts in the bargain." [58]

"Jack came in as quite a visionary," says David Morse, who was working as circulation development manager when Hoagland arrived. "Everyone was terribly impressed with his methodical approach. He was able to relate incredibly well with everyone. He was fixing a lot of things that were broken." Seeing Morse's willingness to work hard and his incisive knowledge of publishing operations, Hoagland quickly made him director of advertising and then assistant manager and marketing director of the Publishing Society.

Driven as Hoagland and all his recruits were, his style still seemed to work well with the quieter church culture. "He was very charismatic in a low-key way," says David Els, who worked as a research analyst at the Publishing Society before becoming circulation director under Hoagland and then publishing director of the *Monitor*. "He tackled major questions without intensity." [59]

Hoagland felt that the Publishing Society was dominated by people stuck in old ways of thinking. At the same time, Wood was concerned that the church membership was aging, shrinking, and way too narrow in its view of the world. Together, they were excited that the *Monitor* could perhaps be a means of reviving the church. If there was one thing that people who otherwise derided Christian Science, as being weirdly obsessed with spiritual healing, respected, it was the *Monitor*. If the paper could be taken out of what they felt was a cocoon and infused with fresh, expansive thinking based on what had proved effective in other media organizations and other businesses, it could help the church reach out to potential new members, people who perhaps had never even heard the name Christian Science. It could also possibly start to turn a profit.

What was in some respects a sleepy institution began quickly to feel the heat. As Hoagland pushed his changes, with Morse's support and the backing of Wood and the Directors, resistance grew among employees, including *Monitor* staffers, as well as among the broader church membership. To Hoagland and his supporters, the resistance was a sign the church desperately needed reform, and it only made them push harder.

For many employees as well as church members, their resistance was not about change but about the way it was being done. Just as Mrs. Eddy had lost her trust in publisher William G. Nixon almost a hundred years before, when he began using "worldly, material means" to increase the circulation of the *Journal*—means she felt might bring in more subscribers but could not hold them—many members began losing their trust in the Directors, believing they were advocating a shift in emphasis from prayer and healing to schemes and personalities. Some objectors acknowledged that the *Monitor* and the church were, in crucial ways, stumbling and needed to change, but, they believed, this was not the way Mrs. Eddy would have approached the issue.

On one level, it was a classic business-versus-nonprofit problem, showing the risk of assuming that management approaches from one sector will work well in the other. The debate was also partly over the future of the newspaper business. Was print dying, or did it just need a rebirth? Was electronic journalism the medium of the future for the news business, eclipsing print, or did print still have a bright future if media organizations like The Christian Science Publishing Society could figure out how best to use it?

But more issues were at work. Church leadership was one of them: Were members and employees supposed to accept whatever the Directors decided was good for the church? Or were they supposed to follow Mrs. Eddy herself, who had plenty to say about how the church was to be run, much of which could be interpreted as opposing the approach of those pushing change. On the other hand, one of her clearest directives was that the church be managed by the Directors, who, as Christian Science teachers, were some of the most experienced church members. She had not intended The Mother Church to be a democratic institution.

On the most fundamental level, although few acknowledged it yet, the growing storm over the paper and the church's direction was actually about the purpose of the *Monitor* itself. Was it mainly a good, public-spirited newspaper that represented a more constructive approach to journalism? If so, perhaps the paper was underselling itself. Perhaps it could be better promoted, and its form and content adjusted, so that it could reach a much larger audience and even fill a commercial niche sizable enough that profits could pour in and the paper's deficit be eliminated. After all, many people inside and outside the church said they wanted media that presented the positive aspects of the news. If that audience truly lay out there, the *Monitor* could be a terrific vehicle with which to develop the niche.

On the other hand, was the *Monitor* part of the church's religious mission, designed to infuse humanity with more spiritual, "scientific" thinking and to help heal problems in public affairs and other arenas, both personal and collective, as a demonstration of the power of God and Christian Science? In this definition, the *Monitor* was not designed to make people comfortable so much as to upgrade how they thought, helping them become less fearful and selfish, more perceptive and generous.

As during the church crisis in the late 1910s and early 1920s, the leading voices on both sides were sincere Christian Scientists. But that didn't keep them from disagreeing passionately.

Without illusions

As he watched what was going on in Boston, Takashi Oka was skeptical. The church needed to update publishing operations, but the nervous energy seemed only to exacerbate the tensions that had been developing since the late 1960s.

Oka had a different understanding of how to move people. Like the sun softening the air on a cold spring morning, he tried to touch *Monitor* readers with a warmth and beauty that opened possibilities. "You have to find the tone that will indicate that you love the person [you are reporting on]," he says, "that you love his country, you love his people." [60]

His time in China was drawing to a close. As he walked for the last time through what was still called Peking by the West, he described what he saw:

> *At Xidan Crossing, I had to wait for the light. Beside me, hordes of cyclists, mostly in blue but many in brighter colors encouraged by the new policies, waited impatiently, some of them darting forward like schools of minnows before the light had really turned. In front of me, pedestrians were scurrying across, almost in solid phalanxes, hurrying toward the department stores further down Xidan Street. An orange bus jammed with people somehow managed to turn from Changan Boulevard into Xidan Street, in the face of both pedestrians and cyclists, its female conductor shrilly warning passers-by that 'the bus is turning.'* [61]

He noticed a billboard that exhorted the people to "Emancipate your thinking," then read on the other side of the street a different message: "Resolutely uphold the socialist road." The tension between the two ideas would shape China for years to come, he knew. Many Chinese were skeptical that the government understood what it was doing, but they kept silent. They had been fooled once during the Cultural Revolution into voicing their opinions, and they would not be fooled again. One young woman told Oka, "One thing I learned [during that time] was to live inside myself. No one can touch me there." Life had to be lived with integrity, and then truth and falsehood would sort themselves out. "To be without illusions does not mean to be without hope," Oka wrote. [62]

As had happened before, Oka's thinking found an echo in DeWitt John's. At home in Lincoln, Massachusetts, John was busy in his retirement, maintaining a healing practice as well as caring for his students in Christian Science. But he kept his eye on what was going on at the church, and he saw the need to try again to raise everyone's sights about the *Monitor*. In 1983, he published an article in the *Christian Science Sentinel* called "Our newspaper—why?"

> *Our newspaper's role is to report calmly and with equity and spiritual insight—without sensationalism or commercialized exploiting of society's evils—the news developments that demand the constructive thought and action of thinking citizens. . . . the* Monitor *views the news with neither a naive optimism nor easy escapism, nor with a cynicism that suggests doom. It faces honestly the appalling ugliness of mortal life as well as the unfolding good in human experience. It approaches the whole earthly scene with a profound conviction that the answer to humanity's difficulties, a practical answer, lies fundamentally in spiritual enlightenment—in the light derived from divine Love.* [63]

Love—practical, tough, and flexible in the way a parent's love has to be when children aren't quite mature—had been John's light in making decisions when he was editor of the *Monitor*. In his book *The Christian Science Way of Life*, published in 1962, while he was still at the Committee on Publication, he had written of Jesus' parable of the prodigal son, and he unwittingly set a stark contrast with other attitudes, before and after him at the *Monitor,* that lashed out at the materialism and sin of members and the world alike:

> *The parable does not end with the son's confession of guilt. If it ended there, or with a confirmation of the guilt by the father, the whole point of the story would be different. But the father repudiates the condemnation and guilt. Here is the affirmation that our heavenly Father looks upon us as sons, and that we should awaken to this true concept of ourselves, right here and right now.* [64]

He quoted Mrs. Eddy: "The more I understand true humanhood, the more I see it to be sinless – as ignorant of sin as is the perfect Maker." [65]

Some sixty years earlier, Frederick Dixon had run into trouble, in part because he did not understand the sinlessness of true humanhood. He and the church had fallen hard as a result.

It was a lesson his troubled newspaper and the church behind it—officials, employees, and members alike—would have to learn again.

10

So Much More is Yet to be Done

Kay Fanning picked up the phone in early 1983 to call her lawyer, Newton Minow, former chairman of the Federal Communications Commission under President Kennedy. She was taking a new job, she told him. He was not surprised:

> *I told her I knew what the new job would be. Kay asked, "How could you know? It is a secret!" I said there was only one job that could persuade her to leave Alaska, and that could only be editor of* The Christian Science Monitor. *Kay said, "You know me so well that you are right; I will become the editor of the* Monitor. [1]

Fanning had tears in her eyes when she told her staff at the *Anchorage Daily News*. But the new job seemed a perfect fit. The *Monitor* represented the big leagues, a chance to prove herself on a global scale. Who could turn that down, especially someone like her with a taste for adventure and an ambition to do good? And to be able to help the church she had come to love, the religion she had found both practical and uplifting. It had saved her life and more.

"She was in awe," says former *Anchorage Daily News* reporter Gail Miller, now a Christian Science practitioner. "Editing the *Monitor* brought together her two great loves, Christian Science and journalism. She said to me something like, 'I don't know if I can do it. We'll see. If it doesn't work I'll be back, but I'll give it a try.' She was very humble about it." [2]

For Jack Hoagland and the Christian Science Board of

Directors, the move also made sense. "She was an outstanding person with enormous appeal and prestige in the newspaper industry," [3] Hoagland says. She was also a rising star in the American Society of Newspaper Editors. She had the editorial skills to produce a credible paper and the publishing perspective to give the bottom line its due. She would be the first woman editor for the *Monitor*, a historic coup, which could help the *Monitor* and its reform team make history. And she was a sincere church member.

"I could do that"

Nearly twenty years earlier, in August 1965, Kay had been on her way to a different kind of challenge.

Recently divorced from her husband, Chicago newspaper publisher Marshall Field IV, she had decided to make a new life for herself and her family in Alaska, a state they scarcely knew. Alaska was the Last Frontier, only six years into statehood, and it promised to be a place where Kay, the only daughter of a Chicago banker, could carve out a new identity for herself that wasn't circumscribed by the word "debutante."

Kay had never held a paying job. She had helped her husband sort out problems at the *Chicago Sun-Times* and *Chicago Daily News,* and more than once had said to herself, "I could do that." But outside of pillow talk and the occasional visit to the management team at Field Enterprises, as her husband's liaison, the closest she had come to newspaper work was as a student worker at her Smith College newspaper.

But journalism was the only field she really knew, so she surveyed the two dailies in Anchorage, where the family had settled, and applied to the smaller *Anchorage Daily News*. The paper was feisty and disrespected. She could identify.

Shoved into an expanded closet in the newsroom, paid two dollars an hour, she cut and filed stories and pictures for the paper's morgue until one day she said to herself again, "I could do that." She contacted the father of one of her children's school friends and wrote a story about his father, who was on trial for promoting a fake cancer drug. It made the paper's front page.

Now officially an *Anchorage Daily News* staff writer, Kay charged ahead. She rode in the bucket of a cherrypicker over the starting line of the World Championship Sled Dog Race, bundled against the frigid air to report on the Fur Rendezvous winter carnival, and listened to sobbing teachers tell about the deaths of two students on Eklutna Glacier. She explored the controversy behind birth control in a state where Alaska Natives had exceptionally high birth and infant mortality rates, and Christian missionaries fought against the practice.

She scarcely had time to turn her notes into stories in the newsroom, let alone at home as a single mother. So she got up at 3:00 A.M. every day and wrote till the children woke up. The birth control series and the coverage of the student deaths won Alaska Press Club awards.

One day, an old acquaintance showed up in Anchorage: Larry Fanning, former editor of the *Chicago Daily News*. Kay's ex-husband, Fanning's boss, had died suddenly, and Fanning had been replaced. He was now looking for work. Knowing Fanning's dream of owning a newspaper, Kay introduced him to the owners of the *Anchorage Daily News*. Rumor had it that they might sell.

As talks moved ahead, so did Kay and Larry's romance, until one day they said, Why don't we buy it together? They married in 1966, and they bought the paper together for nearly half a million dollars in 1967.

The Fannings had hopes but few illusions. The paper was a money loser—the only reason the former owners had made a profit was that they printed the Anchorage telephone book, a contract the owners refused to sell. The printing press was seventy-five years old. The other newspaper in town, the *Anchorage Times*, was much larger and dominated the advertising market. The *Times* owner was as much a community booster as a newspaper owner, and no self-respecting advertiser could avoid appearing in his paper.

The *Daily News*, on the other hand, put little stock in respectability. A favorite spot for informal staff meetings was the China Doll, a local strip club. The paper's politics were so left of center that some business leaders called it "Pravda North." Years later, one prominent banker told Kay that for ten years he had refused loans to any client who advertised in the *Daily News*. [4]

Still, the Fannings were confident they could turn things around, if only by making the *Daily News* a model of good journalism. ". . . [W]e both had a strong sense of the role of a newspaper as a public servant, of an opportunity to make a difference," Kay Fanning wrote later. [5] To her, a newspaper "is not primarily a business but a public trust—truly the fourth estate, whose responsibility is first and foremost to report the news responsibly, to be a watchdog over government, to provide a forum for all sides of the issues, and to spotlight areas of injustice." [6] It was not necessarily what the Anchorage advertising community, less concerned with justice than profits, wanted to hear.

At one point, the Fannings considered buying a television station, but they soon dropped the idea. "To us, television, however powerful and lucrative, could never be the influence for good in a community that a newspaper could," Kay said. [7]

Sticking it to the Times

Once the Fannings took ownership of the *Daily News*, they found out how high the hill was they had to climb. The 18,000 in paid circulation claimed by the owners was actually 9,000. The *Times* claimed 22,000. It was a huge gap to close if advertisers were going to even think about switching—or sharing—their loyalty.

The Fannings worked hard. Kay would go home at night to feed the children dinner, then come back to work till two or three in the morning. What might have made a difference was a new editorial slant that catered to the Anchorage establishment, but that was unthinkable. With Larry as editor and publisher, and Kay as reporter, editor of the Sunday magazine, sometime columnist, advertising saleswoman, and assistant to the publisher, they continued to champion the concerns of Alaska Natives—Eskimos, Indians, and Aleuts—as well as issues such as gun control and environmental conservation.

None of this made the Alaska establishment swoon. As Kay admitted later:

> *We got a rude awakening very quickly. I think Larry was convinced, and so was I, that all it took was good people to put out a good product and put it over the top. . . . It was probably naïve. We took editorial positions which were not compatible with the general Alaskan viewpoint.* [8]

Perhaps it was possible to make a deal with the *Times*, they thought. In other cities, competing papers had entered joint operating agreements and merged some business operations while maintaining separate editorial staffs, thus reducing costs for both. A potential new backer considered putting money into the *Daily News* if an agreement with the *Times* could be reached. But the *Times* resisted, in part because the federal government had begun wondering if newspaper combinations could be monopolistic.

For two years, the Fannings put everything they could into the paper—sometimes they would pay salaries from their own pockets—but it wasn't enough. They finally turned to a source of cash they had wanted to avoid: their children's trust funds, given to them by their father. Kay asked her oldest son, Ted, if he might want to invest some of his money in the *Daily News*. He and his trustees agreed.

For a while, the Fannings breathed a little easier. Staff morale was high. Kay and Larry were more than happy to let their young, idealistic reporters have their heads, pursuing the stories they felt really mattered, while sticking it to the *Times*.

In an attempt to control cash flow, Kay came aboard

full- time, in 1969, as assistant to the publisher, watching every dollar spent and signing every check. She also pestered her husband to pay more attention to the small stories, such as obituaries, that made a difference to many readers.

Still, the relentlessly bad financial news about the *Daily News* continued. The paper lost nearly a half million dollars in 1970. Ted was still willing to take the losses, but the burden was heavy on his mother and stepfather. Then, in January 1971, Larry was in the middle of financial discussions when he had a heart attack and died.

Kay wrote later in her memoir:

> *It was as if the breath was knocked out of me for a moment. Then I rallied. This was the time to prove what I deeply believed, that life is permanent, spiritual, and can never be lost, regardless of appearances. I knew that Larry, although no longer visible to me, would go on being and doing his good work, that nothing spiritual and permanent could really change.* [9]

Kay was a Christian Scientist. She had known about the religion since she was about ten, when her mother had sought Christian Science treatment for health problems. Her mother had never become a Christian Scientist, and Kay did not embrace the religion till years later, but she was impressed by *Science and Health* and kept a copy with her through boarding school and college.

By the time she was an adult, however, she was drinking, smoking two or three packs of cigarettes a day, and taking tranquilizers and sleeping pills. One Saturday afternoon after her divorce, her friend Eppie Lederer, better known as the advice columnist Ann Landers, came over for a visit. Kay offered her a glass of wine.

"You know, Kay, you could be an alcoholic," Lederer said.

Kay was stunned. After her friend left, she took a long walk through the streets of Chicago. "My life felt out of control," she said, "like a San Francisco cable car headed down a steep hill for a crash landing." [10]

When she returned home, she threw out the wine and the pills and—in a few months—stopped smoking. She began studying Christian Science seriously and took an intensive two-week course in Christian Science with Chicago teacher Harvey Wood. She soon realized that she and the family needed a change, and not long afterwards, some friends showed her pictures of their travels to Alaska. Kay was hooked. A few months later, she and the family were on their way north.

Nothing purple

With Larry gone, Kay saw no way to go but forward. At times, she felt lonely as a Christian Scientist among so many who were not, and she was grateful that Illinois Senator Charles Percy and his wife, both members of the church, flew quickly to Anchorage when they heard the news about Larry. "I felt they could share in my way of thinking," Kay said. [11]

Percy began calling advertisers, telling them the paper would continue under Kay's leadership. Despite a sense of doom in the newsroom, Kay assured the staff she would "keep the colors aloft." On the first election night after Larry's death, she set up a bar in her office so everyone could celebrate after finishing the next day's issue. As one reporter put it, "She was a teetotaling Christian Scientist, but she felt it was a memorial to Larry and an act of affection for her staff." [12]

Ted's trustees were skeptical, however, that Kay could handle the job, at least the business end of it. Circulation had barely grown in the four years she and Larry had owned the paper, and none of the major advertisers had come aboard. The pipeline that was supposed to bring Alaska's newly discovered oil to the market had been delayed by the federal government— land rights of Alaska Native peoples was the issue—and the state's economy had stalled. It was not a good time to grow a newspaper.

But Kay, and Ted's trustees, pressed ahead, and they

decided the time was right to renew talks about a joint operating agreement with the *Times*. By 1974, they had a deal. The *Times* would take care of circulation, advertising, and production. The *Anchorage Daily News* would continue its editorial work free from interference.

In the United States, wherever a joint operating agreement (JOA) had been entered into by two papers, the result was usually good for both, at least financially. "I wanted it to work," Kay said later, "but in my heart I knew it wasn't a very good JOA. It lacked an essential element, which was profit pooling. [*The Times* wasn't] really accountable to us in any way. We had no control over our own business affairs, but if there was a loss, we had to pay up." [13]

The *Daily News* lost $650,000 in 1974 and $750,000 in 1975. *Times* publisher Bob Atwood blamed the paper's editorial stances, but Kay wasn't intimidated. When, in 1975, the subject of the Teamsters Union came up in the newsroom—whether the union's political power and heavy-handed tactics served the interests of the state and its people—she didn't hesitate to give her blessing to an investigation.

Chasing the story, the *Daily News* reporters discovered that the much bigger *Los Angeles Times* was pursuing the same subject. Before Kay's staff could complete its work, the California paper published a story, "Crime Wave Strangles Alaska," with the Teamsters at the center. The story provoked outrage in Alaska and caused the *Daily News* to wonder if it was doing the right thing by continuing to plow the same ground.

But where the *Los Angeles Times* told a story of general lawlessness and helplessness, the *Daily News* focused on more concrete details, such as the financial ties between the union and government officials, and the number of convicted felons on the payroll of the union warehouse supplying the trans-Alaska pipeline. Attention to detail was clearly a hallmark of Kay's work.

The American journalistic community was impressed. The series, called "Empire: The Alaska Teamster Story," won the paper the 1976 Pulitzer Prize for Public Service.

The joy in the newsroom was short-lived. A few months after the Pulitzer was announced, Ted Field decided to stop subsidizing the paper. Five million dollars since 1968 was enough. Kay was forced to reduce the editorial staff from twenty-one to twelve.

Circulation by now seemed to be on a steady course downward, but Kay tried to keep the spirits of the staff high. And she did what she could to keep her own courage up. Some people called it her "relentless optimism," others her "graceful tenacity." It showed in the newsroom. It also showed at home, where she planted a flower garden but would not place anything purple or somber in it.

Rescued

Finally, it came time to face the competition head on. After two years of the joint operating agreement that was supposed to save the *Daily News*, the number of subscribers had fallen from 11,600 to 7,580. The *Daily News* sued the *Times* for $16.5 million, claiming breach of contract and unfair competition. The lawsuit alleged, among other things, that when potential advertisers phoned the number listed for *Daily News* advertising, the phone was answered "*Anchorage Times*." Ads for the *Daily News* were sold as an add-on to *Times* ads, meaning advertisers had to buy space in the *Times* first.

The *Daily News* won—sort of. The papers settled out of court, in 1978, with the *Times* paying the *Daily News* $750,000 and giving free printing services for another six months. But the *Times* kept the Sunday paper, and without that and Ted's subsidy, the *Daily News* was even weaker than when it entered the JOA. Kay tried yet again to keep her people's spirits high. "Christian Science has saved this paper before," she told one staffer over lunch, "and it will save it again." [14]

She invested the $750,000 from the *Times* in a new press and production equipment. She went to Governor Jay Hammond, more liberal in his politics than many in the state but in line with Kay's and the *Daily News'* view of things, and asked him to place state ads in her paper. He did. [15]

Meanwhile, Kay searched for investors, but she was coming up dry. Although she didn't tell anyone, she planned to fold the paper by the end of January 1979. [16] But she kept praying. The paper, she was convinced, had to survive. [17]

Then, in one final push, she gave her pitch to the McClatchy Company, owners of profitable California newspapers. They were intrigued by the possibility of owning a statewide newspaper in a growing state—and by Fanning herself. McClatchy purchased eighty percent of the *Daily News*. Fanning agreed to remain as publisher for three more years.

McClatchy immediately put in money, at first losing $5 million to $6 million a year. But the company's commitment was genuine, and with new circulation and advertising experts as well as new editorial ideas, a new layout, new features, even new comic strips, the paper became fatter than ever. By September, circulation was up to 25,000. By 1981, the *Daily News* had a Sunday paper again, and that year, the paper won the top four awards from the Alaska Press Club.

There was no doubt who the final winner was in Anchorage. After the initial excitement and crushing reality of buying a number-two newspaper in a small and struggling city; after watching her husband die and her paper almost do the same; after battling entrenched political and business powers and the tactics of a so-called business partner that amounted, at best, to benign neglect; after the highs and lows of stimulating journalism and painful layoffs, Kay Fanning watched as her rival, the *Anchorage Times,* folded, in 1992.

It happened ten years after she left the paper, but the end of the *Times* was Fanning's final statement that a gentle and idealistic young woman from a privileged family could be as tough and smart as the wiliest operator in a state that was full of them. "Atwood had it within his power to guarantee the *Times'* dominant position in perpetuity," said Howard Weaver, who rose from reporter to become Fanning's managing editor, "but instead forced Fanning into a different course that finally would leave nothing of the *Times* but a fading memory." [18]

By all accounts, Kay Fanning helped make Alaska a different state. "She came to a place that was self-absorbed and inward focused and brought to it, by her presence and participation, a greater vision of the world and of itself," said Weaver, "She did all that through this fierce and abiding affection for the place." [19]

She had other affections, too. Her love for journalism was strong, and in part, she proved in Alaska what she later told the American Society of Newspaper Editors: "In the end, ideas are more powerful than dollars." It didn't hurt, of course, that McClatchy had some powerful dollars to put behind the ideas, but the ideas came first and opened the door.

Her other love was her religion. When she met Ann Landers in the early 1960s, in Chicago, she had no idea where their conversation would take her. If her mettle was eventually tested in the unforgiving climate of Alaskan politics and journalism, it would be doubly tested in the seemingly sunny environment of a church devoted to healing.

"People have no idea what you face when you come to work here," says a high official of the Christian Science church, who prefers to remain anonymous. "The pressure is intense."

Thinking large

The Christian Science Board of Directors greeted Fanning warmly when she arrived in Boston and said they needed her to help put life back into the *Monitor*. Content and design could use refreshing. Team spirit needed a spark.

In November 1983, five months after Fanning's arrival in June, the *Monitor* celebrated its seventy-fifth anniversary, and the *Boston Globe* published an editorial that praised the *Monitor* for its unruffled approach to the news and noted the high esteem in which journalists held the paper. [20]

It was a generous view of the paper, but it didn't mention the big problem that everyone in the industry saw, a problem that Hoagland and his colleagues hoped Fanning could help them solve: The *Monitor* seemed to be walking on tired legs. The median age of its subscriber base was more than sixty, and the base was getting smaller, and people were not turning to the *Monitor* for news in the numbers needed to attract advertisers. To prop up the paper, the church was handing over cash every month in numbers so large that the church's ability to function could eventually be threatened.

But putting the newspaper on a more solid footing financially and editorially was only the beginning. Hoagland was also looking for someone who could be tight with his team, who could help him bring a smarter, more aggressive style to the church publishing business.

"Jack and Kay worked incredibly well together at the beginning," says David Morse. "Kay was feisty and understood the marketing side. She was also articulate and had a practical ability to communicate a vision. And when pushed, she would compromise." [21]

The financial position of the church itself was better than it had been in a long time, and it allowed Harvey Wood and Hoagland to think big. The world's need was so large. Why shouldn't their thinking also be large? And besides, Wood said, on more than one occasion, the church was not a bank, meaning that it was not in the business of accumulating money. It had an obligation to use its surplus for humanity's benefit.

Shortly after Fanning arrived, Hoagland unveiled a new design for the paper. Trying to "build on the existing model and make it work," he poured money into efforts to boost circulation and advertising. "I tried to stay within the bounds of what [the *Monitor*] had been," Hoagland says.

For her part, Fanning worked to instill a new spirit in the editorial staff. She wanted the kind of culture she had had at the *Daily News*—challenging, invigorating, fulfilling, and fun—minus the strip club. "She brought a can-do attitude to the *Monitor*," says Neal Menschel, a photographer at both the *Anchorage Daily News* and the *Monitor*. "She insisted we have value in the world in terms of searching for truth. She made people feel more like journalists."[22]

Fanning knew where to place journalists for maximum impact. "I may not be the sharpest news person at the paper," she told Todd Hoffman, a freelance photojournalist who eventually became photo editor at the paper, "but I do have a knack for seeing talent and getting the right people at the right time in the right spot. This is a big ship and it will take a while to turn it, but that's how we're going to do it." [23]

Clay Jones, who was deputy international editor and eventually assistant managing editor and Asia correspondent under Fanning, found the new culture liberating. "She let her employees have the freedom to do their jobs and be creative," he says. "You could go into her office and chat things up. She was aware that her strengths were in leadership and management and restructuring and bringing the *Monitor* into a new place." [24]

Women especially were ecstatic. Many had never worked under a female editor. "I went to the bathroom one day," says reporter Sara Terry. "And omigosh, there's Kay Fanning washing her hands at the sink. And it hit me, men encounter their boss all the time in the washroom, but I never had. My boss is a woman! She had worked in a man's world, and now she was coming to us."[25]

"She was warm and kind and loving, but tough," says staff photographer Melanie Stetson Freeman. "You felt you were working for someone who had vision. It was such an honor. We were headed somewhere, and it was a good place. We felt, the *Monitor* felt, so distinct. We knew who we were, what our voice was." [26]

Fanning's willingness to listen and learn impressed journalists accustomed to less humility from their editors. Hoffman had published photographs in the *Monitor* and had admired the work of chief photographer Gordon Converse for years. But he was disappointed in what he saw as amateurish photo editing—using photographs not as "visual quotes" but simply as ways to break up a page. One morning, he was sitting at a table in the Hilton Boston Back Bay with Neal Menschel, waiting for Fanning to show up for breakfast. Three minutes late, she appeared and slapped a copy of that day's *Monitor* on the table.

"Look," she said. "We have photo problems. I don't know what they are. Can you guys do anything about them?"

Hoffman knew right away it was the editing problem that had bothered him for so long. Fanning didn't understand the problem, he realized, but she knew intuitively that there was one, and she didn't hesitate to ask for help. He was hooked. "It was unbelievably humble," Hoffman says, quite unlike the attitude of what he called "alpha male" editors, who demanded that you never show a weakness. "She was willing to listen and learn." He wrote a critique of the paper she had placed on the table, and he was eventually hired as photo editor.

Fanning wanted to make the paper indispensable to its readers. "When she recruited me she said her goal was to make the *Monitor* a 'must read,'" says Larry Goodrich, who came from the U.S. Foreign Service and worked initially as a staff editor for national news. The paper was considered a "second read," similar to *The Wall Street Journal*, a paper to go through after reading a more general or local one. "We found out through surveys that people didn't have time for that second read," Goodrich says, "so they were cancelling subscriptions. Kay wanted to make the paper more newsy." [27]

One of the biggest problems was deadlines. Because the *Monitor* was distributed by mail, it had never been able to avoid early deadlines, which made the news in the paper slightly out of date. The other national papers, *The Wall Street Journal* and *USA Today*, had many printing plants around the country and could get their papers to readers quickly. The *Monitor* had only four plants and moved much more slowly.

Erwin Canham had partially solved the problem through an analytical or interpretive model—the "stand-up journalism" that made the paper useful even days after publication. But as Clay Jones points out, that approach wasn't working anymore for the *Monitor*. "Newspaper journalism was hit badly by the advent of TV news in the early sixties," he says. "So papers had to adjust by doing something else. Some papers went into long-form analysis, so we had more competition in areas we had been strong in. Baby boomers were more educated and demanded higher levels of journalism, and other papers provided that in the form not only of more analytical writing but also more overseas bureaus."

In an attempt to re-establish the *Monitor*'s distinctiveness, Jack Hoagland sunk some $23 million into marketing and promotion as well as editorial content over the first four years of Fanning's editorship. It was money the Directors hadn't spent on the paper since the DeWitt John and early Hughes eras.

The effect wasn't what he and Fanning had hoped for. Circulation rose to nearly 178,000, the highest it had been for more than a decade. [28] Conversion rates (readers subscribing on a trial basis and then renewing) doubled from twenty percent to forty percent, indicating that people liked the journalism the *Monitor* was producing under Fanning. [29] The median age of readers started to drop. But spending $23 million for about 30,000 subscribers meant the cost of getting and keeping them was more than the revenue they brought in both in circulation income and in advertising. Even more ominously, the *Monitor*'s deficit ballooned from $9.9 million in 1983 to more than $20 million by 1987. [30]

From Hoagland's standpoint, the problem was bigger than circulation and advertising. "To his credit, he foresaw more competition from the digital revolution," Jones says. Fanning and Hoagland visited MIT's Media Lab to try to understand the future of the news business. "The *Monitor*'s niche was getting hit," Jones adds. "Kay was part of the church [visionaries] who recognized that the newspaper had to shift."

It hadn't escaped Hoagland's notice that in 1962, the year the *Monitor* began losing money consistently, television had surpassed newspapers as the source of news preferred by most Americans. When the paper had spent some $70 million on promotions, from 1965 to 1975, he believed that it was only delaying the inevitable. He was sure the news business was moving away from print toward electronic delivery—radio, television and, with the start of CNN in the early 1980s, cable. Somehow the *Monitor* had to keep pace.

Fanning was not against moving into electronic journalism. She just wanted to be sure the paper's valuable franchise wasn't hurt in the process. Hoagland agreed. A respected *Monitor* was key to making a success of any new ventures.

To Live for All Mankind

Hoagland had already taken the *Monitor* forcefully into radio, producing for American Public Radio, starting in 1983, a one-hour weekend program of news, features, and commentary called Monitor Radio, showing off the capabilities of *Monitor* correspondents. "[Kay] liked the idea," says John Yemma, who had just returned from a stint as Middle East correspondent to head the New York Bureau. "She thought the *Monitor* was branching out in ways appropriate for the times. It was very exciting, experimenting with radio." [31]

Sara Terry had been working as Los Angeles correspondent for the *Monitor* and then, briefly, as an editor for the *Journal, Sentinel,* and *Herald* editorial department. She was invited to join Monitor Radio's founding team, and she did.

"Monitor Radio was great," she says. "There was a real love for the *Monitor*. The show was based around the paper. Some people on the newspaper staff criticized everything that wasn't the paper, but radio had a good relationship with print. We won a ton of awards and really rocked the public radio world." Terry herself won an Overseas Press Club award, in 1985, for best radio news or interpretation.

Monitor journalists had participated in radio broadcasts off and on since the 1930s, but this was the first time the church itself had produced a regular news program. Hundreds of thousands more people now had access to *Monitor* journalism. The new listeners, it seemed, were like those who read the *Monitor*, but there were more of them and they were younger. Since the program ran on public radio, therefore without advertising, it was unclear how the church would convert the listeners to revenue. Still, it was an encouraging sign.

Hoagland and Director Harvey Wood were excited. It was a new audience not only for the church's publishing but for the church itself. Communication was the future! In mid-1984, Wood had an inspiration: Create a global teleconference linking church members around the world. When it was finally produced, in December, it was called "To Live for All Mankind," and it was intended to encourage members to reach outside themselves and focus their prayers on the world.

In some respects, "To Live for All Mankind" overlapped the mission of the *Monitor*. Hoagland even compared it to the launch of the newspaper, in 1908. [32] Lasting two hours and costing $3 million, it connected more than a hundred sites worldwide and was translated into nine languages. A panel of *Monitor* journalists, including Fanning, discussed the *Monitor*'s work in the context of world healing. The panel was chaired by Richard Nenneman, who had served as the paper's business and financial editor for nine years, before leaving for Girard Bank in Philadelphia. He had been brought back by Hoagland and installed as managing editor before Fanning arrived.

Publically, Hoagland and the Directors took the position that "To Live for All Mankind" was a "thrilling" success. "It does not escape us that this is an opportunity," Wood told the *Boston Globe*. "Our members tell us you have shown us some leadership, now show us some more." [33]

But the event raised the hackles of many church members in a way neither the building of the church center nor the *Monitor*, for all its controversial political coverage, ever had. With the gaudy expectations surrounding the event, many members felt that the unity and global awareness it tried to create were more manufactured than real. Some believed that they were witnessing a growing sense of personality in church operations, something Mrs. Eddy had tried to avoid, believing it to be the reason that religions eventually disappear. [34] The Directors and Hoagland tried to ignore the squawking. It was just a few religious reactionaries and dissidents, they said.

But they realized that they had a battle on their hands if they were to remake the church and its publishing operations in the way they wanted. More and more it seemed that nothing short of revolution would do.

Wood, Hoagland, and other supporters started meeting at least once a week at a restaurant for lunch, developing strategy and tactics to move the church and publishing forward. [35] They worked cautiously at first, tasking Nenneman with improving business operations at the *Monitor,* while Fanning opened new bureaus and upgraded recruitment and training among editorial staff. The Publishing Society installed a new satellite dish on its roof to transmit images of the daily *Monitor* to remote printing plants, speeding delivery times.

Richard Nenneman was an intelligent and dedicated Christian Scientist with years of experience, but Fanning had always felt uncomfortable with him as managing editor. For one thing, his interests lay in the direction of what one writer called "a more contemplative, laid-back newspaper." [36] According to one former editor, he made no secret of his distaste for "the news." As Nenneman said in his autobiography, "The kind of journalism I liked was more thoughtful [than a daily paper would produce], and although I recognized the importance of daily news, I felt that the Monitor in particular had a more important mission." [37]

His persona also did not work for Fanning. Dubbed "Tombstone" by Geoffrey Godsell, Nenneman did not embody the warmth and command the respect she was looking for in someone who managed her staff. Nenneman, for his part, wrote in his autobiography, "We worked together satisfactorily, but I did not feel she had much of a sense of what the *Monitor* was, and on at least one occasion she told me she had not felt competent to take the job." [38]

By early 1986, Fanning had promoted David Anable to Nenneman's spot. "David was her lynchpin pick as managing editor," Todd Hoffman says. "As international news editor, he had built a cadre of young, energized, competitive guns in his department, and he brought that same eager energy to the entire newsroom as managing editor. Like her, he wanted working at the paper to be fun and energizing, a joyous endeavor."

Anable began holding lively, give-and-take daily briefings about the day's paper, its strengths, weaknesses, and goals, open to any and all newsroom staff who could escape deadlines to participate. Nenneman moved upstairs to become one of Hoagland's assistant managers and director of publishing.

"Every meeting David would pick someone out of the crowd and ask, What day is it?" says Gail Russell Chaddock, a professor of political science whom Kay had recently hired. "It was his way of saying, You have to be alert, in the moment. He would demand that staffers look deeper on subjects like Africa and bring out the fact that there was more going on on the continent than famine and pestilence and war." [39]

Page One conferences, where editors would decide what to feature on the next day's front page, had always been held in a back office. Fanning moved them to a modest table in the center of the newsroom, directly in the flow of work. "Kay and David were ahead of their time," says Paul van Slambrouck, who had come from heading the South Africa bureau to replace Anable as international news editor. "They were open and transparent." [40] Where previous chief editors had run the Page One meeting, Fanning delegated it to Anable, occasionally checking in to share her perspective. She would also walk through the newsroom and stop to read what editors were working on and give comments. But in keeping with her approach of hiring good people and letting them have responsibility, she took a hands-off approach to newsroom management.

By this time, Hoagland and Wood knew where they wanted to go, and it wasn't just toward improving the daily print product. In fact, Hoagland was convinced, the Publishing Society wasn't in the newspaper business. It was in the communication business. Why should it be tied to an old model?

"It really became clear we were moving in a new

world," Hoagland says. "The *Monitor*'s traditional people had kind of shielded themselves from that." He began experimenting with new electronic formats, such as shortwave radio, which he was convinced offered rich possibilities as the largest mass medium in the world. He brought John Hughes back to anchor a monthly half-hour television show, beginning in July 1985, called "The Christian Science Monitor Reports." Then, a half year later, Hoagland started a domestic radio show. In mid-1986, he began a weekly news show for television.

But the opposition that Hoagland and Wood feared grew. Some was coming from the newspaper itself. Reasons varied, from disdain for anything that wasn't print, which came from some traditionally minded journalists, to concern over the attempt to take on so many new media projects at once. The newsroom was already working hard to cooperate with the growing array, and it was taking a larger slice of Anable's time.

"I was enthusiastic about our expansion into radio," he says. "It was a natural fit with print, and we had the resources and skills to do both. But the stampede into so many other new forms of media publishing was putting a strain on the newsroom and beginning to produce enormous administrative and financial strains." [41]

Of even greater concern to Hoagland and Wood, however, was the opposition rising from the "field." After "To Live for All Mankind," Hoagland and church treasurer Don Bowersock, along with other managers, including David Morse, had set out on the road to Christian Science churches to try to raise enthusiasm—and money—for the media future they envisioned. What they found sobered them and led to a fateful decision. David Els remembers talking to Jack Hoagland one night in Jack's office:

He had just returned from a trip with Bowersock, and he looked rather glum. "What happened," I said. "Not well received?" And he said, "Well, it's just not out there." He was talking about both financial and moral support. And then he said, "We're going to do this on our own. The membership won't support it. We have to do this in spite of them." [42]

Morse recalls similar conversations. "I keep going back to a conversation with Jack and Harvey [Wood]," he says, "and the thrust was that they felt the [Christian Science] movement was in difficult shape, losing members, the *Monitor* was not reaching people, and TV was the 'Hail Mary' pass. If we don't do it, they said, we're going to lose the movement anyway."

For their part, what many members saw was a Boston leadership that couldn't be bothered with them because it viewed them as too inflexible, too bound by the past, and too selfish and unthinking in their resistance to new trends. It did not sit well.

Fanning was well aware of what Wood and Hoagland were doing, but she did not get caught up in their pessimism about the *Monitor*'s core audience. She wanted to create a newspaper the church could be proud of.

Charging ahead

As 1986 moved along, electronic media at the church were starting to eclipse the newspaper in the time and money put into them. Some of the thinking was still oriented toward the daily paper: Hoagland experimented with a "black box" that would transmit the newspaper to a receiver in the home, where the subscriber could print the paper at his leisure. Some people saw the idea as being more a newsletter than a newspaper, but Hoagland was convinced it was worth exploring.

TV and radio, though, took the majority of the attention, a development that grated on some of the newspaper staff. "It seemed clear to me that we had to expand our visibility in [other] media," Hoagland says, "position ourselves for things coming. Media were going in a vastly different direction. For people who were steeped in the newspaper, the going was tough."

But it wasn't just print journalists who were concerned.

David Morse, who by this time was assistant manager and marketing director of the Publishing Society, watched the fervor for broadcasting with growing skepticism. "One day I was in London, and I got a call from Jack," he says. "'We're going to buy a TV station,' he told me. I thought it was a terrible idea, and I told him. I also told the Board [of Directors] the church had no business running a TV station."

For one thing, the station would have to make money from advertising, and government rules prohibited banning ads, such as medical ads, that the church would find objectionable. Another problem was that programming purchased from others to fill the time between church material would often have ads embedded, which meant a commercial for Tylenol, for example, couldn't be stripped. There were equal opportunity hiring requirements too, which might run against the church's preference for employees who were church members.

In a short time, Hoagland felt that he had solved the problem. He created a for-profit venture called the Monitor Syndicate, working at arm's length from the church, and placed Morse at the head.

The TV station—Boston UHF station WQTV, Channel 68, which the church bought for $7.5 million—offered Hoagland and his staff hands-on experience in television, giving them a laboratory, a place to preview content, and a showcase for *Monitor* television programming. The syndicate also took over ad sales for all media, including the newspaper. Hoagland located the syndicate's offices some distance from the church in an attempt to distance the operations from the "Chapter 11 mentality" he felt had befallen the Publishing Society.

The attitude continued to lose him friends in the *Monitor* newsroom. Some staffers refused to appear in the electronic media. Others kept trying to help. Fanning was proud that her writers could manage to do print and broadcast, but she was becoming wary of what the increased emphasis on broadcasting was doing to the paper.

Hoagland felt he had to push, and he began to believe that Fanning was not doing all she could to help him. The media were beginning to work in a new landscape, he believed, and the paper had to adapt. "Change is hard," he says. "Kay was a great leader of the newsroom, but she and Anable simply couldn't allow themselves to see what was happening to the media. The *Monitor* has always been a bellwether, but because of our thin, wide distribution we were feeling it first and hardest. Others would feel it shortly thereafter. I kept trying to say that."

David Anable insists that the issue was not the new media. "We certainly were profoundly aware of what was happening in the media world," he says. "But we were increasingly concerned that the management's plunge into new media was poorly planned, its possibilities vastly exaggerated, its financial implications consciously or unconsciously understated, and its impact on the *Monitor*'s identity and founding purpose glossed over."

Hoagland admits that his impatience with what seemed like foot-dragging at the paper might have had unintended consequences. "I obviously didn't do as good a job as I should have," he says. "I failed to keep them comfortable."

With the growing need for news for both television and radio operations, and with what he perceived as increasing resistance from the paper, Hoagland felt that he had no choice but to set up an electronic news operation in parallel with the *Monitor*'s. Some *Monitor* staffers, attracted by the bigger paychecks in television as well as the possibilities of electronic journalism, left the paper and joined Hoagland, increasing the tension with Fanning and her editors.

The editors didn't like losing staff, but what they found harder to swallow was the fact that reporters were being recruited behind their backs. Potential recruits would be told not to tell the editors about the job offer. Even after the editors protested and Hoagland's team promised to end the practice, it continued—to the embarrassment of the reporters involved, who told the editors what was happening.

Hoagland still saw the newspaper as part of the media mix and wanted to do what he could to modernize operations.

The paper had a longstanding community retail advertising program: branch church members, contracted by the *Monitor* around the world, would sell ads to local merchants and then encourage other members to patronize them. He thought the program was confusing and even irritating to new subscribers as well as to advertisers, whom he did not think liked the cluttered appearance of the paper. Besides, it was unprofitable, and the membership, aging and shrinking, as was the *Monitor*'s readership, was not his target audience. Many of them did not even care about the program, so he decided to kill it.

Fanning disagreed with the move. The program was a tangible link between members and the *Monitor*, and any link was a strength for the paper. But signs were growing that her voice was making less and less difference outside the paper.

Children in Darkness

Fanning was as determined as Hoagland to create a new dynamic for church communications. But to her, the newspaper was the key. She and Anable agreed on the need for more urgency in the paper's daily coverage, balanced by powerful investigative series. Again and again, as she did at the *Daily News*, they brought together teams of people who could produce journalism with impact. Where DeWitt John would assign one person to a project, Fanning and her editors would assemble a team and send it off to tackle the subject.

One of half a dozen big projects was a series called "Children in Darkness: the Exploitation of Innocence," which ran in the *Monitor* from June 30 to July 8, 1987. It explored, in the words of its introduction, how "[m]illions of children—and their numbers are growing—are being used by adults as tools, as objects, even as slaves. . . . The damage from such exploitation is incalculable. The urgent need to stop it is only beginning to be realized." [43]

Some of the *Monitor*'s male correspondents in developing countries had been writing to Fanning, pointing out the number of children they were seeing in detestable roles.

Fanning jumped at the idea of investigating, but because the subject was children who were inevitably scarred and scared, she thought the team should have a particular makeup—all women.

She and her editors assembled the team, and over six months starting in late 1986, Sara Terry and Kristen Helmore as reporters and Melanie Stetson Freeman as photographer traveled to a dozen countries from Guatemala and Kenya to India and Thailand, gathering stories under trying circumstances. Terry tells about one:

> *In the Philippines, Melanie and I were trying to find boy prostitutes. There was a very large sex tourism trade there that fed off children who were vulnerable. As we were asking around, we were told of a café where foreign women would pick up teenage boys. When we got there we found a dark room full of French café tables. Boys and young men were sitting at every table.*
>
> *There was no way we would get anywhere if we announced we were reporters, so I had to go in and pretend I was a customer. They put us in chairs in front of the room and asked what type of boy I was looking for, what did I want him to do with me. I was appalled at the situation, but I said, "I want someone who's young." They finally came out with a fourteen-year-old, and I paid. When we got in the car and started driving to the hotel, he tried to take my hand and began treating me as if I was going to be his lover.*

It was one of the most painful times of Terry's life, she says, but she was determined to follow through with the story. They took the boy back to their hotel room:

> *When we got back to the hotel, we had to bring him up to our room—these two white women with a young boy. This was a top-quality hotel, and the porter on our floor knew, or thought he knew, what we were up*

to. The boy spoke only Tagalog, so I went to get a guy from the band in the hotel bar to translate.

When the translator arrived and we told the boy we were journalists, his face collapsed into disappointment and shame. He admitted his parents didn't know what he was doing and that he was trying to get money for schoolbooks. I remember telling him there were children like him around the world who were caught in this situation and that I wouldn't tell his parents. We talked for an hour, as Melanie took pictures. Then we took him back.

At another point, Terry and Freeman were in Thailand and paid for a young girl named Kham Suk. "We bought her a strawberry milkshake, and she giggled at that," Terry says. "She told us how her family had sold her to the brothel, how she had lost her virginity to a Japanese businessman."

Terry believes that the children trusted them because they weren't threatening. "Men were often the perpetrators," she says, "and having women there created a safe place. Child prostitutes came with me because I was a woman."

When the team returned to Boston, they sat down in Fanning's office with her, Anable, and van Slambrouck. Terry began describing what they had gone through. Her voice started to shake. Anable interrupted.

"We don't want to let emotionalism get in the way," he cautioned.

Terry erupted. "Don't you dare equate emotion with emotionalism," she almost shouted. "I defy you to read what I have to write without crying. Don't ever accuse me of emotionalism again!"

She got up and walked out, then headed straight for her desk at the far back corner of the newsroom. In a few minutes, she had written the lead paragraphs of the first article, an overview of the series:

Kham Suk is 13 years old. She is a small child,

with a delicate face. When she giggles, she sounds like any little girl at play. But Kham Suk doesn't have much time for fun. Three months ago, her mother walked her across the border from Burma into Thailand and sold her to a brothel for $80.

Kham Suk's family desperately needed the money. Kham Suk is still paying the price: $4 a trick.

Terry went on to describe a ten-year-old boy she had met later in the trip, who was drafted into the Iranian army as a human minesweeper, surviving miraculously to become prisoner number 8085 in an Iraqi POW camp. She told of a Pakistani boy who had hopped a bus at five years of age to get away from an abusive stepmother and now, at age twelve, slept on the street and worked as a waiter in a grimy teahouse. "When I think of my family," he said, "I go crazy."

These are children who live in darkness, the darkness of poverty, ignorance, and greed—and indifference. There are tens of millions of children like them in the world today. They are the pawns, the possessions, and the products of an adult world that all too often exploits childhood for its own ends. [44]

She sent the lead to Anable, who wrote back, "I can only imagine what it took to do that." Terry appreciated the gesture. "It was his way of saying, I get the emotional cost," she says. "Kay understood. She was tough, but she was a woman. She brought sensitivity and brought it in a judicious way."

Van Slambrouck still remembers the meeting and its aftermath. "It was a great encounter," he says. "That's the way it's supposed to happen. It's only natural that reporters get emotional. They see a lot of stuff in the field. Editors are supposed to keep a certain objectivity. Good journalism needs both of those things."

In a couple of days, Terry had the first article ready. She forwarded it to her editors and waited. Soon Fanning came by her desk. Terry looked up. "'Trick' is too harsh," Fanning said. "How about 'customer'?"

That was the only change she made.

"She was right," Terry says. "I was angry when I wrote that."

Helmore wrote the next piece in the series, on child labor, telling of Shadab, a nine-year-old boy in India, who had spent twelve hours a day since he was six "squatting in semi-darkness on damp ground, polishing little pieces of metal on a high-speed grinding wheel."

Terry wrote the third article, called "When all you have to sell is your body." Reliving the pain of the children she had met, as well as her own humiliation, she suddenly faced writer's block.

Her desk sat next to a big window overlooking Clearway Street. Under it was a wide stone ledge. She climbed out. Tears gushed. "I don't think I'd cried in the course of the series," she says. "But the horror of child prostitution was so intense. To have confronted that kind of evil that close . . . I just fell apart."

She prayed to see how to finish the series, and when she got back inside, she says, she wrote something else. It was a religious article for the *Monitor*, the one that runs every day as "A Christian Science Perspective." It was called "Dissolving the Darkness of Indifference," and it appeared the first day the series ran:

> *Children in darkness—it's a disturbing image. So troubling, in fact, that it might seem a lot easier simply to turn away. . . .*
>
> *But . . . indifference only helps to perpetuate the misery of exploitation. In fact, dissolving indifference may be the most important first step we can take toward finding genuine, lasting solutions.* [45]

After finishing the religious article, which talked about the role of prayer in dissolving indifference, Terry was able to write what she needed for the feature article.

On the last day of the series, Richard Cattani, the *Monitor*'s chief editorial writer, wrote the lead editorial, describing what international institutions, governments, and grass-roots organizations could do about the problem. Then he reached out to readers in the way the *Monitor* at its best always does, appealing for higher, deeper, and more active thinking:

> *This is a moral battle that cries out for more recruits. Our individual thoughts touch directly on universal conditions. Our expectations, as citizens, for how our governments and public organizations treat the world's children are a barometer of our moral coherence and worth.* [46]

Readers loved the series. In one letter the paper published, an organization head called for the creation of a children's lobby to pressure governments. A professor from Ohio said he would use the series in his classroom. [47] Congress used the series to write legislation on child labor, and the United Nation bought printouts and distributed them to everyone working on the Convention on the Rights of the Child.

Fanning's star was higher than ever. She was no longer a regional phenomenon; she was a national and international figure, and the *Monitor*'s prestige was growing again after years of stagnation. "We were accepted in a whole different way than in the past," David Morse says. In 1987, she was elected president of the American Society of Newspaper Editors. It was a huge honor, the first time a woman had been chosen to lead the prestigious organization.

"The deed is done"

After "Children in Darkness," Sara Terry needed a break. Soon the perfect opportunity came along. Singer David Bowie wanted someone to do media relations for his 1987 summer tour, and Terry, whose husband was a rock guitarist, was more than happy to sign on. She took a leave of absence from the *Monitor*, and when the tour was extended to the fall, she asked for a longer leave. Fanning and Anable were not happy but relented.

While she was on tour, Hoagland sneaked her into Boston for a day to audition for a co-anchor role in London for the TV news operation. Hoagland never told Fanning and neither did Terry, a decision Terry came to regret. She was hired, but the poaching from the paper—it was not Hoagland's first, nor was it his last—added to the sour relationship between print and broadcast.

Convinced that the tide was turning toward his model of the new church journalism, Hoagland presented his ideas for the *Monitor* to an all-day meeting with the Trustees on August 17, 1987. Fanning was not invited nor even told about the meeting. Hoagland says he was afraid that informing her would "stir things up."

At the meeting, he outlined his vision of radio as the principal *Monitor* international medium, and television as the main national medium. The daily paper was weak, he said. After all, it had no metropolitan market to serve as a core reader base, as most papers did. Its cost of procuring ads was high and its circulation income modest.

He told the Trustees that Publishing Society deficits would remain around $20 million if the paper continued to be published. The deficits would disappear, he believed, if the paper was terminated and broadcasting took over as the main vehicle for *Monitor* news. Eliminating the daily was only one possible scenario, but he felt obligated to make it plain. [48] He knew that the printed paper had a strong, if small, constituency, and he was not blind to the fact that eliminating it could be explosive. But in his view, broadcasting, along with a glossy monthly magazine he wanted to start, offered better possibilities for reach and profitability, and they could maintain the *Monitor* name and its cause.

In his recommendations to the Trustees, Hoagland asked them to "[a]ccept and not resist the possibilities that have become evident to us to reach more of humanity more rapidly and frequently" and to "[r]ecognize and build on the expanded reach, influence, and effectiveness of new (to us) publishing media." [49]

The Trustees trusted that Hoagland had his numbers right about the relative profitability of broadcasting versus newspaper and decided that they liked what they heard.

In September, Hoagland presented his ideas to both Trustees and Directors. Again, Fanning was not invited or informed. Again, he sketched out his financial projections and made clear that he thought the newspaper's future was bleak. But it wasn't only finances that made him skeptical. The financial losses, he believed, were a message that the paper had distanced itself from humanity and needed a radical new identity. [50] People still wanted what he believed to be the paper's strength—"balanced, unsensational" news—just not, perhaps, in print form. He urged the Directors to decide what they wanted to do.

At a third meeting, at a hotel in a Boston suburb, on October 17, all the parties reached agreement.

David Morse wasn't at the meetings, but he knew they were going on. As soon as the last meeting was over, he says, Don Bowersock called him. "The deed is done," Bowersock said. [51] Morse believed it meant the decision had been made to end the newspaper. The date set for the final issue, in the recollection of Morse and others, was April 30, 1989. [52]

A short time later, a senior Publishing Society executive who did not know about the meetings (and who does not want his name used now because his current organization has ongoing contacts with the church) was asked to come to Hoagland's office. Sitting at the conference table were Hoagland, Richard Nenneman, and Netty Douglass, Hoagland's executive right hand during this time and his eventual successor as Publishing Society manager.

The newspaper will be terminated, Hoagland told the group. The executive was stunned. He looked around the table and noticed Nenneman slowly eating a banana. Everyone else was calm too. They already know, he thought.

"Jack, has it been approved by the Board?" the executive asked.

"Yes," Hoagland said.

Knowing the sensitivity of such a decision, Hoagland reminded everyone to keep it confidential.

Hoagland vigorously objects to characterizing the meetings with the Directors and the Trustees as efforts to kill the newspaper. "This was exactly the opposite of what we were trying to do," he says. "We were trying to build around the paper. We came out of the meetings with some reduction in budget, but it's a bald-faced lie that we ever considered zeroing-out the paper."

Hoagland's former opponents are as strong in their beliefs today as is Hoagland. They are convinced that the paper was indeed targeted for elimination. Morse says that he was in many meetings on the subject where attendees were told not to tell Fanning.

Later in October, Fanning found out what was going on and was livid. She was the editor! She got a videotape of the August meeting from Hoagland, and as she and others on the newspaper staff watched, they realized that the daily print paper could be headed for oblivion.

Fanning was convinced that the newspaper's death was not inevitable, and so were others. "I didn't think we were ready for that," says John Yemma, who was now the paper's business editor. Fanning wanted equal time to prove it.

Knowing her reputation both within and outside the church, Hoagland realized that he would have to go along. She assembled a task force consisting of herself and the "four Davids"—Morse, Els, Anable, and Winder. David Winder had become assistant managing editor, in the summer of 1987. The task force would review the facts and assumptions used in the August 17 meeting and present recommendations "for the future course of the daily paper," including how the paper could reduce its deficit to $10 million the first year and $5 million the second. They had to agree in writing not to disclose the findings of the task force until Hoagland and the Trustees had had a chance to review them.

With the input of Urban and Associates, a leading newspaper consulting firm, the group felt that it had both the editorial and business experience to do a fair study from all angles and to come up with a reasoned justification for continuing the paper in its present form. Hoagland, too, was hopeful, but not for the same reasons. He counted on Morse and Els to support his view that there was no future for the paper, at least without radical changes.

He didn't know Morse and Els as well as he thought. "I had great faith in our task force," Els says. "I had a fairly aggressive circulation plan that I felt would bring the deficit down to $5 million. With the Monitor Endowment Fund contributing about $4 million at that point, the deficit would be down to only $1 million. Looking back on where the newspaper industry was headed, I don't think it would have worked for very long. But we wanted a chance to try." The task force eventually spent about $600,000 of the newspaper's budget to develop a scenario for the *Monitor* to survive as an influential daily newspaper.

Meanwhile, Hoagland quietly asked Nenneman to create a prototype of a new *Monitor* that would quickly bring the deficits down. No one else was to know.

In December, Hoagland met with the newspaper staff, and one person told him that the staff didn't trust him. When word got back to the church administration, Fanning was held accountable. "Why can't you control your newsroom?" she said she was asked. "Why do you allow them to say things like that? Why aren't they on board?" [53]

"These people will pay anything you want"

Hoagland was happy with how everything was shaping up on the broadcast side. He developed a concept for a daily morning TV program, summarizing the previous day's news. He began moving toward a more prestigious evening newscast.

Knowing it was important to keep *Monitor* sensibilities alive in the broadcasting operation, he recruited John Yemma from the newspaper as the program's news editor.

But television was a very different medium from print, with different content and, especially, financial requirements. Some experts insisted that the church was letting ambition outpace wisdom and the size of its reserves, but Hoagland did not believe it. "Jack cut himself off from people who were telling him his strategy was not workable," David Morse says.

Sara Terry, like Yemma, was intrigued by the challenge of television. She had loved working for Monitor Radio in the early days and was looking forward to joining the TV operation in London after her secret audition in Boston.

She discovered, though, that things were different in TV. In part because there were relatively few Christian Scientists with TV experience—something critics said was a sign the church was not ready to plunge deeply into broadcasting— Hoagland had been forced to hire many people from outside the church. As long as top management like himself and Yemma were church members, he reasoned, any problems could be muted. After all, the newspaper itself had a number of non-Christian Scientists on its staff. Using church outsiders also made it easier for Hoagland to make his moves without resistance. He had enough internal critics already without his having to pay them a salary!

The problem was, those from outside the church did not always understand what the *Monitor* was about. One senior manager thought of Mrs. Eddy as "a charismatic mystic" and said that her metaphysics rested on "the power of human consciousness," both untrue. [54] When a Christian Science couple, David and Ginger Twitchell, who had relied on prayer for a sick child, only to have him die, was put on trial for manslaughter, one TV staffer told Terry that he thought hanging was too good for the parents.

Terry was used to working with church outsiders on the paper, where everyone seemed to blend with the *Monitor*'s mission. But she was shocked by what she found in television:

> *The* Monitor *wasn't being appreciated at all. In fact, it was being trashed. Everyone who was a Christian Scientist [was suspect]. There was open hostility to the idea of spiritual healing. I heard producers tell outsiders that the* Monitor *had nothing to do with the church. There was never a clear statement as to what the* Monitor *was. I would say that this or that wasn't what the* Monitor *was all about, and I was repeatedly flown back and forth across the Atlantic and told I was being disruptive and would be fired unless I stopped. I was finally demoted from co-anchor and put on stories about things like free-range pigs.*
>
> *Jack Hoagland treated me kindly. But I think he was lied to. The non-Scientists were doing silly things, like putting alcohol on the [expense account] tab after business dinners. Contractors were told, Don't ask questions, these people will pay anything you want.*

Morse confirms this. "A friend of mine was in the [satellite] transponder business," he says. "We were at a high-school reunion in California, and he was laughing at us, how much money we were spending. It was a joke in the industry. You don't ask questions, you just collect your pay. I don't think anyone looked at [what we were doing] as a business."

Terry's sense of integrity was offended. "[Hoagland and the Directors] were telling church members that TV was rooted in our ideals," she says, "while the reality of TV was so night-and-day different. This had nothing to do with Mrs. Eddy's *Monitor*. If it had been grounded in that, I don't see why it couldn't have made it."

Hoagland believes that the objections to the attitudes among broadcasting personnel came from people determined to find things wrong. "We pulled together the most marvelous staff of people who wanted to work with the *Monitor*," he says. "In my father's era, much of his staff, especially in production, was non-Scientists. I get a little weary fighting that stuff. I didn't respond as vigorously as I should have."

Like Terry, Yemma had taken up his new job with enthusiasm. But he lasted only a short time:

> *I got cold feet about four months into it. I didn't feel it was developing in the right way. And I had some questions about the whole model. I felt it was expanding in an unsustainable way. People were coming in way too fast. Every morning there was a new idea, a new idea for a show, new expansion. That could be an indication of wonderful progress. But I'm practically minded. That can also be an indication that things are running in a way that doesn't have enough careful thought, especially when dealing with a value system as important as the Monitor's.*

Unlike some others who left the television operation noisily voicing their criticisms, Yemma departed quietly. "Jack and Netty felt their model made sense," he says. "I [preferred to] remove myself from a situation I didn't feel wholly invested in. I didn't want to oppose it in a subterranean way." He asked to return to the Monitor newsroom, and Fanning gave him back his old job as business editor.

David Cook, who succeeded Yemma as editor of radio and television, defends the broadcast operations. "Did [the people from outside the church] understand every nuance about the *Monitor* and the church? No," he says. "Did they respect the values? Yes. Were there some mercenaries? Yes, but there are mercenary Christian Scientists too. Levels of commitment and values varied widely across newspaper as well as TV and radio." [55]

Hoagland grew more and more dismissive of criticism, insisting that all was well and that millions of viewers were begging for what the church would offer in broadcasting. He put encouraging projections before the Trustees and Directors as well as the members.

Prospects seemed promising at first. Hoagland signed NBC and CBS veteran John Hart as anchor for the daily news show "World Monitor News," with former CBS senior producer Sandy Socolow as producer. His team pursued cable networks as distributors and settled on the Discovery Channel.

Hoagland didn't rule out print from the new church media universe, but he wanted a substantially different product. He invited Earl Foell back to edit the monthly magazine, *World Monitor*, which would be written, "not by *Monitor* staffers, but by opinion-leaders for opinion-leaders, with special emphasis on issues of global import." [56] The first issue, which came out in the fall of 1988, was led by statements from former American presidents Jimmy Carter and Gerald Ford.

But criticism from *Monitor* staff and church members continued, and in April, the Directors felt it necessary to publish a long letter in the *Journal* called "The pathfinding mission of *The Christian Science Monitor*." The letter began with the encouraging observation that "the *Monitor*'s pathfinding mission includes the overcoming of divisions, whether they be national, racial, religious or cultural." By the end, though, it noted that "...we are particularly appreciative of the continuing support that is being given to this endeavor by loyal Christian Scientists everywhere." That last sentence seemed to imply that those who questioned the media ventures were disloyal to the church and Mrs. Eddy. Substantial support did not pour in from the field.

Hoagland was still convinced that church members who disliked what he was doing were too backward to bother with. "We can't continue writing just for a small elite—that's not what it's all about," he told the *Boston Globe*. "That's why we have to open up our thinking. . . . Any change in a very traditional organization with a strong sense of history is difficult. . . . We're praying that we succeed." [57]

In passing, he told the interviewer that "exactly what the print newspaper will eventually be, none of us knows." It confirmed the worst fears of many *Monitor* staffers. What was he planning?

As 1988 moved along, resistance to his moves continued to build. Then, in David Morse's words, "everyone shut down the conversation," and, he says, Hoagland denied that a decision to close the newspaper had ever been made.

Then the rumor began circulating that what Hoagland was planning was no longer a complete shutdown but a radical redesign of the paper. It would have only sixteen pages, carry no advertising, and operate with a much smaller staff. Costs would drop and the subsidy would shrink to under $10 million. According to Morse, ads would be eliminated because "these only caused issues [among church members]."

The "new *Monitor*" would be the "crown jewel" of the church, Morse says, and circulation would decline to what Hoagland felt was its "natural level," around 120,000. Morse was skeptical. "There is no such concept in the publishing world [as a 'natural level' for circulation]," Morse says.

Morse shared what he was hearing about the new design with Fanning, who took it to Hoagland. Hoagland denied the rumor. He then chastised Morse for talking, and Morse says, at that point he understood that he "was there to push TV, not the newspaper." Late in August, however, Nenneman confirmed to Fanning that there was indeed a new prototype. Hoagland now calls it "a modestly alternative design for readability."

As head of the syndicate, Morse was becoming concerned. He was still sure there was no way the TV station could turn a profit if it was owned by the church. In the summer of 1988, he went to Hoagland and Don Bowersock, the church treasurer, and with his chief financial officer, presented a spreadsheet that showed the revenue and expense lines of the TV station never crossing. The station could not break even with the church strategy, he said, and the church would be on the hook perpetually for millions of dollars. Afterwards, Morse's CFO was pleased.

"We just saved the church," he said to Morse.

"No," Morse shot back. "We just won't be invited back to the next meeting." Morse proved to be right. "We were never included in any further business meetings" on Hoagland's plans for television, he says.

But Morse could not let the matter rest. He met with

Bowersock and suggested that the church sell the TV station. In fact, Morse said, I'll put together a group to buy it, and I'll still provide the *Monitor* adequate time for all its programs. At a breakfast at The Ritz-Carlton in late summer, Bowersock gave the go-ahead, and Morse formed Exeter Communications, Inc. He presented a purchase package of $25 million to the church, $10 million in cash and the remainder paid out over time. A decision on whether the church would accept the offer was deferred.

Morse couldn't wait, however, and watch what he felt was a sinking ship. In September, more convinced than ever that a financial debacle was coming, he handed Hoagland his resignation. Hoagland rejected it for the moment and asked Morse to stay on at least until after Fanning's task force had presented its report. Morse agreed to do so.

David Cook, who later served as editor of the newspaper, believes he understands the challenge both Fanning and Hoagland were facing:

> *When you're editor of the* Monitor, *you feel an enormous responsibility that nothing bad happen to the* Monitor *on your watch. You have a sense of all the people over the years who have sacrificed and loved that thing. You know about the sacrifices, you know what people [gave up]. You have this enormously powerful sense that something precious has been handed to you to shepherd. And you don't want anything bad to happen.*
>
> *If you're Kay Fanning and you love the* Monitor *enormously and they are talking about trimming back print and spending more on broadcasting, you see it as an attack on this thing you're responsible for. I think Kay felt Jack and the Trustees and Directors were not always open with her as to what they were planning.*
>
> *If you're in Jack's position and you look at the business side of the* Monitor, *and you've tried everything you could and spent tons of money and couldn't get the needle to move, you cut back on the*

paper and put the money in broadcasting, with the chance that you may be able to cover costs.

"Something was all wrong"

On October 31, 1988, Fanning and the task force walked into the Directors' conference room to face the Directors, the Trustees, and assorted others on the Hoagland team. She was momentarily stunned by the tension in the room. "Something was all wrong," she told Neal Menschel later. But she took a deep breath and kept moving.

Apparently sensing the strain the Fanning team was under, one of the Trustees leaned over and whispered to David Winder, "We're with you." [58] The team, though, was concerned.

"We knew that the outcome of the meeting had been pretty much fixed in advance, and that it was going to be a long shot to get a fair and open hearing," says David Anable. "But I could not believe that the Board would be so misguided as to go with the management plan, in effect destroying the daily paper, when we had a well-documented and thoroughly researched proposal that would enable the daily paper to grow and flourish."

David Els was more hopeful. "Going in, I thought we would get a fair hearing," he says.

Individual members of the team presented parts of the 150-page task-force plan. The newspaper's contribution to the Publishing Society deficit would drop from $20 million in fiscal year 1987, to $10.5 million by fiscal year 1988, and to $8.5 million in the following years. The editorial budget would be cut by $2 million and staff reduced by thirty-eight to a level lower than at any time since the 1920s. Overseas bureaus would be retained. Further cuts, the task force believed, would jeopardize the paper's standing as a legitimate international daily newspaper. Systems would be set up to control costs, although costs were already lower than other similar publications.

Urban and Associates insisted that new technology, such

as the "black box," would not help relieve the *Monitor*'s financial difficulties before the twenty-first century.

Els quickly saw that the meeting was not going as he had hoped:

> *As [the presentation] progressed, things deteriorated. People were taking what we said more lightly than I thought appropriate. I had what I thought was a good argument that the paper was having a strong influence, as shown in the pass-along rate, which was two to three times circulation. It was an idea we had come up with after lots of research. It meant the actual readership was more than half a million. But I got a flurry of questions. Basically, it was "Oh, that's ridiculous." They were not about to accept what I was saying. Their position was that there were no more options for the paper. I knew then that this wasn't going anywhere.*

During a break, one of the Directors came up to David Morse. Despite the assurance of the Trustee to Winder, there were other forces at work. "You'd better duck," the Director said. "This isn't going to happen." [59]

As the presentation ended, Hoagland congratulated the task force but insisted that the consulting firm's skepticism about the value of the new technology was off base. Harvey Wood, as the Directors' liaison with the paper, was more blunt. He criticized the task force for not finding a way to reduce the deficit to $5 million.

At the end of the meeting, as the Trustees and Directors departed, Morse noticed that most of them left the report and supporting materials on the table.

That night, Hoagland called Morse, questioning what the task force had insisted was a unanimous opinion that the paper could be saved. It couldn't be unanimous with you and Els there, could it? Hoagland asked. "I clearly was expected to be opposed to Kay," Morse says. "I never knew why."

When Morse insisted that the conclusion was indeed unanimous, Hoagland had had enough. "You're all gonna go,"[60] he said.

Morse called a director, Richard Bergenheim, who would later serve as *Monitor* editor. "This is going to come to blows and Kay's going to walk," Morse told him. "And as Kay goes, so goes the [Christian Science] movement. People are going to go with her, and their financial support will go with them." Bergenheim, however, declined to intervene.

The next morning, Hoagland tried once more to turn Morse, telling him to "quit burning all your bridges."[61] But for Morse, it was not about his career. He was incensed that no one seemed concerned about the church's finances or the schism the TV effort was causing in the church. "I knew it was over," he says.

The Directors quickly rejected the task-force ideas. "Everything was falling apart," Els says. Morse adds, "They just wanted Kay out. They had already printed the new prototype."

Hoagland then presented Fanning with the Nenneman design and told her it would be implemented. It indeed had no ads and would include only three national and three international stories of at most 800 words each, with roughly half the number of news pages. Some material would be picked up from Monitor Television and put into print, thus reducing the need for newspaper staff, which would also be cut in half from 175 to 88. The *Monitor* would be produced on heavy paper, in what Anable called a "desktop version" of the newspaper. Richard Nenneman himself called the new design a "daily magazine." [62] The subscription price would rise from $144 to $200, and circulation would be allowed to drop to the "natural level" of 120,000. The aim was to make the paper self-sufficient in a few years.

Then, in a move that shocked Fanning, Hoagland said the *Monitor* editor would no longer report to the Directors or even be appointed by them. She would work under a publishing director, which meant that business interests would be paramount. The publishing director would report to Nenneman, who was responsible not only for the newspaper but also for TV and radio content. Nenneman, in turn, would answer to the manager, Hoagland. Despite his distance from the newspaper in the hierarchy, Hoagland would be actively involved in shaping the content and would appear more frequently in the newsroom.

Hoagland presented Fanning with a diagram of the new structure of the Publishing Society:

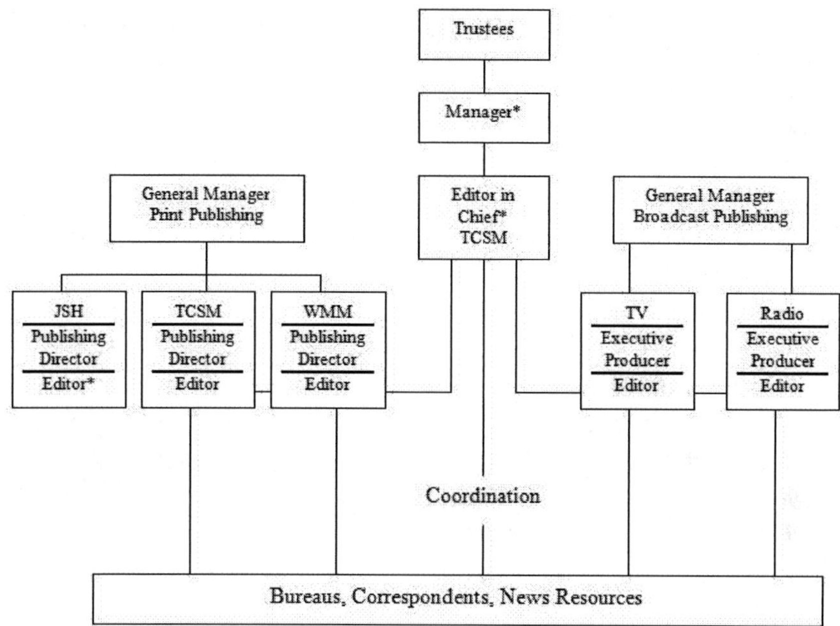

Fanning was knocked back on her heels. Not only would she now report at least two levels below the Directors, but she would have no control over her staff. All newspaper journalists would report to Nenneman and Hoagland and would be shared by TV and radio, creating inevitable friction and confusion over who worked for whom. The "coordination" the diagram called for seemed just a vague hope, as there was no mechanism, aside from management's good will, to achieve it.

Fanning turned immediately to the Directors, and on

Thursday, November 10, explained to them why she could not accept the new structure. ". . . [T]here are certain minimal conditions an editor needs to enable him or her to function as editor," she pointed out. [63]

Her first condition was editorial independence and integrity. She did not mean by this that she wanted to act independently of the church's mission. No editor of the *Monitor* could do that. But at the same time, she knew that some people outside the church "search for evidence that the paper is not a real newspaper." She understood that having an editor of integrity who could be counted on by outsiders to think for herself, and by insiders to think for herself *and* like a Christian Scientist, was the best protection for the paper and the church.

Fanning's second condition was hierarchical. There should be no Publishing Society "chief executive," she said. She pointed to the fact that Mrs. Eddy's *Church Manual* named the manager as the senior business official and, when listing the editor and manager together, placed the manager second.

Her third condition involved working with a sympathetic publishing director. She understood the importance of keeping an eye on the bottom line. But she knew from her experience in Alaska that a paper controlled mainly by business interests, as was the rival *Anchorage Times*, would inevitably sacrifice the joy and problem-solving zeal that made the *Anchorage Daily News* competitive and such fun to work for, and that made the *Monitor* under her an inspiration for many staffers.

Finally, Fanning insisted that there be a serious negotiation for compromise between Nenneman's prototype and her task-force proposal. She objected strongly to the fact that Nenneman's paper cut back so severely on content and staff, and had not been put through market testing.

Fanning reminded the Directors that, in giving authority over the *Monitor* to the Publishing Society, they would essentially be reversing the court decision in the 1920s that made the Directors the primary governing body of the church.

The Directors gave no answer and asked her to think

about things over the weekend.

The next day, Fanning, Anable, and Winder met for lunch at the Hyatt Regency hotel in Cambridge. "We knew by this time there was no future for us at the *Monitor*," says Winder. "They were already planning our replacements. So we looked at all the options." One was walking out. Winder realized that Kay was independently wealthy and could afford to leave. He and Anable were not in that position. For all of them, it would mean losing everything they had worked so hard to build in their careers.

But there were certain advantages to quitting now, Winder felt. Resigning offered them at least a platform from which to make their positions clear and to warn others that things were not right.

Anable was inclined in the same direction. He felt that the rush into new media was out of control, buttressed by misleading statistics, and heading for financial disaster. He had no desire to be involved with what he saw as the near-destruction of the daily newspaper as well as the elimination of half its staff. He was also concerned that, if Fanning alone resigned, she would be painted by critics as an emotional woman who could not cope with the strains of change.

Fanning expressed concern for the future of her two editors. But Anable and Winder agreed that, as Anable puts it, "it would send an important message if all three of us went together."

Winder leaned forward. "I think we have no other recourse," he said. Fanning wanted to think about it and try once more to find a solution everyone could live with.

Back at the newsroom, Paul van Slambrouck stopped by Fanning's office. He was scheduled to leave for Eastern Europe over the weekend to meet with Czech dissident Vaclav Havel and other news sources. He had heard rumblings. "Is there anything happening here that I need to know about?" he asked.

Fanning smiled at him. "You should probably cancel the trip," [64] she said.

On Sunday, Harvey Wood called her at home and asked

her to put in writing what she wanted in terms of editorial control over the paper. She wrote a memo explaining her four minimum requirements and, on Monday morning, November 14, presented it to the Board chairman, John Selover, shortly after 8 A.M. He told her that everything was still open for discussion except the reporting relationship. Discouraged, she returned to the newsroom, and by noon, she received a call saying that the Directors were not willing to discuss things further.

Sadness and regret

That morning, the editors held their normal Page One meeting to decide what to feature the next day on the front page. An hour or so later, a memo came around. There would be a staff meeting after lunch. Neal Menschel was in the newsroom:

> *It was dark, hugely dark. Everyone knew something was up. There were rumors. There was a handful of people, less than five percent, who trusted Jack Hoagland. They felt he was out there doing his thing, leaving everyone in the dark.*

Shortly after noon, Fanning asked her senior editors to join her in her office. Anable and Winder were already there. She closed the door. "We're going to resign," she told the group.

"It was one of those moments when you go numb," van Slambrouck says. "We stood around staring at each other in disbelief. I couldn't believe this institution couldn't find a better way. We'd all witnessed this slow-moving train wreck for a while, but it was still a shock. There were some tears, but no one cried. We were just numb."

At one o'clock, Fanning emerged from her office and walked to the center of the newsroom. When she announced that she, Anable, and Winder were leaving immediately, there were audible gasps. She read from a letter she would be sending to the Directors that day:

> *Serving the church and the mission of* The Christian Science Monitor *has been the greatest experience of my life. I am deeply grateful for the opportunity to contribute to the church and newspaper I love so much.*
>
> *Sadly, I feel that it is as much my duty to resign as Editor today as it was to accept your invitation to come to the* Monitor *five and a half years ago. The assignment from you then was to invigorate the content and form of the paper and to build a team spirit. This I feel we have done—and yet there is so much more that is yet to be done that could strengthen the* Monitor *in its rightful place as a world class newspaper, blessing mankind, not only through the million plus persons it reaches every week, but more importantly through the ideas it spreads.*
>
> *The decisions that are being made now will not have that effect. Instead they will undo the efforts of the last five years—indeed those of the past 80 years. I am convinced that the downsizing, downgrading of the* Monitor *will be seen in time as a tragic mistake, a serious blow to the church, and a step away from Mrs. Eddy's vision for her movement.* [65]

She was departing, she said, without rancor. But she wanted the Directors to know why she was taking such a drastic step. It was not only because of the money that was being taken from the paper to fund broadcasting. It was not only because the Publishing Society was being restructured. More than anything, she said, it was "because of the manner in which these things are being done."

> *The working atmosphere in the Publishing Society, and the relationships with the leadership of the church are totally unlike anything I have encountered in secular organizations and utterly incomprehensible in a*

church. A spirit of mutual trust, candor, openness, and genuine tolerance of diverse viewpoints—even encouragement of them—are essential for any organization to progress. Unfortunately, today we have an atmosphere of secrecy, lack of communication, antagonism, suspicion, instability, and general chaos. [66]

She spoke of the "disdain" with which the task-force report was received and the refusal to consult with her about the future of the paper. "No responsible editor could remain under such conditions," she said.

I had hoped to stay here until the inevitable awakening to the fallacy of such methods, but the latest sequence of events makes it clear that this is the right time to depart. . . .

From the sidelines now, holding no ill feeling, I'll continue to love and pray for the Church, the Board of Directors and The Christian Science Monitor. *If there comes a time that I can again serve—in a more normal atmosphere of openness and mutual trust—I stand ready.* [67]

David Anable and David Winder read from their own letters to the Directors, Anable insisting that the decision to produce a new and much smaller paper was "neither wise, nor well thought out, nor necessary." [68] Winder called the church employees being fired, while TV was expanding, "sacrificial lambs for camouflaging the runaway costs of television." [69]

By the end, much of the staff were beside themselves. Some wanted to walk out with the newsroom leadership or at least go on strike. Others were unsure if that was the right thing to do. Someone asked Fanning, "How can we support you on this? Should we all walk out?"

No, Fanning said. You can't all leave. You have to put out the *Monitor*. We can't do our jobs, but you have to ask yourselves if you can do yours.

Most of the staff decided to remain, at least for the time being. If they all walked out, many reasoned, "they" would just shut the paper down. "We decided we had to keep it going," says photographer Melanie Stetson Freeman. "I kind of wanted to walk out with her. For a long time afterwards, we would have meetings and talk about what to do. Everyone, every day, for years, asked, Should I stay or should I go? I just decided, I work for Mrs. Eddy's paper. I'm going to stay."

Elizabeth Pond, though, was too angry. The reporter who had been held captive in Cambodia, when DeWitt John was editor, announced the next day that she, too, was resigning. She decried the state of church finances in the face of growing TV operations and wondered if management now thought Mrs. Eddy's vision for the *Monitor* was outmoded. [70]

Ed Girardet, who had covered the war in Afghanistan, was also angry. "I . . . should like to congratulate the Board of Directors on destroying what was once considered to be one of the finest journalistic institutions in North America, if not the world," he said in a letter to the Directors. He told them he would leave the paper once his contract expired in May. [71]

Anger soon turned to sadness. Columnist Joseph Harsch wrote the Directors, "The immediate prospect ahead would, for me, be like going back from playing with the Boston Symphony to the local high school band, or from playing with the Boston Red Sox to the Toledo Mud Hens. After those five years of the Fanning-Anable-Winder era I cannot bring myself to stay on with a half *Monitor* at half staff." [72]

"It was one of the saddest moments in the history of the *Monitor*," David Morse says. "But ironically, it was also one of the most significant. It held up standards of ethics that editors would maintain. They would not compromise for personal gain."

David Cook, as excruciatingly neutral now as he was during this time, believes that Fanning had no choice but to resign. "I regret to say, reading the history of the time, I do think they made it so she had to quit," he says. "They were asking her to agree to a management structure that I don't think any editor could agree to. You can be put in a position where you have to resign to keep people from doing unhelpful things."

The rest of the media world knew quickly about the departures. "It was Kay's journalistic sense that helped her make sure her message wasn't squashed," John Yemma says. "She made sure people in other news organizations were aware. So what could have become an internal happening, which could have been controlled and glossed over by Jack's PR people, [became public news]. That meant her resignation had more impact. It may have helped the *Monitor*."

Cook agrees. "By doing what she did," he says, "she bought the *Monitor* additional years as a newspaper. It made getting rid of the *Monitor* toxic for a number of years."

As for Fanning, she had been through too much in her life to succumb to anger. "There was no animosity," says Freeman. "Never a bad word about anyone."

Morse says Fanning handled her resignation "with the most profound spiritual grace I have ever seen. I would walk away from her house shaking my head. She was never resentful of Harvey or Jack, never said an unkind word." A few years later, at a critically low point for the paper, she would return to the newsroom to try to rally the staff, and in 1996, she would be instrumental in persuading the Pulitzer committee to award the prize for international reporting to *Monitor* reporter David Rohde.

Hoagland admits that he was surprised by the turn of events. "It was a tremendous disappointment," he says. "The whole thing got out of hand. I always felt badly. [Kay's] departure was very damaging."

Moving on

A short time after Fanning and the Davids left the newsroom, Hoagland and several directors, including Harvey Wood, walked in. The staff waited silently. The Directors announced that chief editorial writer Richard Cattani would be the new editor. "It wasn't a surprise," van Slambrouck says. "It was like the other shoe dropping."

Cattani had not been the Directors' first choice for editor. When Fanning suddenly resigned, Richard Nenneman was hastily offered a choice between editor of the paper or editor in chief over all media ventures, including the newspaper, the monthly magazine, television, and domestic and international radio services. He chose the latter. As he wrote in his autobiography, "I was not really that interested at this point in running the paper and hoped to get on with [writing] the biography [of Mary Baker Eddy] I had now begun." [73]

In many ways, however, Cattani was a logical choice. A Harvard-educated former public relations executive in Detroit, he had worked at the paper since 1968. He was admired in the newsroom for his deft hand at writing editorials, but he was not easy to talk to.

Neal Menschel likens the reception Cattani received to that of a labor scab. No one applauded. One of the Directors scolded the staff for not being more welcoming to their colleague. "Cattani was a smart guy and a good person," Menschel says. "It was tough on him."

Frederic Hunter, the former Africa correspondent who had been hired on a one-year contract as editor of the Home Forum page, raised his hand at the meeting. "I came to Boston to work for *The Christian Science Monitor*," he said. "Can you tell me where the Christian Science is in TV and everything else we're doing here now?" [74] It was a direct challenge to the church officials.

Harvey Wood passed the question around the visiting group. No one wanted to handle the hot potato. Then Wood turned it back on Hunter, asking him what he thought the religious purpose of the paper was. Hunter cited the daily religious article and contrasted that with the lack of a religious element in TV news or the monthly magazine. It was a weak answer, and Wood pounced, saying that other *Monitor* writers might be offended that "their great spiritual input" was not being acknowledged.

As a loyal Christian Scientist, Hunter was quickly

aghast at what he had done. After the meeting, he wandered the streets of Boston, then went to the Directors' office to deliver an apology. He breathed easier until, a short time later, Wood told church members that the Directors' critics were now apologizing. Hunter says he was "infuriated" at how a sincere attempt to be a faithful member had been twisted into humiliating obeisance.

At the first major meeting in the newsroom after Cattani had taken over, the new stripped-down prototype was passed around. "It was like *The Wall Street Journal* with mug shots," Todd Hoffman says. "It was boring." The reaction was similar throughout the newsroom.

The prototype went back for further work, and a short time later, a new all-color format emerged. "The Directors decided they had to make a show of support to the paper" and so switched to color, Larry Goodrich concludes.

Meanwhile, church security guards told *Monitor* staff that the guards had "been ordered to police photocopy machines to prevent copying and distribution of documents about the *Monitor* changes." [75] An office manager was accosted by Cattani after she had made copies of the Fanning task force materials and asked if she was loyal to him. When she said she was loyal to the *Monitor* and the church, she was asked to think over her actions and sent home. The next day, Saturday, Cattani called her and told her not to come back to work. A day later, Nenneman called to say that she was not fired after all. She resigned anyway.

In a meeting with the *Monitor*'s Washington bureau on November 16, two days after the resignations, Wood, Hoagland, and others from Boston implied that Fanning's decision to resign was simply pique over having to report to someone else. The group insisted that opposing what the Trustees and Directors wanted to do was working "against the *[Church] Manual*." [76]

As David Morse had predicted, consternation grew among church members. Clay Jones agrees that the resignations, along with the controversy that had gone before, upset a lot of people. "The dispute over the direction of the *Monitor* cast a pall over the movement," he says, "not as big as the litigation of the 1920s, but things were seen as not right in Boston."

The Directors were concerned enough that they took the unusual step of summoning Christian Science teachers to Boston to talk about the media issue. Together with church employees, the teachers gathered on November 21, a week after the resignations, to hear the Directors' side of things.

The resignations were all unnecessary and arose from a "deep misunderstanding," the Directors said:

> The Monitor *is NOT being shut down.*
> *The price for a subscription is NOT going up.*
> The Monitor *is NOT being changed into a newsletter.*
> *The upcoming changes are NOT the first steps towards its eventual closing.*
> *Broadcasting never has and never will deprive the paper of needed revenue.*
> *The editorial integrity and independence of the paper are NOT being taken away.* [77]

As in their meeting with the Washington bureau, the Directors seemed to be saying that Fanning and others at the paper had been so blinded either by personal ambition or misinformation that they had resigned over something that was not and never had been true. Those who knew the facts were not pleased with what they saw as a twisting of the truth.

Outside observers were also disappointed. A small newspaper in Maryland wrote morbidly:

> *This week we are writing a eulogy to one of our best friends. . . . This friend, who has spent her life being a model of integrity and fairness, is about to be euthanized in the name of progress. . . .* The Christian Science Monitor, *America's best newspaper, is about to die.*

The newspaper, which has thoughtfully informed presidents, diplomats, world leaders and all those who love a gentle, objective approach to the issues of the day, is being sacrificed in the name of television. [78]

Among *Monitor* staff, the mood was gloomy. The feeling has not completely dissipated, even today. "It's all extremely painful," says Melanie Stetson Freeman, who is still a *Monitor* photographer. "We had the best editor, the best managing editor, they were doing great things for journalism and the church. It's such a shame their time was cut short."

The concern, however, was not just among the newspaper staff. The Directors and Trustees still faced the daunting challenge of substantially reducing the church's annual subsidy of the *Monitor*, which was running at about $20 million. To all appearances, failure to resolve the challenge of the annual operating budget could bankrupt the church.

11

Regret

Surprised at the turn of events but determined to finish the job he had started, still backed by the Directors, Jack Hoagland pushed ahead. He had rejected David Morse's resignation at first; now he accepted it. "We're taking over the TV station," he told Morse. "We're terminating you." [1]

Hoagland and his team began appearing on the newsroom floor almost daily, making editorial decisions. Todd Hoffman was finding that after he had left for the night, someone was going into his photo files, and in late January 1989, he resigned. [2]

Richard Cattani's budget had been slashed from $10 million to $7.7 million, and the paper had shrunk from thirty-two to twenty pages, losing a third of its news space. The deficit dropped, but only to about $13 million a year.

One of the biggest problems was the decision to produce a full-color paper. For one thing, the entire *Monitor* photo archive was in black and white, so for a time, the paper had to rely on outside resources to meet many of its photo needs. But an even bigger challenge was deadlines. The technological demands made them so early—at least eighteen hours between the last story changes and the next day's newspaper—that it became difficult for journalists and readers to stay on top of the news. Editors began to veto articles on major news stories to prevent the *Monitor* from looking out of date by publishing the stories two days later. Editors also informed correspondents they would receive less editing attention from Boston, causing correspondents to turn increasingly to soft feature stories. The *Monitor* won several design awards. But it didn't stop people from calling the paper "USA Yesterday."

To try to correct the deadline problem, Cattani was told to return the paper to the Canham model of interpretive journalism. Investigative pieces were cut back. "He really had no choice," Larry Goodrich says. "He was locked into a terrible situation." [3]

Cameron Barr, a correspondent who eventually left the paper for *The Washington Post*, sees Cattani as having been immensely frustrated. "He was constantly rearranging [newsroom] furniture," he says. "I took it as a product of his inability to make larger changes." [4]

The deadline problem only added to what was already a tense newsroom environment. People dealt with emotions in different ways. Some vented. Eighty-seven staffers signed a letter to the Directors opposing "the drastic contraction of the current newspaper" and urging them to reconsider. [5] There were no changes, however, and the exodus of reporters and editors continued. In Cattani's first few months, several dozen people left the paper, either through resignation or early retirement.

Paul Van Slambrouck was one. He didn't see where his next step would be at the *Monitor*, and he wanted to get back to California to be near his family. By the spring, he had taken a position as national and foreign editor with the *San Jose Mercury-News*.

Frederic Hunter was another who left. In a short resignation letter, he told Cattani: "I deeply love the *Monitor* idea. I have found it stimulating to serve the *Monitor* as Africa Correspondent and special feature writer some 15 years ago and now as Home Forum editor. . . . Since early November we have seen turmoil, corporate infighting and the settling of personal scores. . . . As a result of these actions, the Monitor has lost its purpose, identity and direction." [6]

With resignations, early retirements, other staff cuts, and defections to television, what Fanning had built was largely dismantled. "If you measure an editor's legacy by the people they trained and left behind," says Clay Jones, "the Cattani era wiped out her legacy because so many people were let go." [7]

David Cook calls the staff departures a "catastrophe" for the paper. [8]

The effect on both readers and sources was strong. "I would talk to my regular sources," says one former reporter. "These were some of the most elite policy people in Washington. They would say, 'What have you guys done with your paper? My colleagues and I used to read it. Now we don't.' It was disheartening."

Charlotte Saikowski called the reaction in Washington "heart-rending." A scholar at the Council on Foreign Relations, who disliked what was going on, told her, "We treat [the *Monitor*] as a national treasure. You have an obligation far beyond your church." After what she called "much anguish and prayer," she decided that she could not "go along with . . . the dizzying rush into the electronic media, notably television, at the newspaper's expense" and submitted a request for early retirement.

"As I think about the past few months and years," she said in her letter to Cattani, "it seems to me I have heard little but how much of a problem and burden the *Monitor* is for the church. . . . What I cherish most are my travels to far places of the world and seeing, even in a remote Siberian town, people's faces light up with recognition and admiration when I said, 'I work for *The Christian Science Monitor*.'" [9]

The decisions on whether or not to stay continued to go both ways. For some, the new landscape presented opportunities they couldn't pass up. Marshall Ingwerson, who worked out of Miami as southern bureau chief, was so upset by the Fanning departure that he started sending his resume to other papers. He got several job offers, but when Cattani asked him to move to the Washington bureau, to cover the White House, he decided the *Monitor* really needed him, and he stayed. [10]

Gail Russell Chaddock decided what she needed was simply a change of attitude. "I threw out everything I had collected, the unfair memos, all the gossip," she says. "You just had to put blinders on and think about what needed to be done."

George Moffett, too, tried to shut out the noise from

Boston and do his job. As Middle East correspondent, he heard about the newsroom resignations while preparing to interview Yasser Arafat in Algiers. Monitor Radio wanted to do a set-up piece by phone with Moffett before the interview, and after the engineer made the needed adjustments, the interviewer came on the line. "We have ten seconds and we'll start recording," he said. "By the way, did you know that Kay, David, and David just resigned? Three, two, one. George, tell our listeners what to expect from the meeting tonight."

Moffett caught his breath. "It took a couple of moments to get my bearings to say something intelligent on the air," he admits.[11]

When North and South Yemen announced, in mid-1990, their intention to merge and form the Yemeni Republic, Moffett rushed to Sana, the capital of the republic, on a week's visa, to interview President Ali Abdullah Saleh.

He put in a formal request for the interview to the Ministry of Information and then sat in his hotel room and waited. And waited. His visa was about to expire, and the Ministry seemed to be blocking the request. Discouraged, he did what Oka, Saikowski, Converse, and many other *Monitor* journalists before him had done: He turned to prayer.

He insisted that, despite the evidence of an unresponsive government, he was not, in fact, helpless, because God was in control. He based his prayer on a statement from Mrs. Eddy in *Science and Health*: "Evil is not supreme; good is not helpless; nor are the so-called laws of matter primary, and the law of Spirit secondary." [12]

Christian Scientists often work with statements of Mrs. Eddy's, or passages from the Bible, in their prayers, until they break through whatever fear or other problem seems to stand in the way of complete trust in God. This is what Moffett did, and he began to understand a little of what it meant that good is not helpless and that God's law—not government laws, bureaucrats, or intransigence—was primary. It gave him confidence despite the ticking clock.

In the last few hours of his visa, the dam finally broke.

He was granted interviews with leading parliamentarians and one of the principal Muslim clerics and then, at the end of the day, invited to meet the president. In the article he finally wrote, he used only one cautious quote from Saleh, but the article painted a fair portrait of a country with both hope and lots of challenges. [13]

A different audience

In January 1989, the Directors and Trustees announced that plans were developing to broadcast the *Monitor* on cable TV twenty-four hours a day. The new vehicle, called The Monitor Channel, would be designed for "good men and women everywhere, interested in the betterment of all human conditions."[14]

The church, however, was spending down its fortune. In April 1989, it had $204 million in reserve. A year later, it would have $168 million. Cattani tried to keep the *Monitor* staff together, but in August 1989, the staff was cut drastically from 177 to 103. Once, after visiting the newsroom, the normally impassive Richard Nenneman told Hoagland, in a voice full of emotion, "You can't begin to imagine what it's like down there!" [15]

Hoagland, though, was sure he was on the right track. At annual meeting 1989, he talked of the "modest, quiet, steadfast example of good journalism" that the *Monitor* in all its forms represented. He proudly quoted *The New York Times*, which said, "The sheer integrity of 'World Monitor' is invigorating." He quoted a columnist in the *Minneapolis Star Tribune*, who referred to the *Monitor*'s "journalism of hope." [16]

But since the Fanning resignation, the world outside Boston had been following happenings at the church and the *Monitor*, and the persistence of church critics was beginning to irritate Hoagland. The success of *Monitor* broadcasting depended on industry and public confidence in what he was doing.

Sara Terry, for one, believed that being a loyal member

of the church meant not swallowing her convictions. *Monitor* television was being built on sand, in her view, and she did not want to lend her support to it. "I knew I had to go," she says. "I probably knew more than any other Christian Scientist what was going on in TV. I've never said anything about it till now."[17] By late spring she had resigned.

Other members objected to some of the programming. One program, in January 1990, carried an interview with Dr. Herbert Benson, director of the Mind-Body Institute of Boston's Deaconess Hospital. The intention was to give a respectful ear to a range of ideas, but some members who saw it wondered how the interview could possibly fulfill the mission of the *Monitor*, "to spread . . . Science," when Benson was promoting a "relaxation response" that was more akin to self-hypnosis. The belief that Christian Science preached weird mental gymnastics had bedeviled the church since the beginning. The program, critics felt, would just increase the confusion.

Hoagland kept on. He adopted the phrase "The Monitor Channel: Television for the Global Citizen" to position the new undertaking. As the Publishing Society newsletter for May 1990 put it, "The Monitor Channel's goal is to provide, instantly and continually, everything the viewer needs in order to maintain an enlightened, constructive view of the surrounding world: . . ."[18] There was no hint that the *Monitor* had a religious mission.

The following March, in the continuing effort to reshape the *Monitor*, Netty Douglass described what she hoped would become the *Monitor*'s news standard. "The Christian Science Monitor and its ancillary radio and television news broadcasts were established and are conducted with one purpose: public service," she insisted. [19] "Monitor broadcasts are not a means to propagate Christian Science." [20] Although the statement was meant to convey the idea that the newspaper and broadcasting operations were not designed to proselytize, it was a risky thing to say, when the newspaper's founder had made it clear that the paper was designed "to spread . . . Science."

Meanwhile, church critics were working the press and

making the Hoagland team's efforts to build support in the cable industry increasingly hard. A frustrated Hoagland brashly told the *Boston Globe*, in a comment aimed partly at his church audience, that he was confident of success because the intentions of those behind the new media effort were so high. [21]

The TV operation was hugely expensive to mount—costs for fiscal year 1991 were thirty percent over budget, and church funds dropped to $145 million, $100 million of that restricted in how it could be used—and Hoagland and the Directors became concerned that they would run out of money before their efforts would come to fruition. [22] They tried to raise funds from outside investors, which only inspired more opposition from members, who wondered how a church could sell off part of its publishing activities to secular interests. Some investors were cautiously interested, but with what was happening inside the church, they balked.

At annual meeting 1991, Netty Douglass joined the chorus in pleading for member support, but like Hoagland, she was still convinced changes had to come only from one side. "Isn't it time to close ranks," she asked, "to join hands around the world, to prayerfully support with all our might the utility of these publishing activities as they go forth 'to bless all mankind'?" [23]

But having rejected the members at the beginning as irrelevant, the team was finding it difficult now to gain their backing. It didn't help that members increasingly saw two messages coming from Boston, one aimed at them and praising the *Monitor*'s religious role, the other aimed at the rest of the world—and, presumably, the majority of the broadcasting staff, who were not church members—denying that very role.

Then, in what seemed like an inspired idea, the Directors and Hoagland were reminded of a tantalizing possibility. A former pupil of Mrs. Eddy, Bliss Knapp, had written a book about Mrs. Eddy, which had been privately published in 1947. After Knapp died, his heiress wife had stipulated in her own will that if the church published the book by 1993 as authorized literature and gave it a big boost through its reading rooms, the church would inherit $75 million from her and her heiress sister. The bequest had now grown to $95 million. If the church did not publish and promote the book as instructed, the gift would go to Stanford University and the Los Angeles County Museum.

The problem was, in the view of some church members, part of the book contradicted Christian Science theology about the place of Mrs. Eddy in the religion, essentially deifying her.

For the Directors and Hoagland, the dilemma was easily solved. They announced a new "Twentieth Century Biography Series" on Mrs. Eddy, which would include the Knapp book, even though it was not really a biography. The series would fall in line with the Board's "open-shelf" policy of publishing materials from a variety of writers, even if they didn't always uphold the church's theology and positions. The Directors insisted that it was their fiduciary responsibility to see that the bequest became available to help with church expenses.

The pursuit of the Knapp money caused another firestorm of criticism from members. The editors of the *Journal*, *Sentinel,* and *Herald* resigned, and some members encouraged Stanford and the Los Angeles County Museum to dispute the church's claim. They did, and the case ended up in court. Hoagland and the team were devastated. The church eventually received $53 million from the bequest, but not until five years later.

Amidst the turmoil, The Monitor Channel finally launched on May 15, 1991, as "the full expression of the *Monitor* in television form." At annual meeting three weeks later, Douglass challenged the members, "Are we ready to step boldly into the next century, . . ."[24]

The launch went smoothly, and Hoagland soon came up with a new positioning statement—"The Monitor Channel: The Journalism of Ideas." It was a nicely neutral formulation. Any ideas would work.

Despair

The newspaper had a moment of glory in June 1990 when, early one Sunday morning, Nelson Mandela showed up unannounced at the church plaza. He had recently been released from prison in South Africa and had spoken the day before to a huge crowd along the Charles River.

A *Monitor* staffer who was walking by saw him and stopped. Mandela smiled and motioned her over. He said he had come to the church because he wanted to see the place where "that famous lady" started a religion and a newspaper.

The staff member quickly ran to the newsroom to tell Cattani. He threw on his jacket and rushed out to greet Mandela and give him a tour of the church. Mandela told Cattani that the *Monitor* was the only international paper he had been allowed to read in prison and that it had helped sustain him in his long years there. [25]

The Mandela visit, however, was only a brief respite in what Clay Jones calls the "trough of despair in the Cattani years." The *Monitor* staff resented what they saw as their increasing irrelevance. In the summer of 1991, just as The Monitor Channel launched, an unsigned memo was circulated on *Monitor* letterhead, complaining that the paper was being published only to supplement the Monitor Channel and as a way to placate critics within the church. [26]

Hoagland tried to stay positive, but his troubles were mounting. John Hart resigned as anchor of "World Monitor News." The Discovery Channel renounced its agreement to carry The Monitor Channel. His back to the wall, Hoagland got permission in September to use $20 million in principal borrowed from the Monitor Endowment Fund. The money was repaid five months later, then the same amount was borrowed from the church pension fund. When news of the transactions came out, another volley of criticism hurtled in from the members. The Directors insisted that all borrowings were legal, and outside auditors agreed.

On February 27, 1992, the confidential monthly

Treasurer's Narrative, its distribution limited to a few church officers and staff, announced that income in the first nine months of the fiscal year stood at $52.3 million and expenses at $107 million, twelve percent over budget. [27] Despite its confidentiality, the report ended up in the hands of a *Boston Globe* reporter. [28]

The television team did not want to appear discouraged, but the most promising potential investor, The Providence Journal Company, of Rhode Island, was getting cold feet. Wood refused to concede. "Be assured our resolve is unwavering," he said in a news release. A memo from Hoagland and Douglass to all employees of the Publishing Society and Monitor Television on March 3, 1992, called "Staying the Course," insisted that after ten months of operation, "the Monitor Channel is well on its way to achieving its first-year goal of 4.75 million households in the United States, not including the additional 2 million households which receive the channel through station WQTV in Boston." [29] The two million households Hoagland referred to were those that received the WQTV signal. Only a fraction were actual watchers of The Monitor Channel. It was the "fast and loose" use of such data, David Morse says, that made criticism of the television effort "easy." [30]

Even if they did not have the inside knowledge Morse did, many church members sensed a lack of integrity in the numbers. The rosy projections did not "click" with the arrogance and manipulation they felt from Boston, and they refused to let up on their disapproval.

Hoagland and Douglass had hoped "Staying the Course" would rally support to their efforts. They complained of "an all-out assault on the television activities of the *Monitor*, the purposes of which are not entirely clear, . . ." They decried the fact that investors were being scared away. ". . . [W]henever a progressive step has become known," they said, "well organized resistance by a relative small group who oppose the *Monitor*'s entry into television has heightened and disrupted, to a greater or lesser degree, the work in progress." [31]

They reiterated what they saw as the purpose of the

television venture:

> *[It is] to report the news of the world in a clear, factual, accurate, and calm manner, free of the sensational or inflammatory elements to which television can fall prey. . . . Our programs serve as a monitor for audiences with a generous, committed, and constructive interest in the world around them and in the needs and aspirations of people throughout the world.* [32]

The memo showed little understanding of why opposition was so strong.

Four days later, on March 7, the team decided they were out of options, and they made a tactical move they had planned if the going got too rough. Harvey Wood, who had become a lightning rod of sorts, resigned as a director, and Hoagland, Douglass, and Don Bowersock left their posts. But the latter three only moved to less visible positions, Bowersock taking a new position as managing treasurer, Douglass becoming executive producer for radio and television, and Hoagland continuing as chairman and CEO of Monitor Television and The Monitor Channel. They all kept trying to raise money from investors to keep the operation afloat.

The Directors themselves took over the highest roles in church management, a move they positioned as creating cohesiveness and unity in church operations. An editor-in-chief role for the Publishing Society was created and filled by Director Richard Bergenheim. Other Directors became Publishing Society manager, church treasurer, and head of the Committee on Publication office.

Opponents were not sidetracked. Having pursued courses both insightful and crude in their efforts to stop what they saw as the hijacking of the church and its publishing operation, they began putting forth a simple argument, to devastating effect: The religious purpose of the *Monitor* needed to be preserved at all costs. It wasn't about numbers or prestige, money or technology. It wasn't about what medium the *Monitor* used to convey the news. It was about religion.

It was the last thing that Hoagland's supporters inside the church and potential investors outside wanted to hear.

The *Boston Globe* talked to some of the opponents. Some believed that selling an interest in the *Monitor*, whether broadcast or print, was like selling an interest in the church. [33] Others complained that officials had used the paper's purpose, to "bless all mankind," as a mandate to make public service its mission instead of healing. "The purpose of the Monitor is clearly missionary," said an unnamed member. Kay Fanning told *The Wall Street Journal* that most members just want their church back, and they don't see what a global media empire has to do with the church's mission. [34]

Many of the non-Christian-Science employees of the media ventures were unnerved by the article, which seemed to undermine what they thought was the independence of Monitor Television. One *Monitor* television executive, who later wrote a book about the television venture, accused Fanning of undermining the *Monitor*'s decades-long fight for credibility. [35]

For opponents, however, it was a statement of why the *Monitor* had built credibility in the first place. Mrs. Eddy herself, in a comment in the *Sentinel* in 1909, had told an admiring *Monitor* reader, referring to *Science and Health*, "Stick to your text, and you will stick to your newspaper, and text and paper will carry you onward and upward." [36] In every practical sense, the church and the newspaper were one in purpose.

That idea had been opposed vigorously, sometimes desperately, for years, and by people on both sides of the debate. Now it was front and center, and there was no denying its power. As in the type of healing Christian Scientists experience, when a clear, spiritual idea bursts through and overwhelms the credibility of the physical evidence of disease, the ground on which the whole argument over media had been fought, along with what seemed to be a solid reality of fear, dishonesty, and human will, collapsed.

At ten o'clock on March 8, the morning the *Globe* article appeared, Hoagland faced a somber group of Directors in their conference room. The end was at hand. The Monitor Channel would be sold or shut down. Hoagland had tears in his eyes. His nose started bleeding. [37]

Wood's departure had changed the dynamics within the Board, but the decision was still not arrived at easily. "To the world it looked like failure, and Christian Scientists don't like to fail," says one person who was closely involved. But the Board concluded that the move was unavoidable, even if some Board members still felt that television could succeed if given more time.

Hoagland now says that he agreed with the decision, believing that the damage to the church from the controversy was too much. "The church is a delicate mechanism," he says, "and it was taking a tremendous shaking." But he still blames the "hammering" of church critics, along with intense coverage in the *Boston Globe*, which he sees as motivated by its own corporate and competitive interests to oppose efforts by the *Monitor* to expand into broadcasting, for forcing the channel's closure.

The next day, the Trustees, of which Hoagland was still a member, issued a bitter statement. Decrying "opposition to television from within our own ranks," the Trustees also complained about incessant coverage from "a hostile local press," which had then spilled over to a trade press that had previously been positive about The Monitor Channel's future. From there, investors had been spooked.

In the statement, the Trustees insisted the *Monitor* had an essentially secular purpose. It was a tacit acknowledgment that the whole struggle had come down to the mission of the newspaper:

> *Yesterday's press coverage, quoting unnamed members of our Church, raises further challenges for us in two ways: by trying to reinterpret the very purpose of* The Christian Science Monitor *that was so clearly*

established in 1908—to be an independent, unbiased source of the most objective, in-depth journalism—thus raising doubts about our greatest asset, our journalistic integrity; and by signaling a determined opposition to the principle of partnerships in this enterprise—an opposition which has already proved capable, on occasion, of disrupting our normal business operations. . . . Given the prospects of continuing opposition within our Church ranks, we must now face the necessity of an outright sale of The Monitor Channel to an outside party, no later than June 15, 1992. [38]

Soon after the statement came out, Hoagland resigned as a trustee, and a month later, he gave up his position as chairman and CEO of Monitor Television.

Why?

On June 28, 1992, The Monitor Channel went dark, laying off four hundred workers. Monitor Television had won Emmys and other awards, but the channel had only five million subscribers and needed twenty-five million to break even. *World Monitor* magazine published its last issue in May 1993, after losing almost $40 million. WQTV sold for $3.8 million in June 1993, far below the $25 million that Morse had offered for it. (Ironically, the buyer was Boston University, where David Anable was now chair of the School of Journalism.) Monitor Radio eventually closed in June 1997, after reaching 1.1 million listeners but losing about $8 million a year. The total loss from all new media ventures, outside the print newspaper, was about $500 million. [39]

After WQTV sold, Morse got a call from one of the Directors. "They asked if I had ever made an offer," he says. He told them he had. "They had never heard of it. I had enough conversations with Board members after I left to realize that many members of the Board didn't have a clue what was going on. Many people, including me, were quick to blame the Board, but there appeared to be a whole set of decisions being made elsewhere."

There is no end of theories about why television didn't work for the *Monitor*. For some people, the issue was timing and reading of the marketplace. "They tried to do too much," says Larry Goodrich. "The channel was launched at a bad time in the development of the cable industry because a lot of systems hadn't upgraded to fiber optics. They couldn't carry a lot of channels and were at capacity."

David Cook agrees that the church overreached. "There's no question the values of the *Monitor* can be expressed in TV," he says. "We just tried to do too much. We probably could have sustained Monitor Radio. We could have sustained a weekly TV show, maybe. But nightly and a 24-hour cable channel really taxed our resources."

He also sees several other factors undermining the broadcast effort: the amount of money required; the lack of enough Christian Scientists "with the needed experience and bedrock ideals" to supervise operations; and the fact that broadcasting got caught up in the "intramural church fight."

Melanie Stetson Freeman thinks it wasn't the market, the money, or the personnel so much as simple desperation. "People just got this crazy idea that they would save the religion by doing television," she says.

One thing most people agree on is that it wasn't really about Jack Hoagland. To those who know him, he is a sincere and gentle man. "He came in with a wonderful vision," says Morse, who likes the man personally. "He had the purest of desires." Sara Terry adds: "He was always kind and tried to protect me. His greatest error was that he wouldn't listen to people who tried to tell him the truth."

Cook, who was closer to Hoagland than most people, understands what he went through:

> *He loved the* Monitor *and gave up a lot for it. The same with Harvey Wood. They saw a vision for what the* Monitor *might be in a multimedia world.*

Jack is a brilliant guy and a visionary. He's also a complicated guy. He had watched the work [at the Publishing Society] kill his father. He gave up a successful career and came and gave it his all.

Twenty years later, Hoagland still seems shell-shocked from the experience. "I've got to admit I've tried to be a loyal church member since I left," he says. "It's a tough challenge, always was and probably always will be. I've tried to be supportive of everything they've done." He insists that during his time at the Publishing Society, he "never made a move without prior approval."

He now admits it was a mistake to try to push the church so strongly into electronic media. "The church should have waited till it had to do it," he says. He has refrained from publically criticizing anyone, and when his wife, a rock for him through the most trying times, died, in 1999, he admits he "went into hiding." In 2002, he married Netty Douglass.

But no amount of personal drive or noble qualities could make up for a misreading of the *Monitor*'s mission. "The mistake is always to separate the newspaper from the church," Terry says. "It was during Kay's time that I came to grips with why it was called *The Christian Science Monitor*. We got clear enough and transparent enough that the mission of the *Monitor* took us over."

Fanning herself, when The Monitor Channel ended, said she hoped it was "a first step toward restoring the church to its central mission of spiritual healing." [40]

Apology

Some of the lessons were eventually learned. One was the importance of respecting church members. After the closing of The Monitor Channel had been announced but before it had been implemented, the Directors were already insisting that the idea behind TV and radio was right and might come back again in a new form. But they maintained that next time "we will find a way to do it—together." [41]

In 1993, the Directors went a step further toward making amends. In a statement read by Richard Bergenheim at annual meeting, they acknowledged that Mrs. Eddy's demand that motives and acts of all church members be Christly applied as much to them as anyone. "The Board of Directors realizes that the demand to answer to Principle is just as important for us as it is for anyone else," he said. [42]

The Directors acknowledged that they had been under fire but that it was pointless to demean the motives of either side:

> *. . . differences of opinion are not evidence of disloyalty, and neither are they evidence of deceit by decisionmakers.*

"Still," Bergenheim continued, "we could never claim that no mistakes have been made." It was the passive political voice, with no attempt to specify the mistakes or hold anyone accountable, at least publically, but it seemed to come close to an apology:

> *No man or woman, no institution, no board of directors, has yet demonstrated a way free of all mistakes. And like anyone else, we regret them, we regret them deeply. We seek to learn from them, and pray each day to partake more humbly of Christ's spirit of love, compassion, and forgiveness, . . .* [43]

Finally, the Directors asked for member support for themselves, an extraordinary change in tone from the previous years:

> *. . . this Board needs your help. The Old Testament tells us that even Moses could not do everything required of him on his own. The children of Israel engaged Aaron and Hur to help hold up his arms (see Ex. 17:10-12).*

Will you hold up the arms of your fellow church workers as we go forward together? [44]

The members had already, in many ways, done this. Had no one objected to the forced march into television, the newspaper might have disappeared, and with it Mrs. Eddy's idea for how to make her church a more powerful force for good in the world. The Directors might have had an even greater disaster on their hands.

The key question was whether the Directors would now return the favor. Would they hold up the arms of members in the way that Mrs. Eddy intended, by providing them an even better newspaper, one of such insight and inspiration that it would become a powerful tool for them in spreading the healing power of Christ in the world?

12

Seeking the Practitioner-Journalist

"Holy $#%&!"

John Yemma stared out the window of the high-rise office building in Dallas, Texas. Across the railroad yards to the east, a massive fireball was scorching the night sky. A tank car had just exploded.

On his mind was the downstate hostage drama he had been watching all day, the ongoing political tensions in Austin, and the sordid ins and outs of much of the daily news in Texas and the surrounding states. Now, right in his line of sight, the world, or at least his part of it, was going to hell.

For a young wire-service reporter, it was the perfect ending to a perfect day.

It was a Sunday, in the early spring of 1977, and Yemma worked long into the night to put the tank car story to bed. He had been at United Press International for more than two years now, and he had risen fast since arriving as a refugee from the *San Antonio Express* and *News*, whose parent company had been bought by Rupert Murdoch's News Corporation. Under Murdoch, the only story Yemma had ever placed on the front page was one about a decision by the city of San Antonio to charge the suburbs for services they had been getting for free. Yemma's byline led the afternoon paper, but the headline had been rewritten by the city editor: "CITY DECLARES WAR ON SUBURBS!"

At UPI, at least he didn't have to distort the news. He was already a shift supervisor in charge of a half dozen reporters covering seven states. He would write and rewrite stories for regional distribution and then make the decision on which ones to send to New York for the national wire.

His life was far from quiet, but that went with the territory. He lived the borderline chaos of a wire-service journalist with what seemed like a deadline every minute. On the other hand, he was learning to write and edit under pressure. Catastrophe and weirdness were his daily diet, and it made for cynical days and, occasionally, sleepless nights, but his work appeared all over the country. He was building clips and a reputation.

He was also in love.

Robin Jareaux was a special projects designer at the *Dallas Morning News* and one of the most creative people he had met. She was good-looking and funny, and had a quiet way of engaging with the deep questions of life.

They had met when John's younger brother Mark, who was a photographer at the *Dallas Morning News*, had a few people over to see his latest pictures. Toward the end of the evening, John pulled out the UPI obituary list and began entertaining everyone with the prepared obits of some still-living people. Robin thought he was funny and upbeat. She also liked that he had standards and managed to keep a sense of joy about him, despite the fact that his daily work menu comprised mostly bad news.

Several weeks after they met, he was browsing the reading material in her downtown Dallas apartment and came across something he hadn't expected: literature on Christian Science. He had been in Christian Science Reading Rooms before. They were quiet places to catch up on that pretty-good newspaper, *The Christian Science Monitor,* while waiting for a bus. He'd never cared much one way or the other about the religion. But this girl had flair, and she was a lifelong Christian Scientist and loved it. Maybe it was worth exploring.

Robin wasn't eager to talk about religion at that point in the relationship. But she was intrigued that John seemed interested. She gave him *Science and Health* and, she was happy to learn, he actually read it. In her first marriage, she had barely been able to discuss religion.

What she told him about Christian Science made sense to John. "I had seen enough things," he says, "that I knew the way you look at the world makes all the difference. And there was this concept in Christian Science that one of the synonyms for God is Truth. That resonated for me as a journalist. Even the most secular journalist believes he's fighting for truth. I really was absolutely taken by it." [1]

The night of the tank-car explosion, alone in his apartment, John couldn't sleep. It was more than his usual climb-down from daily intensity, and it was more than thinking about Robin. It was closer to that nadir people hit when their world view has reached its limit. As he later described the moment:

> *Helplessness swept over me. I saw a cold, cruel, out-of-control universe, an absurd life of breakdown and disorder. I would not have been surprised in the next moment to have had to jump out of bed to dodge a falling meteorite!* [2]

He began comparing what he was doing with his life to what he was thinking, and what he was thinking to what Christian Science said about reality. "Christian Science was beginning to give me a framework for thinking things through," he says. Could the way a person thinks be not just a factor but the factor in what kind of life he lives? "I could actually start to feel the logic of that creep in," he says.

It was one of the multiple epiphanies everyone has over time. In the spring of 1977, his epiphany was this: "Get control of your thought and see what that does to your experience."
The next day, he talked to Robin about what had happened. She took him a step further, talked about the good as being normal and more powerful than the aberrant.

His whole life became calmer. He felt his dominion over things grow, and instead of watching for the next shocking thing to write about, he began wanting to write about things with meaning. "I noticed my life beginning to improve," he says. "Without becoming a Pollyanna, I was becoming less an unthinking chronicler of catastrophe and more an intelligent writer." For the first time in his adult life, his cynicism vanished.

A few months later, a position as a feature writer at the *Dallas Morning News* Sunday magazine opened up, and he thought, Here's a chance to step back from the cliff. He took the job, and he and Robin would sneak off for long lunches together. Things got cozy between them over the next year, and they moved in together. At the same time, John was working with a Christian Science practitioner as he gained more familiarity with Christian Science, and he became convinced that abiding by moral law was crucial in bringing his life into harmony with God's law. "John had this moral thing that just compelled him to take the high road," Robin says. [3] One day he literally got down on one knee and proposed, and she was charmed. From separate business trips, in July 1978, they flew to St. Louis and got married in her parents' home. They laughed about the preacher-for-hire with the white shoes and white belt.

John liked working for the magazine, but Robin wanted more. She was a known talent in the newspaper design field and was soon recruited by the *Washington Post* as associate art director. The couple moved to Washington, and it wasn't long before John was reporting from the Washington bureau of the *Monitor*.

After a year, during the summer of 1980, David Anable called him. There was a position open in the Middle East. Would he be interested? Without a doubt. Robin was feeling stifled by the corporate conservatism of the *Post* and was ready for a change.

They moved to Nicosia, Cyprus, and John and Robin would sometimes attend events together. It dismayed Robin when they would be in a room full of journalists and several stringers would have name badges saying "Reporter for *The Christian Science Monitor*." John, after all, was the only full-time *Monitor* reporter in the region. But he refused to get angry.

For three years, he flew around, sometimes for weeks at a time, what he calls the "hauntingly beautiful" Middle East. Then, in June 1982, just as Israeli troops were crossing the border into Lebanon, John caught the last flight into Beirut.

In July, Beirut came under siege, and by August, Robin was tired of listening to the BBC and trying to guess what her husband was up to. She told him she wanted to join him, and he agreed. She found a boat going to the port of Jouneih, Lebanon, and after a night bobbing on the waves, waiting to pass through the Israeli blockade, they met at the Alexandre Hotel in Beirut.

John was gone most of the time chasing stories, and Robin would sit on the roof of the hotel watching the shelling of East Beirut. It wasn't enough. She wanted to see what he saw. There were reports that the Israelis were using cluster bombs near the airport, and John prepared to go look for evidence for a possible story. Let me come, Robin said. Why not? They grabbed a UPI photographer and headed south.

When they arrived, they began walking north along Israeli tank treads, the only route where they were sure that land mines had already exploded. They found spent cluster bombs, picked one up, and photographed others with the charge still in them. When they returned to their hotel, they had to pick their way through a lobby covered with broken glass. The hotel had been car-bombed while they were out.

John was grateful he could finally share some of his intense experiences with Robin, but by 1983, they were ready for another change. The job of New York correspondent for the *Monitor* was open, and editor Earl Foell agreed to give it to John. He and Robin headed back to the States and started apartment hunting in New York City.

Life got complicated, though, when Kay Fanning arrived in Boston and offered Robin a position as the *Monitor*'s design director. How could she say no?

She took a room in a Boston hotel, and for five months, she and John saw each other on weekends. Finally, in November 1983, the business editor position opened and John moved to Boston. Managing editor Richard Nenneman became John's mentor for financial and economic writing.

Robin loved the atmosphere in Fanning's newsroom—where else would you tell the editor you were perplexed about something and the editor would give you an assignment to read an article by Mary Baker Eddy? John, too, was in his element. He began doing radio, as many *Monitor* staffers did, and when Nenneman moved to Jack Hoagland's side of the operation, they kept up their relationship. TV continued to grow, and Nenneman offered John the position of news editor for television.

He was eager to embrace the new opportunity, but after four months, he was disenchanted with TV and returned to the newspaper. When Fanning resigned, John didn't leave right away, but he quietly made other arrangements, finally taking a job as assistant editor of the *Boston Globe Sunday Magazine*. He quickly built relationships at the *Globe* and was put into more and more demanding positions, from covering the first Gulf War to foreign editor, to reporter on ideas and culture, to deputy managing editor for the *Sunday Globe*, to national political editor. Robin saw John's managerial skills sharpen and his self-confidence build. She was grateful that his gentleness remained untouched.

John kept in contact with *Monitor* people and went to lunch once or twice a year with the current editor. They'd ask his advice on various things, even tried to get him to come back. But his *Globe* career was solid, and as he watched the *Monitor* struggle with its identity, its circulation continuing to plummet, he saw no place where he and the paper could grow together.

Reconstituting the Family

On a Monday morning in July 1994, while Yemma, who was now the *Globe*'s foreign editor, was busy preparing the paper's international coverage for the next day, David Cook took a call in the broadcast newsroom in the Colonnade Building at the Christian Science Center. Cook was editor of the

Monitor Radio news operation. Tony Periton, a member of the Board of Directors, asked him to come to the Administration Building for a meeting.

When Cook arrived, all five Directors were there. They got right to the point: Would he take over as *Monitor* editor?

Cook gulped. He hadn't been in the newsroom for some time. People there were still on edge. But the loyal worker and church member couldn't say no. Just give me a week to get ready, he said. The Directors grumbled at the delay but agreed.

The Board saw Cook as a bridge between the newspaper and broadcasting, and wanted him to help resolve the remaining tensions. Too, after what they'd been through with previous editors, the Board was mindful that Cook was likely to take their advice and direction without pushback.

They had also had enough of Cattani. His relationship with his staff had become so strained that a group of them had threatened to walk out at annual meeting—the time of maximum sensitivity for the Directors—unless he was removed. The Directors had asked him to install their own choice as managing editor—Stephen Gray, head of his family's newspaper company, in Michigan, and instigator of an award-winning culture of employee involvement at the paper. Cattani had refused. He was also ill.

"Toward the end, Cattani was not himself," Cook says gently. "He was emotionally spent." [4]

Being editor of the *Monitor* is "a brutal job," in the words of one former editor. Cattani was not the first to have severe physical problems. "The expectations and ambitions are so high," the former editor says, "the resources so meager, and you are often caught between journalists, who want one thing, and the Board, all Christian Science teachers, who want another. They have very different perspectives."

Cook is generous in his estimation of Cattani. "He could be very difficult to deal with," he says, "but he was fiercely devoted to the *Monitor*. In my view, he was a *Monitor* hero. He had to run a paper with a lot of stars having left."

Despite Cook's history with the broadcasting arm of the

church, the staff applauded when he entered the newsroom as editor, on July 21, 1994. They were relieved he wasn't Cattani, but they were also aware of Cook's reputation as someone they could talk to. "I tried to bring compassion for staff and love of excellence," Cook says. "You get much better results when people feel they are loved and taken care of. I tried to make it a happy place again."

In a brief speech to the staff, he began his attempt to instill a sense of family. "For those of us in management, the matter of injuring no man includes striving to ensure that our stewardship of the *Monitor* does not damage any of you," he said. "Not just physical damage or career damage but also damage to your sense of the possibilities of this wonderful place and the value of your contribution to it."

After the speech, he went to his new office, and a frustrated Gail Russell Chaddock soon walked in. She had been slated to go to Paris as the *Monitor*'s correspondent there, and her husband had quit a job he loved so the family could be together. But that very morning, Cattani, in one of his final acts as editor, had changed his mind and assigned someone else to Paris, leaving Chaddock's family in turmoil.

"I'm not going to start this job by screwing someone's family," Cook told her. "You are going to France."

He set immediately to work trying to persuade some of the people who had left in anger to return to the paper. It wasn't easy, especially since the broadcasting arm had just laid off hundreds of people when the TV operation folded. But using offers of increased pay approved by the Directors as well as not a little guilt, he got some good reporters and editors to give the paper another chance. He brought back Earl Foell as chief editorial writer and Foell's former managing editor, John Dillin, as his managing editor.

With the calm Cook restored to the newsroom, correspondents could focus on their stories, and the old courage and reporting skill resurfaced more and more.

Genocide in the Balkans

On August 18, 1995, the *Monitor* confirmed some of the world's worst fears. "An on-the-spot investigation by *The Christian Science Monitor*," a front page story said, "has uncovered strong evidence that a massacre of Bosnian Muslim prisoners took place last month." [5]

The writer was David Rohde, a former production assistant with ABC News, who had been hired by the *Monitor* in 1994. "I had always admired the *Monitor* for its foreign coverage," Rohde says, "how in-depth it was and how it didn't focus on disasters. I liked that it tried to show some of the positive things happening overseas." [6]

Hired as a copy editor and reporter for the culture desk, Rohde worked hard to keep his writing in front of the international team. Finally, in November 1994, a slot for a reporter to cover the developing war in Bosnia opened, and Rohde found himself in Zagreb, Croatia, as the *Monitor*'s Eastern Europe correspondent.

He had heard rumors of a massacre in Srebnica, and in July 1995, he visited American officials and collected satellite photos of the alleged mass graves. Soon afterwards, he entered Bosnian Serb territory and headed for the press center, supposedly for another story. When he was sure he wasn't being watched, he veered off to see what he could find on the massacres.

> *Nearing the Serb-held village of Nova Kasaba in Bosnia, I stared at a blurry, faxed copy of a US spy satellite photo. Were there really mass graves in the fields near this road, as US officials alleged from the photo?*
>
> *Another photo, taken earlier, reportedly showed a soccer field half mile away where Muslim prisoners had been held, just before the alleged graves showed up in the later photos. . . .*
>
> *The soccer field, now filled with grazing cows*

and horses, rolled by on my right. Bosnian Serb soldiers at a military command post eyed my car warily. I turned back and parked my car on a dirt road where it could not be seen. I left my Serb driver and interpreter in the car. [7]

He spent two hours exploring the area on foot, at times hearing bullets whiz by his head, until he found a young Muslim boy's primary-school diploma and some photos with Muslim names on the back in the grass. Then he came upon prayer beads, a bullet, and papers. Finally, he spotted something white jutting from a plot of freshly dug earth. It was two long, thin bones that could only have been human.

Six weeks later, after further research, he filed another report that began:

Bosnian Serb soldiers systematically executed as many as 2,000 Muslim prisoners after taking the UN "safe area" of Srebrenica in July, according to credible eyewitness accounts newly obtained by The Christian Science Monitor. *Nine Muslim men who say they are survivors of mass executions gave separate, corroborating accounts of what could be one of the greatest single war crimes of Bosnia's brutal 3½ year conflict.* [8]

Later in October, he visited Serb-held territory again and found two more grave sites. Just as he was about to take a photo of human bones, he was arrested by a Bosnian Serb watchman. Over a period of ten days, he was held by the government, put on trial, and threatened with execution.

Back in Boston, the *Monitor* family that Cook had reconstituted pulled together. "Dave Cook was fantastic," Rohde says. "He flew to the Dayton peace talks with ten members of my family to try to pressure the Serbs to get me released. My family worked closely with the newsroom. We're all still very grateful to the *Monitor*." Others, including U.S.

Secretary of State Warren Christopher, also intervened with the Bosnian Serb government on Rohde's behalf.

Rohde was finally "pardoned" by Bosnian Serb leader Radovan Karadzic and freed.

For his bravery, determination, and ability to write a gripping story that helped change world events, Rohde was awarded the *Monitor*'s sixth Pulitzer, the 1996 award for international reporting.

Cook, knowledgeable about *Monitor* history, knew how much it meant for the paper to be back on top after more than twenty-five years and the despair of the Fanning and Cattani eras. "We are grateful to the Pulitzer Prize Board for recognizing David Rohde's work," Cook said in a statement. "His reporting was relentless, courageous, and compassionate. It is a worthy addition to the Monitor's 88-year commitment to unselfish, comprehensive, international reporting." [9]

Kay Fanning had helped lobby the Pulitzer committee to give the prize to Rohde, and putting more parts of the family back together, Cook invited her and David Anable back to the newsroom for lunch. It was the first time either had returned since resigning.

Then, before he had even collected his award, Rohde bolted to *The New York Times*. Cook was angry, and Rohde's action still galls him. If there's one thing Cook expects and gives, it's loyalty. It wasn't the first time a star reporter had left the paper for better pay and more prestige, but the way it was done, suddenly and after so much had been invested to save his life, was jarring.

For his part, Rohde says he had been in touch with the *Times* for several years and had already received an offer before he got word that he had won the Pulitzer. "I thought it was my one chance to go to the *Times*," he says.

In looking back at his career—which includes another Pulitzer, for the *Times*, in 2008—he is happy to give the *Monitor* its due. "At the *Monitor*, you have a freedom to look at stories off the news," he says. "For the *Times*, you are working with lots of other people and have a lot more resources [but] you focus on the straight story of the day, the whole paper-of-record thing. It's much looser with the *Monitor*. In some ways, the *Monitor* is more creative in its coverage."

Exhausted

The *Monitor* was getting noticed again. Circulation, however, continued to drop. By 1997, the paper's paid subscriptions stood at 77,000, a third of its historic high. Deficits hovered at about $17 million a year. Advertising continued to be low.

After the spanking they had received from the membership, the Directors were not going to let the paper fold. They agreed to join the rest of the newspaper industry and to begin exploring what the World Wide Web could do, and the paper started its own website at CSMonitor.com, in 1996. In 1998, there was another attempt to reform the paper's content and appearance through a new design and new sections. "It was a more modest and humble approach," Clay Jones says. "None of the grand gestures and movements of the 1980s." [10]

News of more changes, though, didn't impress the newspaper industry, which seemed again to be preparing the paper's obituary. Fanning gave Cook a vote of support, telling the *Boston Globe* that she was confident he had the *Monitor*'s best interests at heart. But the *Globe* just saw the move as a sign of desperation. [11] The new design fell flat. If there was to be a future for the *Monitor*, there would have to be more than cosmetic changes.

In the spring of 2001, the Directors told Cook his time was up. He admits that the news was a surprise. "[The Directors and I] had had no trouble," he says. He tried to be generous. "While six months ago, I did not expect to be standing here as the soon-to-be-former editor of the *Monitor*," he told the newsroom on May 19, 2001, when the decision was announced, "I feel the Board's decision is the right one for the *Monitor,* and for me and my family. Different times call for different editors. We offer the gifts we have to give when they are needed."

Cook admits he was exhausted, and he prefers to look at the decision now as one of compassion. "The Board was being kind to me," he says. "I did the job for seven years, and radio and TV before that. Being editor is very different from other jobs. You tend to get calls like, 'We need ideas for a million dollars in cuts in the next two hours.'" He was sure he wouldn't miss that part.

He moved to Washington to become chief of the paper's bureau there and host of the Monitor Breakfasts started by Budge Sperling.

The right questions

In his place, the Directors appointed former international news editor Paul van Slambrouck. In 1997, he had returned from the *San Jose Mercury-News*, where he had been deputy managing editor in charge of daily news meetings and Page One decisions for the Sunday paper. Since 1997, he had been the *Monitor*'s San Francisco bureau chief.

"I felt I was pretty prepared for the job," he says. As one of his first acts, he gathered the main editorial team, with a consultant, in the auditorium of the church's Sunday School for a half-day retreat. "What's our story?" was the theme. Each member of the team was asked to tell why he or she worked at the *Monitor*. Then the group discussed what made the *Monitor* special and how that affected its work. "What are we going to give our readers that's unique?" van Slambrouck asked them. [12] There was no conclusion, but he stressed that asking the right questions was important.

If the *Monitor* was going to make it out of the wilderness alive, it was going to have to bring more than conventional management exercises to the task. But van Slambrouck understood that it was time for the *Monitor* to step up again. Coming together as a family had been vital for its survival, but it was not enough to make a great newspaper.

More reporters began returning. "Paul was permission for other people to come back," Gail Russell Chaddock says.

"We could rebuild on the stone that was rejected." [13]

But the evidence of decline was still strong. Circulation was now a little over 71,000. Numbers didn't tell a completely negative story: 600,000 visitors were now coming to CSMonitor.com every month, viewing millions of pages. But a decade after the paper had almost died, it was still not clear why it deserved to live.

Cartoons and disasters

On September 11, 2001, Clay Bennett had been awake since 5 A.M., drawing the *Monitor*'s editorial cartoon for the next issue. The TV in his home was tuned to CNN.

Bennett was a veteran of the business. He had spent, as he puts it, "Eleven wonderful years at the *St. Petersburg Times*. Unfortunately I was there thirteen." [14] When a new editor came along with more conservative politics, the two could not coexist, and Bennett was fired, in 1994.

"I quickly realized there weren't any papers lining up to hire me," he says. Working out of a downtown studio in St. Petersburg, Florida, he began taking on freelance assignments and training students at an art institute in the basics of animation and Photoshop. Then, out of frustration, he stopped drawing altogether. "I did everything shy of squeegeeing people's windshields," he says. He was sure his career in newspapers was over.

In early 1997, he heard that the *Monitor*'s cartoonist had quit, and he submitted his resume. After months of waiting, he was invited for an interview.

After his experience with the *St. Petersburg Times*, he was prepared for questions about his politics. But the *Monitor* was more interested in the kind of person he was and the kind of life he was leading. He didn't pretend to be a Christian Scientist or to understand the religion, but having read the newspaper for years, he felt comfortable with its spirit.

I'm not a mean guy. I'm a very nice guy. There

> *were a lot of things we didn't share, but there were a lot of things we did share. . . . I trust that man can do better and will do better. In a way we were very kindred, though maybe not in our lifestyles.*

He wanted the job badly. "Look, Dave," he told Cook, "I can tell you right off the bat, I drink and I smoke and I cuss right out loud. I may not be the perfect person for this job. But I may very well be the perfect cartoonist for this job."

Cook agreed. What he and his colleagues saw in Bennett was someone who was issue-oriented, who wouldn't engage in character assassination and cheap shots.

The day after Christmas, a FedEx delivery man rang the bell of Bennett's mother's house in Huntsville, Alabama, where he was spending the holidays. In his hand was a contract from the *Monitor*. Bennett is still in awe. "That was the day my career was saved," he says. "They showed a lot of faith in me. I worked harder than I ever worked in a job. If I was going to fail, it wasn't going to be because of lack of effort."

By 2001, Bennett was a veteran *Monitor* staffer. He had come to see that the challenge in working for the *Monitor* wasn't the cartooning itself. It was the *Monitor*'s approach to the news:

> *I had been reading the paper for years. What surprised me wasn't the limitations they put on you, it was the restrictions. There were things you couldn't do. They didn't like the sense of hopelessness, or doom and gloom, or sensationalism. I wasn't above a good gut punch. But you had to be very clever in the way you went about that at the* Monitor.

He couldn't use certain medical images as metaphors, such as a syringe. He had to avoid images of death—no grim reapers or even graves. About one in ten of his cartoons was killed. By contrast, at the *St. Petersburg Times*, one in fifty of his cartoons had been rejected.

"[A rejection at the *Monitor*] was a very small percentage of the time about politics," he says. "It was almost always not about what I was addressing but how I was addressing it. It was about the tone of the cartoon. Injure no man."

Precisely what "injure no man" meant constantly eluded him. "What is injuring?" he would ask people, half jokingly. "If the guy gets over it in a week or two, has he been injured? Is it no harm, no foul?"

His philosophy became "let me draw what I want to draw, and you publish what you want to publish. As long as the disparity is not too great we can work with this." He learned to accept the process and wanted others to understand his reaction when his ideas were killed. "I'm just upset," he would tell people. "Give me a few minutes and I'll be back to normal."

Bennett never resented the process. "It most definitely made me a better cartoonist," he says.

> *Every day wasn't a delight. Self-censorship was the hardest. I didn't draw some things I wanted to. The worst part was the uncertainty. But I respected the reasons my cartoons were killed. I respected them more than I respected why they were killed at other papers. At other papers, it was pure politics. At the* Monitor, *they were committed to a higher form of journalism.*

Religion itself rarely entered into the discussion, he says. He would have theological conversations with other staffers, joke about whether time was real and if not, why are we so obsessed with deadlines? But he found the religious touch in the newsroom light. "Even the daily article on Christian Science wasn't real preachy or proselytizing," he says. "Where the Christian Science philosophy was woven into other pieces it was an undercurrent, very subtly, beautifully done.

Catching the right tone

A little after 9 A.M. on the morning of September 11, Bennett was distracted by CNN's reports of a passenger plane crashing into the North Tower of the World Trade Center. He put his pen down and watched, puzzled. It must have been a horrific accident, he thought, like the bomber that hit the Empire State Building, in 1945. But that morning was foggy. This day, the sky was blue.

Then the second plane hit. Now he was stunned. It had to be terrorism, he thought. He switched gears on the day's cartoon and began thinking about how to treat what he saw in front of him. Experience told him there was a logical approach:

> *As a cartoonist, drawing about a national tragedy is always difficult. The first cartoon you draw should never be angry or analytical, but instead simply an expression of sorrow or loss. If you can simply depict what happened and the grief related to it, you've earned your keep for that day.*

What came out of his pen was an American flag, its stripes extending upward. The last two stripes resembled the smoldering towers of the World Trade Center. The flag itself appeared to be burning. The image was raw and full of sorrow, exactly what Bennett was aiming for.

He finished the line art, scanned it into his computer, applied the finishing touches in Photoshop, and emailed it to his editors.

"I never have a backup cartoon," he says. "If you have a backup cartoon the chances you'll kill my cartoon are increased. I wanted there to be a cost to rejecting one of my cartoons."

The Directors, who see every cartoon before it runs and who rarely explain their decisions, were willing to pay the cost. They rejected the drawing, and the editors ran a syndicated cartoon from another artist. Sorrow and loss were not the tone the Directors were looking for.

The next day, his cartoon made it into the paper. In the middle of a smoking pile of stones and steel stood a simple building, untouched and unintimidated. It was labeled "Resolve."

On day three, Bennett drew a cartoon attacking the easiest target of all, the terrorists. Who could object? A teacher was standing at the blackboard in front of a biology class. "Microbes are the lowest form of life," she had written on the board. But in her hand was a newspaper about September 11, and she was changing the sentence on the board to read "Microbes are the *second* lowest form of life."

That one was killed. "Injure no man" had to apply to terrorists as well.

Bennett struggled with his emotions. He had been nominated for a Pulitzer Prize four years in a row now without winning, and when the week had begun, he had his hopes up:

> *I knew everything in journalism [that year] was going to be judged by what happened after September 11, and [all but one] of my cartoons had been rejected outright. I thought for sure any chance I had for a Pulitzer that year went out the window. I remember getting Clay Jones [now editorial page editor] on the phone, and I'm bitching at him. "You guys are ruining my chance of winning a Pulitzer!" And Clay said, "You don't work for the Pulitzer Prize, you work for* The Christian Science Monitor.*" He was right. I calmed down.*

Bennett kept trying to find the right approach that still had some bite. On September 20, he drew an American family at home, peering out of what looked like a prison window. "I guess it was easier than putting the terrorists behind bars," read the caption. The cartoon's target was the restrictions on civil liberties, in the name of safety, which had grown since September 11. That one ran.

The next day, he took on the perversion of Islam,

showing rows of men in simple white robes bowed in prayer, with one man facing the opposite direction, weapons strapped to his back. That one was accepted too. He addressed hate crimes, the missing smiles of Americans, and the Bush Administration's attempts to get the economy moving again by urging people to go shopping. In October, he attacked the Patriot Act, which permitted increased government intrusion on Americans' privacy. "The *Monitor* let me jump all over that," he says. "Looking back, you didn't see too many cartoons decrying terrorism, but a lot decrying the reflexive action toward terrorism."

Finally

On the afternoon of Monday, April 8, 2002, Bennett sat with his wife, Cindy, in Clay Jones's office. The announcement of the 2001 Pulitzer winners would come at 3 P.M. To his surprise, Bennett was one of the finalists again, and he was nervous. An hour before, he had gone out for coffee. As he crossed Massachusetts Avenue to return to the office, he was extra careful. Wouldn't want to get run over by a car right before winning the Pulitzer, he thought.

The time dragged. No one talked to him, as if he were a baseball pitcher with a no-hitter in the works. At three o'clock, Jones pulled up the Associated Press wire service feed on his computer and started reading the results. Finally, Jones read Bennett's name, then leaped from his chair and hugged his cartoonist. In a year when every cartoonist had tackled the same profound issues, Bennett had come out on top. He was in a daze.

Jones immediately marched me out to the newsroom where the Monitor *staff awaited. Speeches were made, and much sparkling water was consumed. They sure know how to throw a party in Boston.*

Life as a cartoonist changed for him. It wasn't the

recognition. No one stops a Pulitzer-winning cartoonist on Boylston Street and asks for his autograph. It was the expectation he put on himself. "I felt an incredible responsibility to prove the Pulitzer judges right," he says. "I would never approach a cartoon in quite the same way again." There came a constant pressure to produce work at the highest level every day.

He stayed around for five more years, but in 2007, he was offered a job he couldn't turn down, at the *Chattanooga Times Free Press* in Chattanooga, Tennessee. He would be living close to his parents, and he was anxious for the opportunity to deal again with the simple straightforwardness of local news. He would also have freedom he could only dream about at the *Monitor*.

On his last day at the *Monitor,* he stood up in the newsroom. "I'm really looking forward to injuring man again," he told the staff to laughter. "When I first got here, I didn't really understand the limitations, but now, ten years later, I still don't understand."

Reflecting on his time at the *Monitor*, he is grateful. "I was an odd duck there, but I really liked all those people," he says. "Maybe I was the weird uncle that embarrassed them at the family outing, but they really took me in as family."

"Why do they hate us?"

For the *Monitor* to really shine, it has to take on the big crises of humanity with the kind of bold love that heals. Not every attempt works. When September 11, 2001, arrived, Bennett struggled to get the approach right. But for him and the senior editors at the paper, it was clear what the day meant. "There was a strong feeling that this was the kind of story we were here to do," says Marshall Ingwerson, who had come from covering the White House to serve as managing editor. [15]

Van Slambrouck reminded the staff of what he had told them when he arrived. "In early press coverage [of 9/11] everyone was asking who did it," he says, "how will we get them, the number of bodies. But we decided to put our stamp on things by asking the right questions."

The key question, he and his senior editors decided, was not what happened, but why. Specifically, why is America so hated? Realizing that there was a lot of support around the world for what the terrorists had done, they dispatched *Monitor* correspondents to the slums of Pakistan, the dusty villages of Palestine, and the mosques of London to find out what Muslims really thought about America. The aim was to help heal the fear and hate that had exploded.

The answers that came back were surprising. It wasn't a revelation that many Muslims resented the United States. It was how far this resentment had spread into the educated parts of Muslim society, especially to those who also had reason to like America.

"There was a certain satisfaction that someone had taken a swing at the U.S.," van Slambrouck recalls. "Someone had kicked the bully in the shins. We decided that was the real story. [Knowing what Muslims really thought] could help prevent something like this in the future. Our readers would be best served by understanding the currents running beneath the surface."

"Let's do something simple and do it well," he told the staff.

A little more than a week after September 11, President Bush addressed a joint session of Congress and put forward the same question the *Monitor* was contemplating:

> *Americans are asking "Why do they hate us?"*
> *They hate what they see right here in this chamber: a democratically elected government. Their leaders are self-appointed. They hate our freedoms: our freedom of religion, our freedom of speech, our freedom to vote and assemble and disagree with each other. . . .*
> *We're not deceived by their pretenses to piety.*
> *We have seen their kind before. They're the heirs of all the murderous ideologies of the 20th century.* [16]

The speech tried for hope and resolve; it ended with venom, feeding the compulsion to begin attacking the Muslim world.

The *Monitor* tried to steer things in a different direction. Discovering that hatred for the United States was more ambivalent and yet deeper than the thin veneer of terrorism, it concluded that not vengeance but light was needed.

On September 27, the paper published a long article called "Why do they hate us?" It was reported by correspondents around the world and written mainly by staff writer Peter Ford:

> *The vast majority of Muslims in the Middle East were as shocked and horrified as any American by what they saw happening on their TV screens. And they are frightened of being lumped together in the popular American imagination with the perpetrators of the attack.*
>
> *But from Jakarta to Cairo, Muslims and Arabs say that on reflection, they are not surprised by it. And they do not share Mr. Bush's view that the perpetrators did what they did because "they hate our freedoms."*
>
> *Rather, they say, a mood of resentment toward America and its behavior around the world has become so commonplace in their countries that it was bound to breed hostility, and even hatred.* [17]

Two of the people the *Monitor* talked to were Saniya and Bassem Ghussein, a mother and father in Beirut who loved the United States. Bassem had worked for an American company for twenty years and took the family on vacations to Disney World.

They had been living in Tripoli, Libya, in 1986, when the United States started dropping bombs in response to the bombing of a disco in Berlin, Germany, ten days before. Sixty-three American soldiers had been killed, and the Reagan Administration blamed Libyan leader Muammar Quaddafi.

During one horrendous night, the Ghussein's home was leveled, and Bassem found himself trapped beneath the rubble. Saniya rushed to check on one of their daughters, and Bassem received the news he most feared:

> *"Bassem," she cried. "Raafat has gone."*
> *. . . Bassem heard his wife's words, and he felt a deep sense of anger and resentment well up inside him. His life and that of his family had been shattered, and nothing would ever be the same again.* [18]

Bassem and Saniya held America responsible for their daughter's death, and for sixteen years they had refused to return to a country they loved. They hated religious extremism and condemned the September 11 attacks, but they blamed America's "arrogant" policies in the Middle East for giving rise to the resentment behind the attacks.

Further on, the article described how people lined up every day outside the American embassy in Sana, Yemen, to apply for visas. Yet the ambivalence of Yeminis was clear:

> *"When you go there, you really love the United States," says Murad al-Murayri, a US-trained physicist. "You are treated like a human being, much better than in your own country. But when you go back home, you find the US applies justice and fairness to its own people, but not abroad. In this era of globalization, that cannot stand."* [19]

Al-Murayri, the Ghusseins, and many others interviewed were people who liked the United States and appreciated at least some of its values. Like Americans, they cringed when they saw the mayhem of September 11. But for years, they had felt their love for America unrequited, their voices ignored, and their talents pushed away.

The article's theme was "Love your enemies," and readers came away, not with fear and loathing, not wondering at the strangeness of Muslim passions or agape at the hatred that killed multitudes, but with a compassion for the many people who had suffered and seen their loved ones—and their own ideals—die.

And, suddenly, there was the *Monitor*. What on prior days had tended toward an ordinary, sometimes boring newspaper had turned to some degree into a deeply understanding, compassionate, and religious one, and it seemed the lightning might start flashing again. The sense of prophecy that Takashi Oka had looked for, with the spiritual view of reality overwhelming the material, had reappeared. A tone of confidence showed itself, as if the paper knew it had what humanity needed. Wrestling with the unleashed fears and hatred that the U.S. government was encouraging, trying to find the love that would bring some measure of healing to American and world thought, the *Monitor* was looking like itself again.

Questions return

The Christian Science Monitor News Service, sending published articles to other news outlets for reuse, showed a burst of success after September 11, as other news organizations latched onto the *Monitor*'s expertise in foreign news.

But as 9/11 faded from the front pages, the *Monitor* found itself back in its old quandary. The causes and effects of the tragedy still lurked, bursting out in more suicide bombings and in the American invasion of Iraq. The world still needed the confident, incisive, and calming influence of the *Monitor*. But the paper's deficit still hovered around $20 million a year, making it difficult to respond to the need with any consistency or depth. And high-priced church projects, including a new $50 million Mary Baker Eddy Library and a $55 million renovation of the church grounds, were again sucking cash. "We were always able to do the biggest right thing we had to do," insists van Slambrouck. But resources were thin.

The Directors instituted more cuts in operations. For the church as a whole, 125 jobs were eliminated, nearly a quarter of its staff. The paper's budget was reduced for reporters' travel expenses, and its page count was taken down from twenty-four to twenty. Van Slambrouck bravely told the *Boston Globe* that the aim was to energize the paper, not diminish it. But the signs were not encouraging. [20]

The paper was far from alone in its financial struggles. Circulation of English-language newspapers was down eleven percent since 1990. Television network news was down thirty-four percent since 1994. Cable news, which once had such a promising future, was flat. All the news media were beginning to realize that their business models had fundamental weaknesses.

But the *Monitor* faced deeper problems. Despite the brilliance of "Why do they hate us," the paper still struggled to escape the mire into which it had fallen after Fanning left. Cook had brought back a sense of family, but the sense of maturity that had consistently characterized the paper under DeWitt John and, to some degree, Fanning—the gentle encouragement and insight, punctuated by breakthrough articles and series that illuminated some problem in ways that could bring healing—largely eluded the paper.

One indication of where the *Monitor* stood was the fact that some of its staff had an uncertain understanding of the paper's mission. An article published toward the end of 2004, detailing the environmental problems growing in Iraq after the American invasion the year before, concluded graphically that people were getting sick. It was an odd story for the *Monitor*:

> *At the landfill, atop a cinder block, four-year-old Muhammad sits playing with a salvaged aluminum knife. His father roots for scrap metal.*
>
> *Muhammad has a cough from the smoke, but he likes the landfill. His father says the cough is just a cold: he doesn't know that burning plastic releases dioxin, or that the greasy smoke they breathe all day could hurt his son's lungs.*
>
> *"Someone, somewhere, pays the price of*

development," says [environmental engineer Amin] Barzanji. "In the short term, these people will be paying the price. In the long term, everyone will. [21]

After so much effort spent eliciting understanding and love for the Muslim world in response to 9/11, the *Monitor* was now fastening an image of inevitable illness and death on one slice of it. For Christian Scientists, it was close to malpractice, injuring mankind much more than blessing it.

Correspondent Charlotte Saikowski had been healed of an illness when she realized she had absorbed fears about the health consequences of pollution. But Saikowski and other veterans were long gone, and the *Monitor* now struggled to maintain a consistent message. There was news to report, and much healing to accomplish, on environmental problems in Iraq. The *Monitor* was not pulling its weight.

Finances, however, were what dominated the conversation at the church. The Directors told van Slambrouck that the paper had to break even by 2008 and be profitable by 2009.[22] They tasked the Trustees with finding a way to cut costs while sacrificing as little as possible of the *Monitor*'s value. Both boards were as concerned as ever that the deficits could bankrupt the church.

The Trustees hired John Hughes as a consultant, along with newspaper consulting firm Urban and Associates of Boston, the one that had advised Fanning and her task force. They brought several members of the *Monitor*'s senior staff into the process, creating another task force on the *Monitor*'s future.

"The Trustees were clearly under the gun by the Directors," Hughes says. "The first thing they wanted to do was make an appraisal of the staff." [23] Hughes conducted interviews, giving staffers a promise of anonymity. He got the honesty he was looking for:

> *They admitted morale was dreadful. There was a slender tier of people who knew what the* Monitor *was about at the top, [and towards the bottom] there were a*

*lot of young guys who had not been employees for long
and were punching a card before going on to other
things. Between the two there was not much in the way
of staff.*

"You've got a serious rebuilding job to do," he told the Trustees.

The task force also conducted an extensive financial analysis of the daily and what it would take to eliminate the deficit, along with a market analysis and focus groups on a print weekly, eventually creating two prototypes.

A solution for the persistently high costs began to emerge. Hughes looked again and again at the figures, but he couldn't avoid what he calls a "distressing" conclusion. "I never thought I would say this," he told the Trustees, "but you don't have any option but to go all Web."

Backed into a corner after decades of unsolved financial problems, having already chosen to cut loose hundreds of years of experience for the sake of a risky and failed pursuit of television, the church had to face the conclusion that the *Monitor* was now only occasionally its former self. In desperation, it was being forced to consider cutting costs in the only way it could see, by eliminating the printed daily paper. Here they were again, at the same crossroads of two decades before: replacing the daily with a new media venture.

It might be the final blow for a proud institution, or if it was done right this time, and if other problems, notably the quality of its staff, could be solved, it might mean its rebirth.

A practitioner on the case

One member of the task force was former director Richard Bergenheim, who had been the director chosen to read the Board's near-apology to the church, in 1993. He had left the Board in 1994 and returned to his Christian Science teaching and healing practice in New York.

The Directors had kept in touch with Bergenheim and

respected his views on the *Monitor*. They also saw the paper struggling and felt that it needed more full-time spiritual guidance. Bergenheim made a presentation to them on the *Monitor*, which so impressed them that they began thinking he might be an answer to a lot of their problems.

"The Board felt we needed a [Christian Science] practitioner on the case," says Mary Trammell. [24] A former professor of English literature, she had been a full-time practitioner herself since 1983 and had served as editor of the *Journal, Sentinel,* and *Herald* before joining the Board in 2001. In 2004, still a director, she had also become editor in chief of The Christian Science Publishing Society, serving as Board liaison for the *Monitor* and the other publications.

"The *Monitor* was bringing the church into a difficult financial situation," she says. "It had great potential, but the debt was increasing, and we needed someone who could really pray his way through the situation."

By May 2005, Bergenheim was the new editor of the *Monitor*. Trammell announced the change in the newsroom, welcoming Bergenheim and giving van Slambrouck a generous send-off as "an immensely skillful steward of the *Monitor* during a remarkably eventful period in world history." The Board seemed to have learned that speaking "kindly when we meet and part"—the words of a poem by Mrs. Eddy—went a long way toward developing good feelings for the *Monitor* inside the church. [25] It was an encouraging sign that, this time, things might be different.

Van Slambrouck, for his part, tried to be a good soldier. "All I can say is that the Board's highest sense of what the *Monitor* needed led to that change at that time," he says. "Therefore it was the right thing."

Bergenheim's relationship with the paper was as much personal as professional. His father, Robert, had been a *Monitor* reporter who had won a Neiman Fellowship at Harvard and then risen to manager of the Publishing Society, the same job Jack Hoagland and his father had held. Robert expected at one point to be named editor, but he eventually became publisher of the

Boston Herald and started the *Boston Business Journal*. For Richard, being asked to be editor was "an emotionally charged moment," according to David Cook, who knew him well.

Richard had worked briefly as a *Monitor* copy kid in the 1960s, his only experience in a newsroom. He had gone on to earn a master's degree from the Shakespeare Institute at England's University of Birmingham and worked as an English teacher before becoming a Christian Science practitioner, in 1974. As a director, he had served as editor in chief of the Publishing Society, largely an oversight role. He was the fourth Christian Science teacher to serve as *Monitor* editor.

"He could be very warm," says Marshall Ingwerson, who served him as managing editor, as he had served van Slambrouck. "When people had problems, he treated them like a [Christian Science] practitioner. He went straight into [prayer] mode. He was very, very kind, very human."

He was not a journalist, however, nor was he a strong manager. "Richard wasn't the sort of guy who spelled out a strategic vision," says Ingwerson. "He was very tactical. He was always taking off from where we are today. He would throw out ideas in machine-gun fashion, and he would drive some people crazy."

Running the newsroom somewhat like a high-school classroom, the only other place where he had been in charge of a group of people, Bergenheim would come up with an idea for a story or a way to pursue one, then push it until people responded. If anyone raised problems with his idea, he would often take it on himself to find a way to solve the problems, even if the problems had only been raised to try to get him to back off. He didn't mind people questioning him. The one thing he hated was being ignored. Reporters and editors called his forays into the newsroom "drive-bys."

Ingwerson respected Bergenheim's intensity. "He had a phenomenal mental energy," he says. Bergenheim would arrive at work each morning having read a number of American and foreign news sources online, including blogs. And he wouldn't just read. Staffers would get emails from him any hour of the night about a story idea or something he'd come across.

Besides his own challenges as a manager, Bergenheim faced the ever-present budgetary problems. Given the Board's mandate to break even in three years, Bergenheim had to lay off about a dozen staff members. The money saved went into the business side. A new head of advertising sales and a new director of business development were hired.

Prayer in action

On January 10, 2006, the *Monitor* published an extraordinary notice on its front page:

> *Jill Carroll, a freelance journalist currently on assignment for* The Christian Science Monitor, *was abducted by unknown gunmen in Baghdad Saturday morning. Her Iraqi interpreter was killed during the kidnapping. . . .*
>
> *The body of the interpreter, Allan Enwiyah, 32, was later found in the same neighborhood. He had been shot twice in the head, law enforcement officials said. There has been no word yet on Carroll's whereabouts.* [26]

Carroll and Enwiyah had just visited Adnan al-Dulaimi, a Sunni politician, for a prescheduled interview. When the interview was postponed, they left for Carroll's next appointment. As they started to drive away, they were stopped, and the brutal kidnapping began.

About an hour later—4:30 A.M. Boston time—someone from CBS News in New York called Marshall Ingwerson at home, asking for confirmation of the incident. Ingwerson got dressed quickly and headed to the office to meet international editor David Scott. Scott had already heard from the *Monitor*'s Baghdad reporter, Scott Peterson. Bergenheim was in Mexico on vacation and couldn't be reached.

Talking through what to do, Ingwerson and Scott decided they had to throw everything they could at saving

Carroll. They launched "Team Jill."

About two hours after Ingwerson and Scott arrived at the *Monitor* office, TV trucks stormed the church plaza. Editors of other papers called to offer advice. An FBI special agent told Ingwerson she was on the way to help him and the staff prepare in case a ransom call came in.

When Bergenheim finally heard the news, he cut short his vacation and flew back to Boston. By early Sunday morning, he was at his desk.

One of his first acts was to hire Carroll *in absentia*. As a freelancer, she received no benefits. As an employee, however, she would be able to receive medical care as well as time off to recuperate when she was released. Not only was the act compassionate, but it showed where Bergenheim's prayers were going. Carrying the confidence he had built up over many years of healing people through prayer, he expected her to be released.

For two days, there was no word about the kidnapping in any news media. On the advice of a network of Iraq correspondents, the *Monitor* had asked other news organizations to hold information about Carroll to see if a quick resolution might come while the atmosphere was still relatively calm. By Monday, however, CNN and the Associated Press said they had to go with the story. Ingwerson asked for one more hour, during which the *Monitor* put the basic details of the kidnapping on its website and prepared a statement from Bergenheim.

Meanwhile, Team Jill became a focal point for the Boston newsroom. Working from early morning to close to midnight every day, keeping in touch with the FBI, CIA, and other government offices, Jordanian intelligence, a security firm in Baghdad, and various local contacts in Iraq, *Monitor* staffers did what they could to help find Carroll. With Bergenheim's permission, Iraq correspondents Scott Peterson and Dan Murphy put aside much of their reporting duties to chase down leads.

After a few weeks, the intensity died down, but as with David Rohde in Bosnia and Elizabeth Pond in Cambodia,

Carroll was now part of the family. Bergenheim was not going to let her die. He was going to try to flood any fear out of the environment with aggressive, positive reporting as well as his own forceful involvement and relentless prayer.

The paper published stories about Carroll as well as her interpreter, painting a portrait of someone who was not only a dedicated and objective reporter but a passionate ally of Iraq and Iraqis. Carroll had written a story about a poor Iraqi family, which had prompted *Monitor* readers to send money, and she had personally delivered the money to the family. Ingwerson called a Baghdad TV station and told the owner about the story and the contributions, and the station sent a crew to film the family. Carroll became known throughout Iraq.

On January 19, twelve days after the kidnapping, with Carroll under a public death threat with a deadline, the *Monitor* published an anonymous religious article that defined explicitly what the paper was asking of its readers. "I ask myself," the writer said, "What will I—an avid consumer of news and a newly minted fan of Jill's work, but far from the scene of events—do with these remaining hours and minutes? I resolve: I will not squander them. I will not give these moments over to fear, to despair, and definitely not over to anger or vengeance. But can I consecrate these moments to prayer? Yes, I can." [27]

In print and online, the *Monitor* continued to publish frequent updates on Carroll's situation, along with coverage of events about her, such as a mass rally in Paris on her behalf. Wanting to be sure everyone was embraced in prayers, the paper quoted Muslim leaders who decried the kidnapping and published an article about three kidnapped activists who were found unguarded and alone, but safe. Carroll was not among them, but the article carried a tone of rejoicing for those freed.

The result that everyone labored for finally came. On March 30, Carroll walked into the Sunni Iraqi Islamic Party in Western Baghdad, freed by her kidnappers.

The *Monitor*'s editorial that day took the same tone of gratitude and hope that the paper's coverage had taken throughout the ordeal. It spoke of the courage not only of

Carroll but also of her family and those who had helped, including Muslim clerics. It praised the courage of those who stood "for freedom of expression, freedom of religion, freedom of association, and for lives free from oppression and violence."[28]

The Carroll coverage was, in a way, a bookend to "Why do they hate us?" It brought the universality and power of the affection for humanity expressed in the 9/11 article down to the level of practical freedom for an individual.

After her return to the *Monitor*, Carroll became a reporter again, covering issues involving the war, the military, the Middle East, and anti-terrorism efforts. On July 23, 2008, she wrote her last article for the paper, then resigned to become a firefighter in Fairfax County, Virginia. To this day, she refuses to talk for publication about her time in Iraq.

The Carroll story was the highlight of Bergenheim's tenure as editor. As the Directors seemed to sense from the beginning, his qualities as a Christian Science practitioner were what the paper needed, and he gave another push to the development of a pattern for *Monitor* effectiveness that could work independently of financial conditions: Take a crisis and let the urgency of focused prayer shape the response. It had been hinted at in Takashi Oka's "The World's Struggle for Resources" and given profound definition in "Why do they hate us?" Bergenheim had applied it in the most practical terms on behalf of a frightened woman at the center of the world's attention.

Now the paper needed to create the same sense of urgency, not just for crises but for every day.

Web first

By 2005, it had become evident that the Internet was an inescapable part of the future for newspapers. Late that year, John Yemma took the job of deputy managing editor for multimedia at the *Boston Globe*, in charge of the editorial operations of the paper's website. He set to work building the

Globe's online video capacity and encouraged reporters and editors to become involved in the multimedia efforts. Diplomatic and determined, Yemma helped the *Globe* make the transition to the new digital era.

As he had with other *Monitor* editors, Yemma would come over from the *Globe* and have lunch from time to time with Bergenheim. He was always open to helping the *Monitor*, even as he was building up the Web operations of the crosstown *Globe*. The papers were in the same city, but their readerships were very different, and they did not see each other as direct competitors.

"Richard was brilliant," Yemma says, "such a forward thinker. We would compare notes [about where the *Monitor* was going digitally]."

Bergenheim was convinced that the *Monitor*'s future lay mainly on the Internet. Twenty years earlier, he had been a quiet champion of the efforts to give the *Monitor* a strong electronic identity, and he had lost none of his enthusiasm over the years. Where Harvey Wood and Jack Hoagland had tried to muscle the church into the new media era, Bergenheim worked more genially to make it acceptable for church members to embrace the future. In his first month on the job, he called the million-plus visitors to the *Monitor*'s website "probably the most significant development in the history of the *Monitor*."

In the spring of 2008, Yemma had one of his lunches with Bergenheim. Yemma was used to propositions to rejoin the *Monitor*, and when Bergenheim broached the subject, Yemma told him again that he'd love to but was happy at the *Globe*.

A few days later, Bergenheim asked him to lunch again. This time, he told him the *Monitor* was doing another strategic analysis of its future. Would he be willing to have lunch with the Board of Trustees?

Soon he was sitting with the Trustees and Director Mary Trammell, and looking at two prototypes of the print weekly that had been developed by the Hughes task force. If the *Monitor* decided to explore a different direction, Trammel asked him, which one would he think would be the best approach?

"I think these are great," Yemma said diplomatically, "but this is a false choice. The choice has to be where you are digitally. You can't put print first." He recommended going with the least-cost option as a temporary measure, but he made it clear that he believed that the days of print were numbered.

The *Monitor*, he said, needed a robust Web strategy, one that saw CSMonitor.com as the daily *Monitor*. After all, he said, a 24-hour Web presence was "more daily than the five-day-a-week print paper could hope to be both in frequency and timeliness. The Web allowed *Monitor* journalism to be in the moment, to respond to the immediate human need when thought can be most fearful because of a breaking news event or a media report."

A few weeks later, he was sitting again with Trammell and the chairman of the Board of Trustees, Walter Jones. What would make it worth Yemma's while to come back to the *Monitor* as editor? they asked. Yemma was still reluctant. His *Globe* career was solid. His wife, Robin, urged him to stay put.

But he didn't like shutting doors. He approached Bergenheim, who confirmed that he didn't want to be editor any longer and would rather go back to New York and resume his teaching and healing practice. "I'm not sure that was the full story," Yemma says, "but that is how he cast it."

Bergenheim left no doubt as to what the Directors wanted. "If anyone should succeed me," he said, "it should be you."

Yemma thought about it, prayed about it, talked to Robin about it. At the *Globe*, he had been working in many of the areas that the *Monitor* was starting to explore. If any paper should make the transition to the Web, he reasoned, the *Monitor* should. Unlike the *Globe*, it had no geographical circulation area to protect, and it had a history of delivery problems. The online era made physical distribution highly anachronistic, Yemma reasoned.

He knew firsthand about the *Monitor*'s painful past in electronic journalism. "Jack and Netty's hearts were in the right place," he says. "If their methods proved not to work, it may have been they were before their time. [With] the conversation happening more and more on the Internet, the *Monitor* seemed the perfect news organization in a networked world."

Yemma was also tired of the layers of people he had to wade through every time he wanted to do something different at the *Globe*—owners at *The New York Times*, *Globe* editors, staff, middle management. At the *Monitor*, by contrast, he would have a much more streamlined hierarchy to work with and could presumably make changes faster. He also had reached as high as he felt he could at the *Globe*.

He had watched news organizations struggle with the new era of online news, and he had ideas on what they should do. He liked the idea of leading change, not just being part of it. "The *Monitor* was ready," he says. "It just seemed as though things aligned."

Robin finally agreed that John should try. "It felt like a sacrifice," she says, "but lots of people sacrifice for a worthy cause. It seemed right, timely, necessary."

On June 9, 2008, the Directors made it official: John Yemma would become the new editor in mid-July. Bergenheim would become president of The Mother Church, an honorary position, for one year, often given to those who have contributed significantly to the church.

David Cook knew Bergenheim well, and he knows that leaving was neither voluntary nor happy for him. "After giving your whole heart to the task, being replaced is a searing experience," Cook says, "even if the removal is handled with kindness, as it certainly was in both Richard's and my case."

On Bergenheim's last day in the newsroom, Marshall Ingwerson gave him a send-off with special praise for bringing the *Monitor* closer to a digital future. "Richard was nodding vigorously," Ingwerson says.

Bergenheim soon set out on a six-week tour of Christian Science churches to encourage support for the *Monitor* and other church publications. On July 20, he and his wife, Phebe, were in Kansas City. The next day, Yemma would assume the editorship. It was Bergenheim's last official night in a position he cherished and for which he felt a calling. He went to sleep, looking toward the future and what he could do to help the *Monitor* embrace it, then got up early the next morning to work. About eight o'clock, Phebe awoke and saw him sitting motionless on the hotel room sofa. He had died. [29]

Cook wrote a tribute in the *Monitor* that ended with an excerpt from a talk Bergenheim had given to college students:

> *Think of the world as filled with friends. We don't let our friends be in trouble without trying to figure out how to help them. We care. And part of what the* Monitor *exists to do is increase the caring capacity of our hearts.* [30]

Bergenheim led the paper, and his life, with his heart.

The deed is (really) done

After Jack Hoagland left the Publishing Society, in 1992, he told a reporter from *Boston* magazine, referring to an electronic future for the *Monitor*, "I believe we'll get there, . . . Maybe not for years. But there's still a niche out there for what we were doing." [31]

By the fall of 2008, the problems with the business model for daily printed newspapers—increasingly expensive printing and distribution costs; online advertising vehicles that were often better than newspapers for reaching consumers; and, most of all, plenty of news and other information available for free on the Internet—made it apparent that print was not, or at least was not exclusively, the future of the news business. Yemma and the Directors decided that the *Monitor* finally had to move.

Yemma brought together ideas that had been put forward by the Hughes task force, the Trustees, and others, added his own, and got sign-off for a range of *Monitor*-related products he was confident would be sustainable: a print weekly distributed by mail; an emailed Daily News Briefing, a short version of the paper designed mainly for older readers who were intimidated by websites and wanted something they could print out; and CSMonitor.com, the *Monitor*'s website.

For many financial reasons, it seemed a good time to make dramatic changes. The paper's deficit, still around $15 million a year, showed no signs of falling. But church membership was falling, and it didn't appear wise to continue tolerating red ink, with contributions to the church possibly diminishing in the future. The paper's circulation was down to 56,000, and no one had any good ideas how to raise it again without massive spending on marketing, something that made little sense when it seemed a big part of the future might not be in print. The paper was spending massively on distribution by mail to a relatively small audience, and advertisers were still skeptical about the value of its older readers.

Going to the Web offered a tantalizing way to cut some major costs quickly and increase the size of the audience and, presumably, the advertising revenue it could bring. The news audience on the Web skewed younger than the audience for print products. Distribution would be much cheaper online. Although charging viewers for reading the paper electronically did not make sense for now, there were possibilities for packaging the news in creative ways that readers would pay for. One was the Daily News Briefing.

The *Monitor* had historically been appreciated most by people with time and an inclination for thoughtful reading as well as an interest in the kind of perspective that most dailies found hard to provide. The weekly, mailed out so readers would have it in time for more leisurely weekend reading, seemed to fit well with that part of the *Monitor*'s nature, especially when there was still a daily—or, more precisely, a minute-by-minute—product that could handle the increasingly rapid pace of news in the twenty-first century.

After a carefully orchestrated communication campaign, so that, this time, members wouldn't be blindsided by changes and would feel that they had been included rather than shunted aside, the Directors told members outright, in the October 29,

2008, *Monitor,* that the print daily would fold.

This time, almost twenty years after a threatened end for the paper produced one of the biggest crises in the history of the church, there was some nostalgia, but few tears. It did not mean that no one cared or that everyone thought the *Monitor* would now be a better news source. But public relations had been done well, and people could see that the times called for change. They were willing to give the paper a chance to adapt.

When the last issue finally came, on March 27, 2009, Yemma wrote an enthusiastic message to readers:

> *As of today, we are shedding print on a daily basis. But the* Monitor *itself—the century-old journalistic enterprise chronicling the world's challenges and progress—is becoming more daily than ever. And with the launch of our new weekly print edition, the* Monitor *is becoming more vital than ever.*
>
> *No longer inked on wood pulp, no longer trucked from printing plants to your mailbox, no longer published only five days a week, the daily Monitor is now a dynamic online newspaper on all days.* [32]

He described how the paper had been moving toward online publishing for more than a decade since CSMonitor.com first appeared. The site now had about two million unique visitors each month. He assured readers that the new *Monitor* was the same as the old one, only in different clothes. "We are making this shift to keep the *Monitor* relevant," he wrote, "and to move our journalistic mission toward financial sustainability." 33

Readers seemed to like what they saw. Ninety-one percent of subscribers to the daily converted their subscriptions to the weekly. Yemma took it as a vote of confidence in the new direction.

Nothing in the *Monitor*'s new look was really new. Richard Nenneman and others had advocated a weekly for years, and it had been experimented with several times. Jack

Hoagland had pushed his "black box" idea for printing an electronic version of the paper in the home, a product similar to the Daily News Briefing. And of course, Hoagland had tried to create a 24-hour version of the *Monitor* that people received simply by turning on a machine with a screen. This time it was not on television but on computers.

It was as if the *Monitor*'s history was coming full circle, and it helped make the changes seem inevitable.

Cutting the costs of printing and distributing the daily *Monitor* didn't mean the end of the deficits. "We lose money," Yemma said, a little over a year into the new venture. "Nothing we do makes money." But he worked with Publishing Society Manager Jonathan Wells, crafting a plan to cut the deficits progressively, and the coordination Hoagland had wanted for the *Monitor*'s editorial and business operations began happening without drama.

"Over a multiple-year period, we will lose less money every year till we break even," Yemma predicted. "So we will have to rely less and less on church funds and more on marketplace revenue."

For fiscal year 2010, which ended in April of that year, Yemma and Wells intended to hit a "contribution margin," or church subsidy, of $15.1 million. [34] They beat that by $500,000. Their aim for fiscal year 2011 was $13.3 million, and they beat it again by almost $700,000, bringing the deficit down to $12.6 million. For fiscal year 2012, during which this book was printed, they were on course to reach $10.8 million. They cut staff costs—the biggest cost category—mainly through attrition, using freelancers where possible. Revenue late in 2011 was mostly from subscriptions to the weekly print paper ($5.4 million a year), Web advertising ($1.1 million), print advertising ($330,000), the Daily News Briefing ($190,000), and syndication ($680,000). Yemma and Wells continued to look for ways to increase it all, and in October 2011, they were confident enough in the weekly to announce a rise in the annual subscription price from $89 to $119, throwing in a free digital edition for subscribers.

The *Monitor*'s midterm deficit goal was $7.2 million, which Yemma and Wells expected to reach by the end of fiscal year 2013. With the Monitor Endowment Fund at around $100 million and producing income of around $6 million a year, that would bring the church subsidy down to only $1.2 million. Using the endowment earnings for current expenses wasn't ideal, Yemma realized, but for the moment, everyone could live with that.

Ultimately, their aim was to see the subsidy drop to zero and the "contribution margin" then go positive, meaning that the *Monitor* would be self-sustaining. "A healthy enterprise should pull its own weight," Yemma said.

The Directors liked that approach. "It's not logical that Mrs. Eddy would start a publication that needed a subsidy," Director and Trustee Michael Pabst said. [35] Not surprisingly, he saw the deficit issue in metaphysical terms. "We are convinced that if you peel away fear, anger, hate," he said, "you'll see the *Monitor* will pay for itself."

Some people on the staff, especially some of those who had been at the *Monitor* since the Fanning-Cattani era, still harbored resentment about the television venture, believing that had it not occurred, the *Monitor* would not be under the financial pressure that led in part to the decision to go all Web. But the paper was under pressure at least a decade before Harvey Wood told the church to "gird up [its] loins," and to say that television was the cause of the problems the paper faced in the twenty-first century was to scapegoat a venture that, while painful in its failure, was more a symptom of the deeper problems Pabst referred to than a cause of lasting harm to the paper.

As they built up speed with the Web-first *Monitor*, Yemma and Wells developed a "unique value proposition," a marketing term that refers to the core value of a product for consumers. "Explaining world news to thoughtful people who care about solutions" is what they came up with—explaining, not just telling; world news, not just American; thoughtful people, not just those seeking sensationalism; solutions, not just problems.

The phrase was devised for internal use, Yemma said, and not to be a motto or to replace "to injure no man, but to bless all mankind," and it applied as much to marketing and advertising as to editorial. It was one of several tools he and Wells used to help manage, in Yemma's words, "a large group of creative people with different skills, motivations, adaptability, and career duration."

The phrase didn't appear to catch any of the paper's lightning, however, and it raised the uncomfortable question of how the *Monitor* was going to get where it still had to go with a phrase, as a principal internal guide, that any number of quality publications could come up with. But at least the *Monitor* now had editorial and business management that was working in the same direction and was willing to listen to what the market was saying. Wells defined the *Monitor*'s value as providing "solution-, progress-, and hope-driven journalism that still covers the reality of the world." [36] While it wasn't so carefully structured as the unique value proposition, it may have captured a little more of the *Monitor*'s uniqueness.

Yemma counted on viewers finding the *Monitor* through search engines and links as well as coming directly to CSMonitor.com. He gave attention to using Google Search and Yahoo! News in creative ways that would increase click-throughs to the *Monitor*'s website. "We embed *Monitor* values into the articles we produce and/or select from partners," he said, "so that readers become familiar with our special approach."

In part, the focus on developing readers through avenues other than the *Monitor*'s website was a way to get around the hesitation some people have about the *Monitor*'s name. Yemma said he hoped readers would see something different in *Monitor* articles and realize that the words "Christian Science" did not connote a proselytizing product or one that slanted the news. It may have been more of an indirect approach to attracting readers, but it was having some success: Eighty percent of readers were now coming through links and search engines.

A particular challenge for Yemma was producing traditional *Monitor* journalism amid the breakneck pace of the Web. With his relatively small staff and limited budget, it was hard to achieve consistent depth and accuracy. "We've shrunk a lot over the years," said staff writer Linda Feldmann, who covers the White House for the *Monitor*. "People are horribly overworked just to keep it all going." [37]

To supplement his staff and keep reporting costs down, Yemma did what editors of other news operations have done: He occasionally contracted with outside organizations, such as the New England Center for Investigative Reporting and the Pulitzer Center on Crisis Reporting, to help fund and produce content. But he insisted that, while these organizations helped in significant ways, the *Monitor* stayed at the center of reporting and editing on every project.

Praise for the new *Monitor* came from both outside and inside the paper. "I think a lot of things they've done with their website are great," said David Rohde, the *Monitor*'s 1996 Pulitzer winner, now with *The New York Times*. "I hope it's one of the publications helped by the Internet."

The *Monitor*'s senior international correspondent, Scott Baldauf, saw the online paper as reaching new heights in its coverage. "I truly believe we are much more vibrant and responsive to news events now than we were in print," he said. [38]

The staff sometimes got frustrated at the tone that online journalism could bring. "When I look at the indices on the website, what is most viewed, lots of times it's about a crocodile eating someone's dog, celebrity-oriented stuff," said Gail Russell Chaddock. "I get discouraged. In D.C. we pull our hair out over political blogs with bitchy, catty attitudes. We think, this wouldn't be printed in the old paper. In the rush to accommodate a new medium, have we lost our culture?"

But she also felt pushed in a good way by the new environment. "If you aren't going to write about Sarah Palin every third day, you have to be so compelling people will read you," she said. "You have to try to write in a way that is delightful and interesting."

Gloria Goodale, who covers primarily arts and culture for the *Monitor* from Los Angeles, refused to accept that the culture of the paper was lost in the transition to the Internet. "I wake up every morning and try to listen for direction," she said. "I try to get people to open their hearts, minds, thoughts, and come out of a story with a deeper sense of humanity, understanding, perspective, vision. I try to do something that will be more powerful for readers so they can say, Now I get it, now I know what I can do in my own life." [39]

That's a part of the *Monitor* culture that didn't change with the Web and probably never will: reporters putting their religion into their work. Baldauf has covered the Taliban in Afghanistan, the recent war in Iraq, and chaotic conflicts in Africa; and he has faced more than one life-threatening situation. "At [moments] like that," he said, "you have to become quiet and listen. You can't entirely make decisions on your own. You can't just follow your gut instincts. You have to search for that voice telling you what to do. For me that's prayer. I highly recommend it."

Working together

Considering what the *Monitor* went through the last time it tried to revolutionize its format, it was hard to imagine the first few years of the Web-first era going much better. A big reason was Yemma's willingness to break down institutional walls of arrogance, insecurity, secrecy, and religious standoffishness in dealing not only with staff but also with readers, the industry, and church members.

"I just try to be open and honest and not sugarcoat the problems we face," he said. "I face up to everything. As a manager, you can't always tell everything in real time, but you can listen to feedback, put things in context. I think the main thing is honesty and some degree of humility. We don't know all the answers."

For Goodale, who worked as a reporter under Kay Fanning as well as a television and radio correspondent under

Jack Hoagland, Yemma was the right person at the right time. "I adore John," she said. "He expresses the heart and soul of the paper so beautifully, he's an excellent journalist, and he knows how to set just the right tone for the staff. We needed someone who understood where journalism was headed and had credibility to place the *Monitor* in the context of the media revolution."

For Goodale, Yemma's importance for the *Monitor* was more than as a leader for the digital era. "It's an incredible sense of healing and progress for John to be brought back now," she said. "He left during a very divisive moment in the *Monitor*'s history, and his return gives the paper a feeling of greater unity."

Yemma and Wells have tried hard to break down the traditional barrier between editorial and business as they have developed their new model for news. They conduct periodic town-hall-style meetings in the newsroom on editorial and business issues. They have created teams that work on all things digital and print. There is a team on metrics and marketing, and one on the practical application of the unique value proposition. Yemma's schedule includes a news budgeting meeting every morning with international, national, and Web editors. He meets with senior *Monitor* editors every weekday to update them on what he knows and to listen to their thinking. Every Friday, he invites correspondents to chat about anything on their minds. He spends extra time in Washington to keep the staff there from "getting their backs up about little things."

The *Monitor* has a Facebook page, and Yemma encourages reporters and editors to develop followings there and on Twitter and other sites. "Like other organizations," he says, "we are only just scratching the surface of social media." He is not yet sure how much of social media is faddishness and how much is truly useful for the *Monitor*, but he is exploring the possibilities. He and Wells have made sure the *Monitor* is on e-readers and tablets, and they plan, in 2012, to bring it to mobile devices.

Goodale sees all the experimentation in a historical

context. "I can't remember any time [at the *Monitor*] when there wasn't a sense of tinkering, new ideas being explored, prototyped, trotted out," she says. "There is no question in my mind that Mrs. Eddy expected all the [church] periodicals to be abreast of the times. Everything she did and planned was in the moment. Today, with pay, free, RSS, podcasts, everything, it's sort of the perfect realization of the fact that the *Monitor* is an idea, and technology is a tool of the idea, reaching people in all ways they live."

The Directors are very much with Yemma. "He had a remarkable record of success managing the transition of the *Globe* from print to online," says Trammell. "He has a gift of explaining world events; he can illuminate issues. He can teach and communicate to the staff. While he is doing all that, he has one eye on the money. And he's a deeply devoted Christian Scientist."

On a Monday morning, in late June 2010, Yemma met with both boards—Directors and Trustees—in a conference room off the newsroom. He was proud of the paper's accomplishments that month: more than 25 million page views, 188th biggest site on the Web, number fourteen among online publishers. [40] He was surprised and pleased when they asked if they could come to the newsroom and applaud the staff. Afterward, he asked the newsroom to applaud the Boards for "setting the table for us."

He clearly understands what it means to manage up. He meets, every week, either by conference call or in person, with representatives of each board to update them on business and editorial issues. Monthly, the whole Board of Trustees looks over the activities of the Publishing Society, asking business, financial, and technological questions.

Every other month Yemma meets with the Directors. The idea that the *Monitor*'s editor would be appointed and overseen by the manager of the Publishing Society is long gone. He often selects a focus for the meetings, bringing along the editor of the weekly edition or the commentary section, or conferencing in senior editor David Cook from Washington.

Trammell reads all the editorials as well as editorial cartoons on behalf of the Directors and signs off on them. "The relationship [with both boards] has been one of mutual respect, I believe," says Yemma. "I have to tell you that, having worked at other places, it is tremendously gratifying to have words like "God" and "love" be part of a boardroom conversation. I absolutely cherish that. It's pretty great to be in a meeting with your bosses, and when you go into a presentation of tough financial issues, there is actually a conversation that deals with this as a metaphysical problem. I find that to be an amazing experience."

The practitioner-journalist

Yemma deserves praise for the way he has managed the transition. The Directors deserve praise for allowing an intelligent and experienced team at the Publishing Society to operate with guidance, but without interference.

But is the *Monitor* closer now to fulfilling its mission than it was before the Web-first strategy kicked in? The jury is still out.

On one hand, despite the ever-present financial challenges, Yemma's team is managing to produce some good journalism, and Yemma praises it highly:

> *We are doing difficult, creative, substantive, even daring work and have, among other things, developed a whole new* Monitor *genre in the weekly "cover story" [in the weekly print edition]. That's not just my admittedly biased opinion. Different readers have praised (to name a few cover stories) "Building Peace," "Taking Back Girlhood," "The Rise of the Global Middle Class," "My Africa," and "How Apple Won Over the World." We led the world with our revelations of the Stuxnet computer worm and exposed the corrupt practices rife in global trading in carbon offsets. Our "Little Bill Clinton" series was a sensitive and revealing*

multiyear examination of the difficulties and triumphs of a refugee family in the U.S. And of course, we have reporters bringing the values of Monitor *journalism to everything from Capitol Hill to Tahrir Square, Athens to Kashmir to tsunami-struck Japan.*

In keeping with Yemma's enthusiastic assessment, it would not be illogical to see the new *Monitor* as building on the best of the recent past, or to use another analogy, cultivating the seeds planted by Oka, van Slambrouck, and others, who helped develop big-problem, big-picture journalism as the model for the paper in resource-thin times.

One example is the cover story in the December 26, 2011, issue, the last weekly edition of that year, called "The (surprisingly upbeat) state of the world." [41] Staff writer Peter Grier picked a few key measurements, including the deadliness of wars, the number of countries considered free, the number of people living in poverty, and the percentage of girls in school, and gave sober and meaningful evidence that the overall trend for mankind is positive. Such a reassuring assessment of the world is not what a reader normally gets from most other media, as the *Monitor* doesn't hesitate to point out in its cover description for the story.

Grier's article, along with the cover stories Yemma mentions, follows the pattern of good *Monitor* journalism of the modern era: bold, fair, and precisely reported, on topics that are on the minds of readers. Yemma's *Monitor* may not always be distinctive in the way the *Monitor* needs to be, producing the calmly urgent, spiritually aware journalism that only the *Monitor* can, but it is making a worthy go of it in the consistent tackling of tough subjects and the effort, in Roscoe Drummond's phrase, to produce reporting with exclusiveness of insight rather than just exclusiveness of information.

Yemma has justification for seeing a special kind of heroism in the work of the *Monitor* under his editorship. "I would argue that it is all the more remarkable," he says, "that we do the kind of work we are doing and that we are systematically decreasing the deficit."

But there is another side to the issue of whether the *Monitor* and its new look constitute progress in the ongoing history of a noble journalistic enterprise: Many church members rarely visit the website or read the weekly, including a number who worked for the *Monitor* in the past. One former reporter admits that he uses CSMonitor.com as his home page both because he feels obliged to as a church member and because it helps boost the number of page views for the *Monitor*. But for serious news reading, he consults other websites more often. The genial disrespect is not a change from the days of the print daily, when (according to knowledgeable sources—no official numbers are available) fewer than twenty percent of members subscribed. Some readers are still looking merely for a paper that supports their political views, but others are waiting to receive a news product that not only informs and clarifies but also inspires. They have seen in past *Monitor* journalism that it can be done.

To inspire its readers is a huge demand for a news organization, but given Mrs. Eddy's intentions for the *Monitor*, it isn't an unfair expectation. If a body of people who believe in what spiritual healing can do for mankind individually and collectively are not inspired by the new *Monitor*, it is a hint that the paper may not yet be doing what it must on a consistent basis.

"Unless our *Monitor* expresses more than business success and wisdom of human minds," William McKenzie wrote Mrs. Eddy back in October 1908, "what is our labor worth? . . . This truly is the purpose of the enterprise, namely, to serve mankind by bringing thought into loving obedience to the Christ-mind." [42] The Christ-mind, to a Christian Scientist, is God, the divine Mind. A journalist who is "[obedient] to the Christ-mind," according to Christian Science, not only is clear-thinking and courageous but also can demonstrate the dominion of good over evil through spiritual healing. Is that too much to ask of a journalist? Maybe not, if he or she wants to help the *Monitor* not only come all the way back but also surge forward in new ways.

Healing is something the Directors seem to have in mind for the *Monitor.* "The qualities that make a good [Christian Science] practitioner make a good editor," says Trammell. "As…our employees strengthen their practitioner qualities, they become more effective."

For Trammell, working as a practitioner means "expressing and living the Christ, divine Truth in action— honesty, purity, clarity, a desire to see everything from God's perspective. That kind of a mindset," she says, "will naturally be inspired to find solutions, will embrace hope and compassion, will have an unshakable faith when confronted with challenges."

She is careful to add that "living a life based on these qualities is not limited to church members."

The aim of such a practitioner-journalist, according to Trammell, is to create an opening for God's communication. "Underpinning every article in the *Monitor* is the basic hope or conviction that an order is in place, a divine order," she says. "A spiritually sensitized person will respond, and it will bring the reader to the point of prayer."

The work of practitioner-journalists may rock boats, as it has throughout the *Monitor*'s history, from Frederick Dixon's diatribes to Erwin Canham's jeremiads. It may spur reform, as with the investigations of DeWitt John and his correspondents, and the wrenching series "Children in Darkness." Like "Why do they hate us?" and Project Jill, it may open a window to a deeper understanding of humanity's commonality. Or it may simply compel readers to be grateful for the immense beauty and resilience of mankind, as in the gentle and insistent writing of Takashi Oka.

Being a practitioner-journalist requires a mindset quite different from that of the average journalist. It demands a breadth of vision that looks both back and forward with spiritual understanding and confidence—in Mrs. Eddy's phrase, a willingness to "[do] the thinking for the ages." [43] It requires a love for humanity that goes beyond caring to blessing. It requires a sense of truth that gives new meaning to the phrase that describes a type of courageous journalism, "speaking truth to power." As Mrs. Eddy wrote in *Science and Health*, "Marvels, calamities, and sin will much more abound as truth urges upon mortals its resisted claims; but the awful daring of sin destroys sin, and foreshadows the triumph of truth. God will overturn, until 'He come whose right it is.'" [44]

The Christian Science church has had something powerful in the *Monitor* for more than a hundred years. Does it finally have the courage, the patience, and the vision to let it fulfill its promise?

■ ■ ■

Acknowledgements

A book like this cannot be produced without people who are willing to contribute their time and knowledge to making sure that the author has the best information possible.

First, there is the library research. Digging up facts, finding quotes, and verifying stories takes experience and not a little patience, and no group of people were more important to this project than Judy Huenneke and her staff at The Mary Baker Eddy Library in Boston. They gave frequent and cheerful help over several years in locating documents, correcting assumptions, and performing a host of other essential details. In addition, Leigh Montgomery of *The Christian Science Monitor* Library assisted in a crucial area – supplying unlimited access to past issues of the *Monitor* – and also gave generously of her time in helping to locate photos for the cover of the book.

Others contributed in vital ways: Longyear Museum in Chestnut Hill, Massachusetts, graciously allowed access to the museum's research library and permitted the use of quotations from the memoirs of Alexander Dodds and a biography of Archibald McLellan; Kenneth Johnson and his colleagues at the Library of Congress assisted in finding, and supplying copies of, the papers of Frederick Dixon; Carra Fenton and Dan Brillman at *Newsweek* helped find information on DeWitt John; John Hoffman and the Illinois History and Lincoln Collections at the University of Illinois Library provided background on the *Monitor*'s first chief editorial writer, John Flinn; and Scott Taylor and Ted Jackson of the Georgetown University Special Collections Research Center not only gave access to the papers of former writer Roscoe Drummond but also helped verify some difficult-to-find quotations when publication deadlines for the book were fast approaching. Finally, Susan Parmentier of Northwestern University gave generously of her time and talents to help track down information from the Audit Bureau of Circulations on *Monitor* circulation numbers.

The library research was essential, but I wanted to tell a story with this book, and for that I had to talk with people who knew the *Monitor* firsthand. In the end, I interviewed more than forty people, and I am very grateful to all of them for being willing to help this book come alive.

John Yemma, the *Monitor*'s current editor, held several long conversations with me, and he never failed to respond to emails or phone calls with relevant and thorough information on how the *Monitor* works. Yemma also permitted me to talk with his staff as much as I wanted to, which was crucial to making this book work. Jonathan Wells, the current manager of the Christian Science Publishing Society, was responsive on questions about the business of the *Monitor*.

In the end, rather than talk to a large part of the *Monitor* staff, I decided to focus on in-depth conversations with a few. Scott Baldauf, Gail Russell Chaddock, Linda Feldmann, Melanie Stetson Freeman, Gloria Goodale, Marshall Ingwerson, and Clay Jones all gave me interesting and insightful material.

There is one staff member whom I want to single out. I have known David Cook, current senior editor and current Washington bureau chief and former chief editor of the *Monitor*, for many years, and I expected that he would provide information that was not only generous and kind—Dave is unfailingly that—but also candid. I was not disappointed. Some of the questions I posed to him were difficult, but he was always honest with his responses. If readers find this book interesting, part of the reason is the quality of the answers that Dave provided.

Current journalists are only part of the story of a hundred-year-old news organization. In the 1980s and 1990s, the paper went through some rough times, and people on both sides of the controversies of the period were willing to talk. I can never express enough gratitude for the help they gave me in understanding that part of the *Monitor*'s history. David Anable and David Winder, who resigned from the *Monitor* in 1988, talked about their experiences openly but without rancor. So did David Morse, David Els, Frederic Hunter, Neal Menschel, and Sara Terry, all of whom played significant roles at the time. My special thanks also go to Gail Miller, who did not work at the *Monitor* but did work for Kay Fanning when she ran the *Anchorage Daily News*. She provided helpful insight into Fanning's thinking and character.

One of the most important and controversial figures during that era was Jack Hoagland, and I finally tracked him down by phone in July of 2010. As were so many of the people I talked with, Jack was gracious and candid about the times and his role in trying to bring the *Monitor* and the church into the modern media age. The *Monitor*'s story would not be complete without his insight, and I want to thank him immensely for being willing to talk about a painful period. This book is much richer because he was willing to go on the record.

I had good conversations with all the former *Monitor* editors who are still around, including not only David Cook but also Paul van Slambrouck and John Hughes. Thank you to them for their time, interest, and perspective.

As noted in the Introduction, the *Monitor* has won many journalistic prizes over the years. For the sake of the story, I focused on the winners of the Pulitzer Prize. In this I was grateful to have the full cooperation of Pulitzer winners Clay Bennett, Howard James, David Rohde, and of course, John Hughes, who, besides serving as editor of the paper, won the 1967 Pulitzer for International Reporting. My talks with all of them were fascinating and substantial. I never laughed so much through an interview as I did with Clay Bennett.

There are two former *Monitor* staffers who deserve special mention: Godfrey "Budge" Sperling, who had a long and illustrious career with the *Monitor*, sat down with me one dark winter afternoon in Washington, D.C., and entertained me with stories of his career, the people he knew, and the institution he started – what is now known as the *Monitor* Breakfast. Thank you, Budge. And there is also Takashi Oka, who was the first person to be interviewed for the book. I had always respected his work, and he provided me with two very long conversations at the Starbuck's in the Barnes and Noble bookstore in Georgetown. Thank you to you, too, Takashi.

Other former staff members helped round out the story with interesting commentary, including Cameron Barr, John Dillin, Judith Frutig, Larry Goodrich, Todd Hoffman, George Moffett, Rod Nordell, and Cynthia Parsons. Allison "Skip" Phinney, who served as editor of the church's magazines as well as head of its Committee on Publication, helped provide perspective on the career of DeWitt John, whom he knew well.

There are many other people I would have liked to talk to, and I regret that I was not able to do so. I know they would have made the book that much richer.

Important information in the book was provided by family members of some former *Monitor* staffers who are deceased, and I am indebted to them for being willing to talk with me. Carolyn Dain, whose father, Erwin Canham, was the longest-serving editor in *Monitor* history, provided helpful insight into her father's character and career; several members of DeWitt John's family, including his widow, Morley, and their two children, Jennifer and DeWitt, Jr., were extremely cooperative in giving insight into DeWitt's time at the *Monitor*. DeWitt, Jr., and his wife even provided a bedroom in their home in Maine so I could ride out a snowstorm after our talk. Edmund Stevens, Jr., gave me a very helpful interview about his father, Edmund, Sr., the *Monitor*'s first Pulitzer winner, and then provided the fascinating memoirs of both his father and his mother. I drew on both. John J. Roche, Sr., contributed stories of his grandfather, John Flinn.

In the category of family members, Robin Jareaux, a former design director of the *Monitor* and wife of current editor John Yemma, gave me not only information about her husband's background and insight into his career but also plenty of laughs.

As also noted in the Introduction, the role of the church is crucial to the *Monitor*, and I wanted to talk to some of those who help lead the church. Two members of the Christian Science Board of Directors, Mary Trammell and Michael Pabst (Pabst is also a member of the Board of Trustees of The Christian Science Publishing Society) were willing to be interviewed, and I thank them greatly for their insight. I have to admit that my admiration for how they oversee the paper grew with the conversations.

The individuals listed above were not the only ones with whom I talked and who provided information on the *Monitor*. Others were interviewed and their insights incorporated, but they have not been named because of the sensitivity of their – or their relatives' – positions with the church. To these people, thank you deeply for your help.

John Kehe, who designed the book's cover, was extraordinarily patient not only in finding a design that would work but also in riding out the complex permissions process. I believe that many people really do judge a book by its cover, and I greatly appreciate John's work.

Finally, I would like to thank George Spitzer and Jane Spitzer of Nebbadoon Press, the book's publisher, for their tireless efforts. Through late nights of painstaking checking of facts, quotes, spelling, grammar, and style, they have contributed immensely to making this book as accurate, fair, and readable as possible.

If the book succeeds as a good history and a good read, the people who helped in so many ways to bring it to life are a big reason why.

Editors

The Christian Science Monitor

Archibald McLellan	1908 – 1914
Frederick Dixon	1914 – 1922
Willis J. Abbot	1922 – 1927
Editorial Board	1927 – 1939
Roland Harrison	1939 – 1941
Erwin Canham	1941 – 1964
DeWitt John	1964 – 1970
John Hughes	1970 – 1979
Earl Foell	1979 – 1983
Katherine W. Fanning	1983 – 1988
Richard Cattani	1988 – 1994
David Cook	1994 – 2001
Paul van Slambrouck	2001 – 2005
Richard Bergenheim	2005 – 2008
John Yemma	2008 – present

Winners of the Pulitzer Prize

The Christian Science Monitor

Edmund Stevens
1950, International Affairs Reporting
"This is Russia—Uncensored"

John Hughes
1967, International Affairs Reporting
Reporting on events in Indonesia

Howard James
1968, National Reporting
"Crisis in the Courts"

Robert Cahn
1969, National Reporting
"Will Success Spoil the National Parks?"

Richard Strout
1978, Special Citation
Distinguished commentary from Washington, DC

David Rohde
1996, International Affairs Reporting
Reporting on Bosnian Serb massacres in Srebrenica

Clay Bennett
2002, Editorial Cartooning
Cartoons throughout 2001

Bibliography

Abbot, Willis J. *Watching the World Go By*. Boston: Little, Brown & Co., 1933.

Bridge, Susan. *Monitoring the News: The Brilliant Launch and Sudden Collapse of The Monitor Channel*. Armonk, New York: M.E. Sharpe, 1998.

Butler, J.R.M. *Lord Lothian (Philip Kerr): 1882-1940*. London: MacMillan & Co., Ltd., 1960.

Canham, Erwin D. *A Christian Scientist's Life*, Prentice-Hall, Inc., Englewood Cliffs, NJ, 1962. (Published in same volume as John, *The Christian Science Way of Life*.)

Canham, Erwin D. and *Monitor* Staff. *Awakening: The World at Mid-Century*. New York: Longmans, Green & Co., 1950.

Canham, Erwin D. *Commitment to Freedom: The Story of The Christian Science Monitor*. Boston: Houghton Mifflin Company, 1958.

Canham, Erwin D., Editor. *Man's Great Future*. New York: Longmans, Green & Co., 1959.

Canham, Erwin D. *New Frontiers for Freedom*. New York: Longmans, Green & Co., 1954.

Eddy, Mary Baker. *Science and Health with Key to the Scriptures*. Boston: The First Church of Christ, Scientist.

Eddy, Mary Baker. *Miscellaneous Writings* and other published works. Boston: The First Church of Christ, Scientist.

Fanning, Kay, with Katherine Field Stephen. *Kay Fanning's Alaska Story*. Kenmore, WA: Epicenter Press, 2006.

Fuller, Linda K. *The Christian Science Monitor: An Evolving Experiment in Journalism*. Santa Barbara, CA: Praeger Publishers, 2011.

Gottschalk, Stephen. *The Emergence of Christian Science in American Religious Life*. Berkeley: University of California Press, 1973.

Heckler, Cheryl. *An Accidental Journalist*. Columbia, MO: University of Missouri Press, 2007.

John, DeWitt. *The Christian Science Way of Life*. Englewood Cliffs, N.J.: Prentice-Hall, Inc., 1962. (Published in same volume as Canham, *A Christian Scientist's Life*.)

Knapp, Bliss. *The Destiny of The Mother Church*. Boston: The Christian Science Publishing Society, 1991.

Manchester, William. *The Last Lion: Winston Spencer Churchill: Alone*. Boston: Little, Brown & Co., 1988.

McKenzie, William P. *Heartsease Hymns*. Chicago: Associated Authors, 1928.

McKenzie, William P. *Voices and Undertones in Song and Poem*. New York: Equity Publishing Co., 1889.

Mosley, Leonard. *Gideon Goes to War*. New York: Charles Scribner's Sons, 1955.

Nenneman, Richard A. *The New Birth of Christianity: Why Religion Persists in a Scientific Age*. San Francisco: Harper San Francisco, 1992.

Nenneman, Richard A. *A Spiritual Journey: Why I Became A Christian Scientist*. Santa Barbara, CA: Nebbadoon Press, 2008.

Peel, Robert. *Mary Baker Eddy: Years of Discovery*. Boston: The Christian Science Publishing Society, 1966.

Peel, Robert. *Mary Baker Eddy: Years of Trial*. New York: Holt, Rinehart and Winston, 1971.

Peel, Robert. *Mary Baker Eddy: Years of Authority*. New York: Holt, Rinehart and Winston, 1977.

Powell, Lyman P. *Mary Baker Eddy: A Life Size Portrait*. Boston: The Christian Science Publishing Society, 1930.

Saucier, Craig E. *Mr. Kerr Goes to Washington: Lord Lothian and the Genesis of the Anglo-American Alliance, 1939-1940*. Dissertation submitted to Louisiana State University, August 2008.

Smith, Clifford P. *Historical Sketches from the Life of Mary Baker Eddy*. Boston: The Christian Science Publishing Society, 1934.

Steele, Rufus. *The City That Is*. San Francisco: A. M. Robertson, 1909.

Tomlinson, Irving C. *Twelve Years with Mary Baker Eddy*. Boston: The Christian Science Publishing Society, 1945.

We Knew Mary Baker Eddy, Expanded Edition, Vol. 1. Boston: The Christian Science Publishing Society, 2011.

Notes and Sources

ABBREVIATIONS

Writings of Mary Baker Eddy:

S&H: *Science and Health with Key to the Scriptures*
Mis.: *Miscellaneous Writings*
Ret.: *Retrospection and Introspection*
Un.: *Unity of Good*
'00: *Message to The Mother Church for 1900*
'02: *Message to The Mother Church for 1902*
Peo.: *The People's Idea of God*
My.: *The First Church of Christ, Scientist, and Miscellany*
Po.: *Poems*
Man.: *Church Manual of The First Church of Christ, Scientist.*

Publications of The Christian Science Publishing Society:

Monitor: The Christian Science Monitor
Journal: The Christian Science Journal
Sentinel: Christian Science Sentinel
Herald: The Herald of Christian Science

Other sources:

Mary Baker Eddy Library (MBE Library): Historical documents from The Mary Baker Eddy Collection and The Mary Baker Eddy Library are generally indicated in the footnotes with an 'L,' 'A,' 'V,' 'or 'IC.'

All other publications and books from any other sources are identified.

INTRODUCTION

[1] "Something in a Name," *Monitor*, November 25, 1908, p. 12. Reprinted in My., p. 353
[2] My., p. 46 and Man., p.17
[3] Beulah M. Roegge, *"The Christian Science Monitor*: Its place in my life," *Journal*, November 1999, p. 44
[4] Comment of Josh Burek, *Monitor* op-ed editor, in "A Century-Young News Mission," *Journal*, November 2008, p. 50
[5] Calvin Frye diary, 1908, EF081
[6] Ibid.
[7] "A Timely Issue," *Journal*, April 14, 1883, p. 3
[8] Mis., p. 4
[9] Letter from Eddy to Directors, July 28, 1908, L00596

CHAPTER 1: JOURNALISM TO HEAL THE NATIONS

[1] Robert Peel, *Mary Baker Eddy: Years of Trial*, p. 275 and p. 376, N4. Based on accounts of Mrs. Eddy from people who knew or observed her, The Mary Baker Eddy Library in Boston believes that Mrs. Eddy "probably" colored her hair for at least part of the 1880s, although there is no conclusive evidence.
[2] S&H, p. 570
[3] Ret., p. 13
[4] Ret., p. 14
[5] Ret., p. 15
[6] "Shade and Sunshine," A10032
[7] "Resolutions for the Day," Po., p. 33
[8] Emma C. Shipman reminiscences, p. 17
[9] Ret., p. 94
[10] "A Timely Issue," *Journal*, April 14, 1883, p. 3, reprinted in somewhat changed form in Mis., p. 7
[11] Irving C. Tomlinson, *Twelve Years with Mary Baker Eddy*, p. 99
[12] Tomlinson, p. 131
[13] Letter from Eddy to McLellan, August 29, 1903, L03064
[14] Letter from Eddy to John F. and Ellen Brown Linscott, May 30, 1898, L05221
[15] "Foreign Exposition on Sunday," *Journal*, October 6, p. 4
[16] *Journal*, October 6, 1883, p. 4
[17] "The People's God: Its Effect on Health and Christianity," *Journal*, June 2, 1883, p. 1, reprinted in slightly altered form in Peo., p. 2
[18] Letter from Eddy to John Carroll Lathrop, May 9, 1906, L04290

---

[19] From Eddy letter to Julia Bartlett, July 21, 1889, quoted in Lyman P. Powell, *Mary Baker Eddy: A Life Size Portrait*, p. 310, N56

[20] Letter from Eddy to Septimus J. and Camilla Hanna, February 24, 1893, L04945

[21] Letter from Eddy to William G. Nixon, March 13, 1892, L02279

[22] Robert Peel, *Mary Baker Eddy: Years of Authority*, pp. 15-16. Undated talk by Mary Baker Eddy between 1889 and 1892, written in Calvin Frye's handwriting, with corrections written in by Mrs. Eddy

[23] Letter from Eddy to William G. Nixon, March 3, 1892, L02278

[24] "Salutatory," *The Christian Science Weekly*, September 1, 1898, p. 1

[25] My., p. 129

[26] Letter from Eddy to Augusta E. Stetson, May 1, 1907, L13516

[27] S&H, p. 340

[28] '00, p. 3

[29] Psalms 68:11

[30] '02, p. 17

[31] William P. McKenzie, quoted in Clifford P. Smith, *Historical Sketches*, p. 101

[32] Cora Reeves Nunn reminiscences, pp. 4-5

[33] Mis., p.116

[34] Alfred Farlow reminiscences, p. 8

[35] Letter from Eddy to Edward A. Kimball, June 3, 1902, L07590

[36] Letter from Eddy to Edward A. and Kate Davidson Kimball, June 22, 1902, L07593

[37] Letter from Hanna to Eddy, January 19, 1901, IC file, Judge S.J. Hanna folder 33d

[38] Abigail Dyer Thompson reminiscences

[39] Letter from William McKenzie to Daisette Stocking, January 6, 1901, quoted in *Years of Authority*, p. 169

[40] Peo., p. 1

[41] William Lyman Johnson, biographical sketch of Archibald McLellan, p. 16

[42] Letter from John L. Wright to Eddy, March 12, 1908, L06998

[43] Ibid.

[44] Letter from Eddy to Archibald McLellan, May 3, 1908, L07146

[45] Letter from Eddy to Directors, July 28, 1908, L00596

[46] My., p. 189

CHAPTER 2: THUNDER AND LIGHTNING

[1] William P. McKenzie, *Voices and Undertones in Song and Poem*, p. 48

[2] Reminiscences of Daisette Stocking McKenzie and William Patrick McKenzie, as recorded by Daisette D. S. McKenzie, pp. 16-17

[3] "One Thing Needful," *Journal*, October 1894, p. 297

[4] Letter from Eddy to McKenzie, October 2, 1894, L04847

[5] McKenzie reminiscences, p. 61

[6] McKenzie reminiscences, p. 20

[7] McKenzie reminiscences, p. 28

[8] McKenzie reminiscences, p. 30

[9] Letter from McKenzie to Eddy, January 21, 1896, IC 13A

[10] McKenzie reminiscences, p. 39

[11] "The Eternal," *Heartsease Hymns,* and *Christian Science Hymnal*, Hymn 359.

[12] Because the church eventually began publishing the *Herold* in other languages than German, the German spelling was changed to the English *Herald* when referring to the magazine in any context other than that of the German-language magazine itself.

[13] Deed of Trust, The Christian Science Publishing Society, January 25, 1898, p. 3

[14] Deed of Trust, p. 4

[15] Deed of Trust, pp. 5-6

[16] Letter from Eddy to Trustees, August 8, 1908, L07268

[17] S&H, p. 583

[18] Letter from Trustees to Eddy, August 11, 1908, IC 94(b)

[19] Letter from Dickey to McLellan, August 12, 1908, L06474

[20] William P. McKenzie, "The Monitor of 1908," *Monitor*, November 20, 1933, p. 27

[21] Letter from Trustees to Eddy, August 13, 1908, IC 94(b)

[22] Letter from Dickey to Trustees, August 14, 1908, L07269

[23] Letter from Trustees to Eddy, August 15, 1908, IC 94(b)

[24] Tomlinson, p. 106

[25] Address by John J. Flinn, December 22, 1926, quoted by Erwin D. Canham in *Commitment to Freedom*, pp. 47-48

[26] "The Christian Science Monitor," *Sentinel*, October 17, 1908, p. 130

[27] Quoted in *Commitment to Freedom*, p. 83

[28] Quoted in *Commitment to Freedom*, p 84

[29] "Newspaper Possibilities," *Sentinel*, October 24, 1908, p. 143

[30] *Commitment to Freedom*, p. 51

[31] *Commitment to Freedom*, p. 52

[32] Quoted in letter from David B. Ogden of The Christian Science Publishing Society to Eddy, November 16, 1908, IC 94(b)

[33] Letter from Dickey to McLellan, November 24, 1908, V03307

[34] Tomlinson, p. 106

[35] Quoted in *Commitment to Freedom*, p. 54

[36] Quoted in Tomlinson, pp.106-107

---

[37] "Construction work rapidly progresses on great dam across the Charles River basin," *Monitor*, November 25, 1908, p. 1

[38] "Cold Comfort for Bosses from Hughes," *The New York Times*, November 25, 1908, p. 1

[39] "Three Men Lynched After 'Legal' Trial," *The New York Times*, November 25, 1908, p. 1

[40] Letter from Bell to Eddy, November 2, 1908, reprinted in *Monitor,* November 25, 1908, p. 12

[41] "Something in a Name," *Monitor*, November 25, 1908, p. 12.

[42] Matthew 5:44

[43] S&H, p. 453

CHAPTER 3: BEYOND CLEAN

[1] Paul S. Deland reminiscences, p. 3

[2] Deland reminiscences, pp. 5-6

[3] S&H, p. 129

[4] Alexander Dodds, Autobiography and Story of the Founding of the Monitor (manuscript), 1917

[5] Deland reminiscences, p. 6

[6] Dodds autobiography, p. 6

[7] Letter from McKenzie to Dodds, August 27, 1908, from Dodds autobiography, no page number

[8] Dodds autobiography. This portion of the autobiography is in Dodds' handwriting, with unnumbered pages.

[9] William Lyman Johnson, "Archibald McLellan, C.S.D.," c. 1927, in Subject File, Archibald McLellan, Addresses by and Biographical Material, MBE Library, p. 3

[10] William D. McCrackan, "Archibald McLellan, C.S.D.," c. 1920-1921, in Subject File, Archibald McLellan, Addresses by and Biographical Material, MBE Library, pp. 1-2

[11] Quoted in "Archibald McLellan, C.S.B.," an anonymous biography in the archives of Longyear Museum, p. 12. This letter is not in the files of the Mary Baker Eddy Library, which has the most complete compilation of Eddy's correspondence. The library, therefore, cannot confirm the authenticity of the quote.

[12] *Commitment to Freedom*, p. 76

[13] Talk on *Monitor* to a group of businessmen in Chicago, October, 1910

[14] "All of Spain Today is Declared Under 'War Law' by King," *Monitor*, July 28, 1909, p. 1

[15] "Spain Verges on Civil War," *The New York Times*, July 29, 1909, p. 1

[16] *We Knew Mary Baker Eddy*, Expanded Edition, Vol. 1, pp. 296-297

[17] From author's interview with John J. Roche, Flinn's grandson, in November 2008

[18] "The Most Troublesome Patient," *Sentinel*, November 26, 1927, p. 244

[19] Ibid.

[20] "Invincible Mind," *Journal*, July, 1928, p. 195

[21] John J. Flinn, address to Mr. Chairman, Ladies and Gentlemen, circa 1910, quoted in *Journal*, February 2005, p. 40

[22] "Emergence from Self," *Sentinel*, September 7, 1929, p. 3

[23] Talk to Chicago businessmen, October 1910

[24] Ibid.

[25] Letter from Eddy to McLellan, January 21, 1909, L03212

[26] Ibid.

[27] *Commitment to Freedom*, p. 75

[28] Letter from William R. Rathvon, Mrs. Eddy's corresponding secretary, to William McKenzie, January 4, 1910, referring to Mrs. Eddy's reaction to McKenzie's letter, L14824

[29] Quoted in Clifford Smith P. Smith, *Historical Sketches*, p. 100

CHAPTER 4: TO THE BARRICADES

[1] "War," *Monitor*, August 3, 1914, p. 16

[2] *Commitment to Freedom*, p. 152

[3] Mis., p. 250

[4] Letter from Directors to Dixon, June 3, 1914, in The Papers of Frederick Dixon, MSS 17127, Reel 1, Manuscript Division, Library of Congress

[5] *Commitment to Freedom*, p. 157

[6] "The Lusitania," *Monitor*, May 10, 1915, p. 18

[7] Letter from Dixon to John V. Dittemore of the Christian Science Board of Directors, June 3, 1914, in Dixon Papers

[8] Letter from Dixon to Adam Dickey, the Christian Science Board of Directors, February 20, 1919, in Dixon Papers

[9] Letter from Dixon to Warner, July 16, 1917, in Dixon Papers

[10] Letter from Warner to Dixon, #119, July 23, 1917, in Dixon Papers

[11] Letter from Dixon to Warner, #205, August 20, 1917, in Dixon Papers

[12] "Feet of Brass," *Monitor*, December 1, 1917, p. 22

[13] Ibid.

[14] Letter from Trustees to Mr. and Mrs. Dixon, February 26, 1918, in Dixon Papers

[15] "Religion and Politics," *Monitor*, March 23, 1918, p. 22

[16] "Religion and Politics," *Sentinel*, April 6, 1918, p. 630

[17] "Kicking Against the Pricks," *Monitor*, November 12, 1918, p. 16

[18] From undated summary of events written after Dixon left the *Monitor*, in Dixon Papers

---

[19] "A Mad World," *Monitor*, October 8, 1918, p. 16

[20] Letter from Dixon to Dickey, March 22, 1919, in Dixon Papers

[21] Letter from Dixon to Bathurst, May 19, 1919, in Dixon Papers

[22] Letter from Dixon to Bathurst, October 6, 1919, in Dixon Papers

[23] Cable from Dixon to Bathurst, October 14, 1919, in Dixon Papers

[24] Letter from Dixon to Bathurst, October 26, 1919, in Dixon Papers. The letter was written after Bathurst was fired but summarizes well where Dixon's thinking was at the time.

[25] Letter from Dixon to Stuart Sessions in the London office, March 13, 1920, in Dixon papers

[26] "Turning to the Gentiles," *Sentinel*, February 4, 1922, p. 360

[27] Ibid.

[28] Ibid., p. 361

[29] Mis., p. 264

[30] Letter from Dixon to Directors, November 1, 1922, in Dixon Papers

[31] "A Thin Red Line," *Time*, March 31, 1924

[32] Letter from Dixon to Directors, March 7, 1923, in Dixon Papers

[33] Letter from Directors to Dixon, April 9, 1923, in Dixon Papers

[34] Letter from Dixon to Directors, May 4, 1923, in Dixon Papers

[35] "Frederick Dixon," *The Interpreter*, November 24, 1923, in Dixon papers

[36] S&H, p. 571

CHAPTER 5: WATCHING THE WORLD GO BY

[1] "Christianity in Business," *Monitor*, January 31, 1922, p. 16

[2] Ibid.

[3] Willis Abbot, *Watching the World Go By*, p. 212

[4] *Watching the World Go By*, p. 214

[5] *Watching the World Go By*, p. 5

[6] *Watching the World Go By*, p. 25

[7] *Watching the World Go By*, p. 33

[8] *Watching the World Go By*, p. 35

[9] *Watching the World Go By*, p. 319

[10] "World Peace and Good-Will," *Monitor*, February 6, 1922, p. 16

[11] *Watching the World Go By*, p. 320

[12] "Army Dirigible Roma Explodes: Falls in Flames Near Hampton Roads Base – Passengers Aboard," *Monitor*, February 21, 1922, p. 1

[13] Letter from Drummond to Erwin Canham, December 6, 1957, from The Roscoe Drummond Papers, Georgetown University Library, Special Collections Division

[14] *Commitment to Freedom*, p. 207

[15] Letter from Drummond to Canham, December 6, 1957, in Drummond papers

[16] "Wet Minority Seeks to Void Nation's Edict," *Monitor*, October 19, 1928, p. 1

[17] *Watching the World Go By*, p. 333

[18] Letter from Drummond to Canham, December 6, 1957, in Drummond papers

[19] "A Night at the Abbey Theater," *Monitor*, December 29, 1923, p. 18

[20] "The Mirage of Easy Wealth," *Monitor*, October 25, 1929, p. 24

[21] "Clearing the Speculative Mists," *Monitor*, October 30, 1929, p. 16

[22] *Commitment to Freedom*, p. 262

[23] Walter W. Cunningham, "A Backward Glance into the Future," *Monitor*, November 25, 1933, p. APS6

[24] Roland R. Harrison, "Publishing in 17 Languages: Surveying the Diversified Activities of the Publishing Society," *Monitor*, November 25, 1933, p. APS2

[25] "The Discovery of Progress," *Monitor*, November 25, 1933, p. 32

CHAPTER 6: THE PROBLEM OF EVIL

[1] From The Roscoe Drummond Papers, Georgetown University Library, Special Collections Division

[2] *Watertown Times*, March 1, 1945, in Drummond Papers

[3] As told to Herbert L. Marx in *Senior Scholastic*, Feb 9, 1948, Drummond Papers

[4] "Peace is Dangerous!" *Monitor*, June 19, 1931, p. 18

[5] "Disarmament: Victory or Defeat," *Monitor*, November 4, 1931, p. 16

[6] "Reading Our Daily Newspaper," *Sentinel*, April 4, 1933, p. 624

[7] "Principle Among the Printing Presses," *Sentinel*, April 26, 1924, p. 685

[8] "The March of the Nations," *Monitor*, September 16, 1931, p. 1

[9] "The March of the Nations," *Monitor*, September 16, 1931, p. 1

[10] "Clipping the Wings of Fear," *Monitor*, August 22, 1934, p. WM1

[11] "The March of the Nations," *Monitor*, December 24, 1935, p. 1

[12] "Rufus Steele Saw Spiritual Values in Affairs of World," *Monitor*, December 26, 1935, p. 3

[13] "Rufus Steele," *Monitor*, December 26, 1935, p. 16

[14] My., p. 353

[15] J.R.M. Butler, *Lord Lothian (Philip Kerr): 1882-1940*, p. 4

[16] Butler, p. 5

[17] Butler, p. 34

[18] Butler, p. 38

[19] Butler, p. 86

[20] Butler, p. 59

[21] Butler, p. 53

[22] Letter from Kerr to Astor, December 10, 1913, quoted in Butler, p. 87

[23] Letter from Kerr to the Clerk of First Church of Christ, Scientist, London, September 18, 1923, quoted in Butler, p. 88

[24] Butler, p. 61

[25] Lloyd George, War Memoirs, quoted in Butler p. 67.

[26] Butler, p. 91

[27] Butler, p. 92

[28] Butler, p. 94

[29] "The Diary of a Political Pilgrim," *Monitor*, January 29, 1925, p. 16

[30] "The Anglo-American Naval Controversy: 1812-1929," *Monitor*, October 4, 1929, p. 22.

[31] Butler, p. 144

[32] Letter from Lothian to Lionel Curtis, May 6, 1933, quoted in Butler, p. 100

[33] "Christian Science and Prosperity," *Journal*, August 1933, p. 251

[34] "Christian Science, Public Affairs, and The Christian Science Monitor," *Journal*, January 1935, p. 508

[35] Ibid.

[36] Ibid., p. 511

[37] Ibid., pp. 511-512

[38] "'Butter' and 'Guns' in Europe," *Monitor*, February 24, 1937, p. WM1

[39] Butler, p. 116

[40] Bliss Knapp, *The Destiny of The Mother Church*, The Christian Science Publishing Society, p. 13

[41] Butler, p. 197

[42] "Germany's Return to Powers' Talks Urged by Lothian," *Monitor*, February 1, 1935, p. 4

[43] Letter to T. W. Lamont, March 29, 1939, quoted in Butler, p. 227

[44] My. p. 213

[45] "The Wide Horizon: Diary of a Political Pilgrim," *Monitor*, December 22, 1938, p. 20

[46] "Britain's New Ambassador," *Monitor*, April 25, 1939, p. 26

[47] Butler, p. 305

[48] Craig E. Saucier, *Mr. Kerr Goes to Washington: Lord Lothian and the Genesis of the Anglo-American Alliance, 1939-1940*, p. 387. Dissertation submitted to Louisiana State University, August 2008

[49] Nicholas John Cull, *Selling War: The British Propaganda Campaign Against American "Neutrality" in World War II.* New York and Oxford: Oxford University Press, 1995, p.123. (Quoted in Saucier, p.391)

[50] "How Are You Going to Vote?" *Monitor*, September 2, 1944, p. 8

[51] *Commitment of Freedom*, p. 275

[52] Letter from Drummond to Erwin Canham, December 6, 1957, in Drummond Papers

---

CHAPTER 7: A PRIZE AND A PROPHET

[1] Erwin D. Canham, *A Christian Scientist's Life*, p. 197.

[2] *A Christian Scientist's Life*, p. 196

[3] *A Christian Scientist's Life*, p. 198

[4] *A Christian Scientist's Life*, p. 214

[5] *A Christian Scientist's Life*, p. 217

[6] "MacDonald, Peace Envoy, Reaches U.S.," *Monitor*, October 4, 1929, p. 1

[7] *A Christian Scientist's Life*, p. 223-224

[8] Convocation Address to Colby College, 1971

[9] "The Washington Bureau of The Christian Science Monitor," *Sentinel*, July 6, 1935, p. 901

[10] Ibid.

[11] "MacDonald Insists on War Debt Action Before 66 Nations," *Monitor*, June 12, 1933, p. 1

[12] *A Christian Scientist's Life*, p. 227

[13] "Down the Middle of the Road: The Outsiders," *Monitor*, December 12, 1941, p. 24

[14] Ibid.

[15] *Commitment to Freedom*, p. 303

[16] *Monitor*, December 7, 1941, p. 1

[17] "Nazi Bombs Kill 8,098," *Monitor*, December 28, 1944, p. 1

[18] "The Art of War in the Jungle," *Monitor*, June 12, 1943, p. WM2

[19] "Shot-by-Shot Story from U.S. Cruiser," *Monitor*, June 8, 1944, p. 1

[20] Ibid.

[21] "Challenge to World Thinking," *Monitor*, May 7, 1945, p. 9

[22] Ibid.

[23] "Down the Middle of the Road: On 1942," *Monitor*, December 29, 1942, p. 20

[24] "At Year's End . . . Down the Middle of the Road," *Monitor*, December 31, 1943, p. 20

[25] "What Liberty Means: Down the Middle of the Road," *Monitor*, August 29, 1944, p. 14

[26] Ibid.

[27] "No Time for Dancing in the Streets," *Monitor*, May 4, 1945, p. 18

[28] "To Realize America's Mission: Down the Middle of the Road," *Monitor*, January 22, 1946, p. 18

[29] Ibid.

[30] Cheryl Heckler, *An Accidental Journalist, The Adventures of Edmund Stevens 1934 – 1945*, p. 1

[31] Nina Andreevna Stevens, Memoirs, p. 88. This and much of the insight on Stevens during the period are from Mrs. Stevens's memoirs.

[32] Nina Stevens memoirs, p. 92

[33] "Baltic Epic Written by Exodus of Germans," *Monitor*, October 11, 1939, p. 1

[34] "Red Invaders Clad in Ragged Uniforms," *Monitor*, December 23, 1939, p. 6

[35] "Modern War Carried Above Arctic Circle," *Monitor*, January 24, 1940, p. 2

[36] "Red bombing of Finnish civilians: Is it a record of brutality in modern warfare?" *Monitor*, February 28, 1940, p. 1

[37] Edmund Stevens, Jr. (son of Edmund Stevens), interview with author, December 2009

[38] "This is Russia Uncensored: Exit of a Reporter: Suspicion Closes In," *Monitor*, October 18, 1949, p. 1

[39] "This is Russia Uncensored: Art for Soviet Sake, Plus American Cars," *Monitor*, October 22, 1949, p. 1

[40] "This is Russia Uncensored: Peasant is Squeezed 'Twixt Quota and Cow," *Monitor*, October 25, 1949, p. 1

[41] Ibid.

[42] "This is Russia Uncensored: Minister of 'Justice' Bares MVD Cruelty," *Monitor*, November 22, 1949, p. 1

[43] "This is Russia Uncensored: Collective Slavery is Seed for Revolt," *Monitor*, January 28, 1950, p. 1

[44] Ibid.

[45] After Stevens died in 1992, controversy arose about whether he continued as a member of the Communist Party during his reporting days, casting doubt on whether he deserved the Pulitzer. But his reporting demonstrated an independence inconsistent with Party membership, and with a strong defense from his family, fellow reporters, and the *Monitor*, the controversy fizzled out.

[46] "The Authentic Revolution: We Are the Great Revolutionaries . . . And Our Revolution is a Spiritual One," *Monitor*, July 15, 1950, p. 1

[47] Ibid.

[48] Ibid.

[49] "The Authentic Revolution: We Are the Great Revolutionaries . . . And Our Revolution is a Spiritual One." The comments of Grace and Stewart were included when the talk was reprinted in pamphlet form.

[50] "The World at Mid-Century," *Monitor*, December 16, 1950, p. 1. The quotation is taken from the article as reprinted in Canham and Monitor Staff, *Awakening, The World at Mid-Century*, p. 1

[51] Ibid., p. WM2

[52] "Hard-Won Gains of Women Leaven Half Century – And Spur World On," *Monitor*, December 20, 1950, p. 9

[53] "Schools in 1951: Spiritual Leaven at Work," *Monitor*, January 8, 1951, p. Sec21

54 "50 Years of Art: Revolution, Experiment – and Achievement," *Monitor*, January 22, 1951, p. 11
55 "Modern Fiction Faces Modern Fact," *Monitor*, January 10, 1951, p. Sec21
56 Canham and Monitor Staff, *Awakening: The World at Mid-Century*, pp. 207-208
57 Undated, quoted in *Commitment to Freedom*, p. 423
58 *A Christian Scientist's Life*, p. 231
59 *A Christian Scientist's Life*, p. 230
60 "How Peace Was Reached," *Monitor*, January 22, 1955, p. 1
61 Ibid.
62 Figures from Audit Bureau of Circulations
63 *Commitment to Freedom*, p. 422
64 "Advertising," *Sentinel*, June 8, 1929, p. 804
65 *Commitment to Freedom*, p. 394
66 *Commitment to Freedom*, p. 405
67 *Commitment to Freedom*, p. 435.
68 "The Tools for Spiritual Citizenship," *Journal*, October 1965, p. 509
69 "Need for Self-Examination Confronts U.S.," *Monitor*, November 26, 1963, p. 9
70 Ibid.
71 "The Tools for Citizenship," *Journal*, October 1965, p. 509, quoted in "President's Fall Convocation Address," by George Moffett, President, Principia College, September 12, 2002
72 "Canham and John named Editors," *Monitor*, May 16, 1964, p. 3
73 Sperling interview with author, January 2009. Unless otherwise noted, all quotations from Sperling are from this interview.

CHAPTER 8: MORE LOVE

1 "Mayor's Fight Takes on New Battle Front," *Monitor*, September 10, 1941, p. 1
2 "Norton Backing Tobin in Hub Race for Mayor," *Monitor*, September 13, 1941, p. 1
3 "Fast Traffic Artery Seen for Back Bay," *Monitor*, February 15, 1941, p. 14
4 "Candy 'Chute Sweetens Air Lift," *Monitor*, October 12, 1948, p. 1
5 "Volksdeutsche – DPs Nobody Wants – Pose Poignant Problem in Austria," *Monitor*, November 16, 1948, p. 9
6 Morley John interview with author, December 2008
7 Phinney interview with author, February 2010
8 "Change at the Monitor," *Newsweek*, March 15, 1965, p. 70
9 Dillin interview with author, February 2010. Unless otherwise noted, all quotations from Dillin are from this interview.

[10] "Change at the Monitor," *Newsweek*, March 15, 1965, p. 70

[11] Hunter interview with author, June 2010. Unless otherwise noted, all quotations from Hunter are from this interview

[12] Sperling interview with author, January 2009

[13] "Deeper than words, the healing Spirit!" *Sentinel*, June 27, 1983, p. 1103

[14] Sperling interview with author, January 2009

[15] John Hughes interview with author, March 2010

[16] "Report on Individual Freedom: Freedom in a Complex World," *Monitor*, January 5, 1965, p. 9

[17] Ibid.

[18] Ibid.

[19] "Report on Individual Freedom: Many march against mankind's prejudices," *Monitor*, March 26, 1965, p. 9

[20] "Report on Individual Freedom: What really makes men free," *Monitor*, April 2, 1965, p. 9

[21] Sperling interview with author, January 2009. Unless otherwise noted, all quotations from Sperling are from this interview.

[22] Clines, Francis X., "At Breakfast With: Godfrey (Budge) Sperling Jr.; Politicians and the Press, Once Over," *The New York Times*, January 10, 1996

[23] "Victory is Assured," *Sentinel*, June 6, 1953, p. 973

[24] "The Simplicity of Reality," *Sentinel*, June 23, 1951, p. 1066

[25] Hughes interview with author, March 2010. Unless otherwise noted, all quotations from Hughes are from this interview or subsequent emails.

[26] "Sukarno: Asian Enigma," *Monitor*, January 6, 1965, p. 1

[27] "Sukarno parries press questions," *Monitor*, October 7, 1965, p. 1

[28] "Campaign snowballs to remove Sukarno," *Monitor*, September 15, 1966, p. 1

[29] "Albee play wins Pulitzer Prize," *Monitor*, May 3, 1967, p. 1

[30] James interview with author, February 2010. Unless otherwise noted, all quotations from James are from this interview.

[31] "A robe doesn't make a judge," *Monitor*, April 12, 1967, p. 13

[32] "Recipe for court reform," *Monitor*, July 5, 1967, p. 9

[33] "Monitor court series wins Pulitzer award," *Monitor*, May 8, 1968, p. 4

[34] "Will success spoil the national parks: U.S. may have to restrict use of public parks," *Monitor*, May 1, 1968, p. 1

[35] "People vs. wildlife," *Monitor*, June 5, 1968, p. 9

[36] "A Message from The Christian Science Board of Directors, read by Inman H. Douglass, Chairman," *Journal*, July 1969, p. 339

[37] "Should U.S. halt Vietnam bombing?" *Monitor*, June 17, 1967, p. 1

[38] "Out from Cambodian captivity: 'Don't shoot, we are international journalists," *Monitor*, June 22, 1970, p. 1

[39] Ibid.

[40] "Last days of captivity: A farewell dinner," *Monitor*, June 25, 1970, p. 1
[41] Ibid.
[42] "Freed journalist's question: 'Why us?'" *Monitor*, June 26, 1970, p. 1
[43] "Our readers write," *Monitor*, July 16, 1970, p. 16
[44] "Correspondents and freedom," *Monitor*, June 20, 1970, p. 16

CHAPTER 9: DEFENSELESS

[1] The conversation has been reconstructed based on the author's conversations with both men.
[2] Frutig interview with author, May 2010. Unless otherwise noted, all quotations from Frutig are from this interview.
[3] Winder interview with author, June 2010. Unless otherwise noted, all quotations from Winder are from this interview.
[4] Van Slambrouck interview with author, July 2010. Unless otherwise noted, all quotations from van Slambrouck are from this interview.
[5] Morse interview with author, April 2010. Unless otherwise noted, all quotations from Morse are from this interview.
[6] Hughes email to author, March 9, 2010
[7] Dillon interview with author, February 2010
[8] Hughes interview with author, March 2010
[9] Parsons interview with author, January 2009. Unless otherwise noted, all quotations from Parsons are from this interview.
[10] "Politics and Private Morality," *Monitor*, August 7, 1974, p. 18
[11] "Mercy and Justice," *Monitor*, September 9, 1974, p. 14
[12] "Report of the Trustees of The Christian Science Publishing Society, read by Howard Palfrey Jones, Chairman," *Journal*, July 1970, p. 342
[13] Ibid.
[14] "Report of the Treasurer, Roy Garrett Watson," *Journal*, August 1972, p. 424
[15] "Report of the Trustees of The Christian Science Publishing Society," *Journal*, August 1972, p. 426
[16] "The world's struggle for resources: Appetite of the wealthy," *Monitor*, June 19, 1974, p. F1
[17] Ibid.
[18] "Need of the hungry," *Monitor*, June 20, 1974, p. F1
[19] Ibid.
[20] "How we warmed to cold-war Russia," *Monitor*, November 24, 2003, p. 22
[21] "An American island in a Japanese sea," *Monitor*, June 24, 1999, p. 22
[22] Oka interviews with author, August and October 2003. Unless otherwise noted, all quotations from Oka are from these interviews.
[23] "Her lessons shape me still," *Monitor*, January 10, 2001, p. 22

[24] "'…the beauty of holiness,'" *Sentinel*, August 14, 1995, p. 18

[25] Oka interview with author, August 2003

[26] "A meeting that set the course of my life," *Monitor*, September 25, 2003

[27] "'The melody of Mind,'" *Journal*, December, 2000, p. 17

[28] Ibid.

[29] "Confronting world problems with spiritual understanding," *Sentinel*, January 21, 1980, p. 91

[30] "God's government and politics," *Sentinel*, June 25, 1979, p. 1105

[31] "The Monitor's Visual Image," *Journal*, October 1972, p. 577

[32] Ibid.

[33] S&H, p. 84

[34] "Report of the Trustees of The Christian Science Publishing Society, read by Robert G. Walker, Chairman," *Journal*, August 1975, p. 425

[35] "Report of the Trustees," *Journal*, August 1975, p. 426

[36] "Report of the Trustees of The Christian Science Publishing Society, read by Glenn A. Evans, Chairman," *Journal*, August 1976, p. 428

[37] "Report of the Treasurer, Marc Engeler," *Journal*, August 1976, p. 424

[38] "Message of The Christian Science Board of Directors, read by DeWitt John, Chairman," *Journal*, August 1978, p. 454

[39] "Report of The Christian Science Board of Directors," *Journal*, August 1978, p. 455

[40] Bridge, Susan. *Monitoring the News: The Brilliant Launch and Sudden Collapse of The Monitor Channel*, p. 40

[41] "Report of The Christian Science Board of Directors, read by Harvey W. Wood, Chairman," *Journal*, August 1979, p. 461

[42] Ibid.

[43] Ibid.

[44] Nordell, "The incomparable Earl," *Monitor*, July 12, 1999, p. 11

[45] "Earl Foell, Senior Editor and Writer at The Monitor," *The New York Times*, July 13, 1999

[46] Man., p. 47

[47] *"The Christian Science Monitor – a prophetic voice,"* *Journal*, May 2001, p. 31

[48] Bridge, p. 42

[49] "Report of the Board of Trustees of The Christian Science Publishing Society, read by Michael A. West, Chairman," *Journal*, August 1980, p. 413

[50] "Report of The Christian Science Board of Directors, read by Hal M. Friesen, outgoing Chairman," *Journal*, August 1982, p. 440

[51] "Report of the Board of Trustees of The Christian Science Publishing Society, read by Frederic C. Owen, Chairman," *Journal*, August 1982, p. 443

[52] "Report of The Christian Science Board of Directors," *Journal*, August 1979, p. 461

[53] "Report of The Christian Science Board of Directors," *Journal*, August 1982, p. 440

[54] "Top editorial posts resigned at The Christian Science Monitor," *Monitor*, May 26, 1983, p. 3

[55] "*The Christian Science Monitor*—an indispensable tool for individual and world salvation," *Journal*, November 1983, p. 658

[56] Ibid., p. 661

[57] Ibid.

[58] Bridge, p. 46

[59] Els interview with author, May 2010. Unless otherwise noted, all quotations from Els are from this interview.

[60] Takashi Oka interview with author, August 2003

[61] "After the Cultural Revolution," *Monitor*, June 22, 1984, p. 14

[62] Ibid.

[63] "Our Newspaper—why?" *Sentinel*, September 19, 1983, pp. 1621-1622

[64] DeWitt John, *The Christian Science Way of Life*, p. 192

[65] Un., p. 49

CHAPTER 10: SO MUCH MORE IS YET TO BE DONE

[1] *Alaska Story*, Reminiscence of Newton Minow, p. 182

[2] Miller interview with author, April 2010

[3] Hoagland interview with author, July 2010. Unless otherwise noted, all quotations from Hoagland are from this interview.

[4] Sheila Toomey, "Former Owner Fanning Dies," *Anchorage Daily News*, October 21, 2000

[5] *Alaska Story*, p. 50

[6] *Alaska Story*, Reminiscence of Jack Roderick, p. 188

[7] *Alaska Story*, p. 50

[8] *Alaska Story*, p. 210

[9] *Alaska Story*, p. 157

[10] *Alaska Story*, p. 18

[11] *Alaska Story*, p. 158

[12] *Alaska Story*, Reminiscence of Allan Dodds Frank, p. 198

[13] *Alaska Story*, Nightingale chapter, p. 211,

[14] *Alaska Story*, Nightingale chapter, p. 214

[15] *Alaska Story*, Interview of Jay Hammond by Pete Spivey, p. 194

[16] *Alaska Story*, Nightingale chapter, p. 217

[17] Irene Sege, "Centerpiece; Stepping Into a World Class Job," *Boston Globe*, June 25, 1983, p. 1

[18] *Alaska Story*, Reminiscence of Howard Weaver, former reporter, columnist, and editor at the *Anchorage Daily News*, p. 228

[19] Sheila Toomey, "Former Owner Fanning Dies," *Anchorage Daily News*,

October 21, 2000

[20] "The Monitor: A Graceful 75," *Boston Globe*, November 25, 1983

[21] Morse interview with author, April 2010. Unless otherwise noted, all quotations from Morse are from this interview.

[22] Menschel interview with author, May 2010. Unless otherwise noted, all quotations from Menschel are from this interview.

[23] Hoffman interview with author, May 2010. Unless otherwise noted, all quotations from Hoffman are from this interview.

[24] Jones interview with author, June 2010. Unless otherwise noted, all quotations from Jones are from this interview.

[25] Terry interview with author, April 2010. Unless otherwise noted, all quotations from Terry are from this interview.

[26] Freeman interview with author, April 2010. Unless otherwise noted, all quotations from Freeman are from this interview.

[27] Goodrich interview with author, May 2010. Unless otherwise noted, all quotations from Goodrich are from this interview.

[28] Audit Bureau of Circulations

[29] Els interview with author, May 2010

[30] Bridge, p. 58 and p. 204

[31] Yemma interview with author, June 2010. Unless otherwise noted, all quotations from Yemma are from this and subsequent interviews through late 2011.

[32] James L. Franklin, "100,000 Christian Scientists; Talk World Peace via Satellite, *Boston Globe*, December 27, 1984, p. 6

[33] Ibid.

[34] My., p. 117

[35] Bridge, p. 47

[36] John Strahinich, "Not Ready for Prime Time," *Boston*, July 1992, p. 51

[37] Richard A. Nenneman, *A Spiritual Journey: Why I Became a Christian Scientist*, p. 225

[38] Ibid., p. 226

[39] Chaddock interview with author, November 2010. Unless otherwise noted, all quotations from Chaddock are from this interview.

[40] Van Slambrouck interview with author, July 2010. Unless otherwise noted, all quotations from van Slambrouck are from this interview.

[41] Anable interview with author, May 2010. Unless otherwise noted, all quotations from Anable are from this interview.

[42] Els interview with author, May 2010. Unless otherwise noted, all quotations from Els are from this interview.

[43] "Children in darkness: The exploitation of innocence: A world where survival is a daily battle," *Monitor*, June 30, 1987, p. B1

[44] Ibid.

[45] "Dissolving the darkness of indifference," *Monitor*, June 30, 1987, p. 35

[46] "Leading children into light," *Monitor*, July 8, 1987, p. 15

[47] "Our readers write," *Monitor*, August 11, 1987, p. 14

[48] In a spreadsheet laying out the cost and revenue of various media for the next few years, Hoagland sketched out an "alternative" scenario for 1989-1990, which zeroed out the newspaper, along with all broadcasting except shortwave radio, daily TV, and religious TV. The cost to the Publishing Society would drop accordingly, and the deficit would disappear as the broadcasting elements grew.

[49] "Presentation to the Board of Trustees, The Christian Science Publishing Society, by The Manager's Office and senior managers, Monday, August 17, 1987"

[50] Bridge p. 60

[51] Morse interview with author, April 2010

[52] This date is the recollection of several people interviewed. Some have said the date was May 1.

[53] John Strahinich, "Not Ready for Prime Time," *Boston*, July 1992, p. 51

[54] Bridge, p. 21, p. 24

[55] Cook interview with author, May 2010. Unless otherwise noted, all quotations from Cook are from this and subsequent interviews.

[56] Bridge, p. 66

[57] Alex Beam, "Christian Scientists Seeking Economic Cure," *Boston Globe*, December 1, 1987, p. 47

[58] Winder interview with author, June 2010

[59] Morse interview with author, April 2010

[60] Morse interview with author, April 2010

[61] Morse interview with author, April 2010

[62] John Strahinich, "Not Ready for Prime Time," *Boston*, July 1992, p. 51

[63] Memo from Fanning to Directors, November 14, 1988

[64] Van Slambrouck interview with author, July 2010

[65] Letter from Fanning to Directors, November 14, 1988

[66] Ibid.

[67] Ibid.

[68] Letter from Anable to Directors, November 14, 1988

[69] Letter from Winder to Directors, November 14, 1988

[70] Memo from Pond to "Paul van Slambrouck and Everyone in International News," November 15, 1988

[71] Letter from Girardet to Directors, January 5, 1988 (actually January 5, 1989)

[72] Letter from Harsch to John Selover of the Christian Science Board of Directors, November 29, 1988

[73] Richard A. Nenneman, *A Spiritual Journey: Why I Became a Christian Scientist*, p. 231

---

[74] Hunter interview with author, June 2010. Unless otherwise noted, all quotations from Hunter are from this interview.
[75] Chronology of The Christian Science Monitor, 1988 Task Force, and 1989 new Monitor, compiled by Elizabeth Pond from interviews and documents, page 15
[76] Ibid.
[77] "Text from Two Important Meetings," letter from the Christian Science Board of Directors, November 29, 1988, regarding statements by Directors and Trustees at all-employee meeting on November 21 and statements of Nenneman and Cattani at meeting of only Christian Science teachers on November 22.
[78] From the *Talbot Banner*, quoted in Pond letter to Directors, February 15, 1988

CHAPTER 11: REGRET

[1] Morse interview with author, April 2010
[2] Hoffman interview with author, May 2010. Unless otherwise noted, all quotations from Hoffman are from this interview.
[3] Goodrich interview with author, May 2010. Unless otherwise noted, all quotations from Goodrich are from this interview.
[4] Barr interview with author, January 2009
[5] Letter from staff members to Board, December 6, 1988
[6] Letter from Frederic Hunter to Richard Cattani, January 19, 1989
[7] Jones interview with author, June 2010. Unless otherwise noted, all quotations from Jones are from this interview.
[8] Cook interview with author, May 2010. Unless otherwise noted, all quotations from Cook are from this and subsequent interviews.
[9] Letter from Saikowski to Cattani, January 3, 1988
[10] Chaddock interview with author, November 2010. Unless otherwise noted, all quotations from Chaddock are from this interview.
[11] Moffett interview with author, June 2010. Unless otherwise noted, all quotations from Moffett are from this interview.
[12] S&H, p. 207
[13] "United Yemen Sorts Out Social, Political Priorities," *Monitor*, June 14, 1990, p. 5
[14] Bridge, p. 85
[15] Bridge, p. 96
[16] "Report of The Christian Science Publishing Society, given by John H. Hoagland, Jr., Manager," *Journal*, September 1989
[17] Terry interview with author, April 2010. Unless otherwise noted, all quotations from Terry are from this interview.
[18] "Monitor Month," May 1990, page 4, quoted in Bridge, pp. 100-101

[19] Bridge p. 116

[20] Douglass, Memo to all Monitor radio and television staff, "Re: Monitor Broadcast News Standards," March 6, 1991, quoted in Bridge, p. 116 and p. 215, N22

[21] Paul Hemp, "The Christian Science Monitor's Big Cable Gamble," *Boston Sunday Globe*, March 24, 1991

[22] Bridge, p. 122

[23] "Report of The Christian Science Publishing Society, read by Netty Douglass, Manager," *Journal*, September 1991, p. 30

[24] Ibid., p. 29

[25] Taken in part from the account of Faye Bowers in "Monitor writers celebrate 'unique' moments," *Monitor*, March 26, 2009

[26] Frederic M. Biddle, "Can the Monitor Regain Past Glory?" *Boston Globe*, March 13, 1992

[27] "Treasurer's Financial Narrative, Fiscal Year 1991/92: Nine Months (May 1, 1991-January 31, 1992), Report 04-B-1, February 27, 1992," cited in Bridge, p. 151

[28] James L. Franklin, "Church Digs Deep for Cash," *Boston Globe*, Feb 29, 1992

[29] James L. Franklin, "Church Officials Defend Loan from Pension Plan," *Boston Globe*, March 4, 1992

[30] Morse interview with author, April 2010. Unless otherwise noted, all quotations from Morse are from this interview.

[31] From The Christian Science Publishing Society (Netty Douglass and Jack Hoagland) to All Employees in The Christian Science Publishing Society and Monitor Television, Inc., March 3, 1992

[32] Ibid.

[33] James L. Franklin, "Christian Science membership sees crisis of identity," *Boston Globe*, March 8, 1992

[34] Ibid.

[35] Bridge, p. 157

[36] "Letters to our Leader," *Sentinel*, December 11, 1909, p. 291

[37] Bridge, p. 157

[38] "From the Board of Trustees and Manager of The Christian Science Publishing Society, to All Employees of the Publishing Society; Re: Television Broadcasting of the Christian Science Monitor," March 9, 1992.

[39] According to a report from the Board of Directors published in the *Journal* of September 1992 (p. 11), the church spent roughly $432 million in net costs on radio and television from 1983 to 1992, including $68.5 million in shutdown costs for The Monitor Channel. The church did not publish reports of media losses after this, but according to the *Boston Globe* [James Franklin, "Christian Science Church to close its newsmagazine," March 27, 1993, p. 1] and *The Wall Street Journal* [Alec Klein, "Christian Science

Monitor Plan Includes New Format, Marketing and Investment," November 17, 1998], the magazine closed in 1993 with about $36 million in losses. With the $8 million in yearly losses from Monitor Radio, cited by both the *Boston Globe* [Jerry Ackerman, "Firm withdraws its bid for Monitor Radio News," June 17, 1997, p. D3] and editor David Cook as quoted in Current.org [Jacqueline Conciatore, "Monitor Radio goes dark at end of this week," June 23, 1997], the number reaches $500 million or above.

[40] John R. Wilke, "Monitor to Sell TV Channel," *The Wall Street Journal*, March 10, 1992

[41] "Report of the Treasurer of The Mother Church, read by John Lewis Selover," *Journal*, September 1992, p. 13

[42] "Annual Meeting Message from The Christian Science Board of Directors," *Journal*, August 1993, pp. 5-6

[44] The issue of whether the Board of Directors admitted mistakes in the TV venture and issued an apology is a controversial one. After the fact, one person who was a strong supporter of the television venture, a senior official in the church and in a position to know, said that church members were accusing the Directors of making mistake after mistake, but that the Board not only didn't consider the television venture a mistake but didn't feel that it had made mistakes at all. The "apology," according to this person, was only issued to let members know that the Board did not consider itself infallible. The statement Bergenheim read, according to this person, was saying that the Board only "regrets our mistakes if history shows they were mistakes" and "we are apologizing for what members have gone through." The author has chosen, however, to take what the Board said publically at face value, as sincere and apologetic, which is what the words Bergenheim read seem to indicate. Any other interpretation would require a cynical view of the motives of all five Directors, which is not consistent with the author's knowledge of the individuals involved and the Board's actions in other areas.

CHAPTER 12: SEEKING THE PRACTITIONER-JOURNALIST

[1] Yemma interview with author, June 2010. Unless otherwise noted, all quotations from Yemma are from this and subsequent interviews through late 2011.

[2] "Through Spirit's lens," *Sentinel*, September 17, 1979, p. 1632

[3] Jareaux interview with author, July 2010. All quotations from Jareaux are from this interview.

[4] Cook interview with author, May 2010. Unless otherwise noted, all quotations from Cook are from this and subsequent interviews.

[5] "Evidence Indicates Bosnia Massacre," *Monitor*, August 18, 1995, p. 1

[6] Rohde interview with author, June 2010. Unless otherwise noted, all quotations from Rohde are from this interview.

[7] "How a Serb Massacre was Exposed," *Monitor*, August 25, 1995, p. 1

[8] "Bosnia Muslims Were Killed by the Truckload," *Monitor*, October 2, 1995, p. 1

[9] "Monitor Correspondent Wins Pulitzer," *Monitor*, April 10, 1996, p. 1

[10] Jones interview with author, June 2010. Unless otherwise noted, all quotations from Jones are from this interview.

[11] Mark Jurkowitz, "Making the Monitor Matter: Will a redesign give this venerable newspaper a renewed relevance?" *Boston Globe*, August 6, 1997, p. C1

[12] Van Slambrouck interview with author, July 2010. Unless otherwise noted, all quotations from van Slambrouck are from this interview.

[13] Chaddock interview with author, November 2010. Unless otherwise noted, all quotations from Chaddock are from this interview.

[14] Bennett interview with author, June 2010. All quotations from Bennett are from this interview and follow-up emails.

[15] Ingwerson interview with author, June 2010. All quotations from Ingwerson are from this interview.

[16] Speech by President George W. Bush before Joint Session of Congress, September 20, 2001

[17] "Why do they hate us?" *Monitor*, September 27, 2001, p. 1

[18] Ibid.

[19] Ibid.

[20] Donovan Slack and Beth Healy, "Costs forcing sharp cuts at Christian Science church," *Boston Globe*, April 3, 2004, p. A1

[21] Annia Ciezadlo, "A toxic threat rises amid northern Iraq's prosperity," *Monitor*, December 24, 2004, p. 7

[22] Donovan Slack, "Christian Science Church Eyes Cuts," *Boston Globe*, February 5, 2004, p. B1

[23] Hughes interview with author, March 2010. Unless otherwise noted, all quotations from Hughes are from this interview or subsequent emails.

[24] Trammell interview with author, August 2010. All quotations from Trammell are from this interview or subsequent emails.

[25] "Love," *Po.*, p. 5

[26] "Reporter Abducted in Iraq," *Monitor*, January 10, 2006, p. 1

[27] "Prayers for a Reporter in Iraq," *Monitor*, January 19, 2006, p. 18

[28] "What it took from the hearts of many people to free Jill Carroll," *Monitor*, March 31, 2006, p. 9

[29] Christine Vendel, "Christian Science leader dies in KC," *The Kansas City Star*, July 21, 2008

[30] "Richard Bergenheim: An Appreciation," *Monitor*, July 22, 2008, p. 9

[31] John Strahinich, "Not Ready for Prime Time," *Boston*, July 1992, p. 51

[32] "Editor's message about changes at the Monitor," *Monitor*, March 27, 2009, p. 1

[33] Ibid.

[34] The contribution margin is calculated by subtracting the *Monitor*'s direct expenses, such as salaries and travel, from revenues. It does not take into account indirect expenses, such as share of Publishing Society energy usage and other overhead, that may be assigned to the *Monitor* by church accountants.

[35] Pabst interview with author, August 2010

[36] Wells interview with author, October 2011

[37] Feldmann interview with author, November 2010

[38] Baldauf interview with author, December 2011

[39] Goodale interview with author, December 2010. All quotations from Goodale are from this interview.

[40] By late 2011, the page views were settling in at an average of 22 million per month, with spikes close to 30 million. The website ranking was from Quantcast and varied from day to day. On a random day in late 2011, it was 243, one rank below the *Los Angeles Times*. The online publisher number was from MediaPost and remained the same (14) in late 2011, between ESPN (13) and Yahoo News (15).

[41] "The (surprisingly upbeat) state of the world," *Monitor*, December 26, 2011, p. 26

[42] Letter from McKenzie to Eddy, October 29, 1908, published in *Sentinel*, November 7, 1908, pp. 191-192

[43] '00, p. 3

[44] S&H, p. 223

Index